THE COMPLETE
Poodle

A well thought out breeding program brings success in many generations. Presiding: Ch. Parade Don't Rain on Mine TP, Group winner. L. to R., Ch. Parade The Right Decision—Specialty BOB winner, Ch. Parade Presentation—Specialty and all-breed BIS winner, Ch. Parade Mud Slide and Ch. Parade Precipitation—Top Producers. *Photo Dave Gossett*

THE COMPLETE
Poodle

Del Dahl

HOWELL
BOOK HOUSE
New York

MACMILLAN • USA

Macmillan General Reference
A Simon & Schuster Macmillan Company
1633 Broadway
New York, NY 10019-6785

Macmillan Publishing Company is part of the Maxwell Communication Group of Companies.

Library of Congress Cataloging-in-Publication Data

Dahl, Del.
  The complete poodle / Del Dahl.
      p.   cm.
    ISBN 0-87605-257-X
    1. Poodles.   I. Title.
  SF429.P85D28   1994
  636.7′2—dc20   93–38104
                                    CIP

10 9 8 7 6 5 4

Printed in the United States of America

Contents

Acknowledgments

WHAT GIVES ANYBODY the right to think they should write "another Poodle book"? I really don't know.

But I do know that the first phone call from my editor at Howell Book House generated a rush of excitement followed by a complex set of reactions, as I wrestled with the many questions that came to the front. Finally, the concept became clear. I should consider writing this book for four reasons:

- I like to write and Poodle people seem to appreciate the writing I've done.
- I've had nearly thirty years of everything associated with the Poodle scene from manning the pooper scoopers to being in the Best in Show ring.
- I've had a battery of teachers—teachers who have become mentors and friends—who helped me learn, knocked me down, propped me up and knocked me down again in so many ways, so many times, that it became apparent I should either work diligently to learn—or quit.
- Finally, I'm a fairly observant soul, and once I got started, I constantly picked up and stole ideas from wherever I found them. I'm happy stealing from friends and from people I don't even know. And the joy of stealing an idea from somebody I don't even care for has absolutely no bounds. And so I decided to do it.

Acknowledgments are essential because they are so much a part of my credentials. So let's begin—and let's begin with the dogs.

Pom Pom, Chou Chou and Pierre triggered the interest that led to my first Poodle, a silver Toy named Monet. She was never shown, but in many ways was the most valuable dog I ever owned. She had a marvelous mind, and every dog since Monet has had to measure up to her. She taught me early on the value of mental soundness in the Poodle. If anything is more important than type, it has to be having a Poodle with a mind.

Little Man came next. He taught me that some dogs just aren't good enough to be satisfying in the ring over time. Ch. Silver Scion of Sassafras confirmed what I'd always thought: Winning is more fun than not winning. He was my first champion.

Then came Ch. Edris Ooh La La. She introduced me to the satisfactions of being a breeder. La La's daughter, Ch. Cutler's Ebony Wysteria only did one thing; she made my reputation. She had the edge because of being my first significant Poodle through her ring career, but she and Ch. Surrey Postmarc really did the most to help me establish my credentials in the breed.

Jug Butt (Ch. Cutler's Ebony Lavender) effectively ran my life for years. Dozens of others contributed, too, as I learned to trim finky fronts and rotten rears and solve dozens of other problems they presented me. They shall remain nameless.

THE BREEDERS

The community of Poodle breeders has long played an important role in helping me think what I think and learn what I've learned. Some names you will recognize; others you won't.

Mockey Chaney—the record will show she bred one champion— was a local mentor at my beginnings. She was a model for integrity and for enjoying and caring for dogs.

Nancy Cutler—no longer breeding dogs—was next. Our association deepened when I got Wysteria and Ooh La La from her. Nancy was a marvelous teacher who demonstrated so much of what she taught. Don't fight over a dog. Groom where you can have company, television and coffee . . . and a host of other common-sense approaches that make breeding and showing dogs a more sustainable activity.

Through the many years that I worked for and showed with handler Peggy Hogg, I was constantly in close association with her many Poodle clients. While I would count many of them among my "teachers," none was more important than Harriett Laws of Mayfield Kennels. She remains a close confidant and friend always willing to share her experiences and to listen to what I'm dealing with—unless she's watching a Bears game.

Beck Mason of Bel Tor judged frequently in the Midwest, and when her assignment was finished, she always found her way to the grooming area. What followed was the equivalent of a seminar on the Poodle, and any dog in the area was apt to be part of what she demonstrated.

Mackey J. Irick of High Heritage Kennels came next, and Mackey instilled in me a need to be a student of the breed and to develop a greater appreciation of the breed's history than I had ever had before.

Nancy and Katey Kinowski deserve special mention for their constant friendship and agitation since old Wysteria was a puppy. They're both excellent breeding strategists, and Katey is my constant reminder that I am growing old. I remember teaching her to trim hind legs when she was a kid. Today, I write about trimming and let her do it.

And finally, there were Jim and Annie Clark. I got acquainted with Annie in the early 1970s regarding a choice of sires for Wysteria. In 1974, when I moved to Washington, D.C., I met Jim and the cast of characters that lived at and passed through Sealark Farms. The first time I visited, I spent the afternoon in the second-floor trimming room (the light was great and the view was perfect), and while Annie trimmed a Standard, I drifted in and out of the conversation as I pored through the scrapbooks on Ch. Fontclair Festoon. That was the first of many sessions on trimming, breeding dogs, training puppies and the host of topics that filled the Clark household each time I was there.

Frankly, life has never been quite the same since, because both have contributed so much that has influenced my thinking about Poodles, about being a Poodle person and about the sport of dogs in general. They never told me what to do, but they gave me a perspective that has greatly influenced not only what I think—but how I think about Poodles.

THE HANDLERS

When I started showing dogs, it became apparent I was not going to be an overnight success. I recall reaching a point when I decided I had to get better or get out. My accidental association with Peggy Hogg is what kept me going, and I will always be indebted to "Mother Hogg" for all the learning opportunities she provided. At our first show together, she trimmed half of Scion and left the rest for me to do (and I've done the same thing to dozens of people since), and the learning process began.

Peggy also helped me develop a businesslike approach to showing dogs, and I have grown to appreciate that more as the years go on.

As Peggy has demonstrated in Lhasa Apsos, Maltese and particularly Shih Tzus, she is a very capable dog breeder. And in my early years, her thinking was very much a part of nearly everything I undertook in my Fontella breeding program. Through her, I gained an inside look at what it is like with a dog at the top. I also learned to close crate doors and lock them each time I took a dog out.

Wendell Sammett, Barbara Humphries, Bud Dickey and Joseph Vergnetti, Paul Edwards, Frank Sabella, Kaz Hosaka, Katey Kinowski, Bill Cunningham and a host of others have always been people whose opinions I valued and from whom I have learned.

When you talk to them or Tim Brazier, Dana Plonkey, Mike Pawasarat, Betsy Leedy, Kay O'Bryant, Gary Wittmeier, Art Montoya, Joan Schilke, Diane Artigues, Carol Cargle, Dennis McCoy, Randy Garren, Sharon Calbrecht, Carol Millar or others, you're talking with people who are not only handlers but are creditable breeders in their own right.

I have to make special mention of the great years I spent traveling with Bob and Jean Walberg and Terry Meyers, during the heyday of Ch. Lou-Gin Kiss Me Kate's record-breaking career. That association was a lot of things, not the least of which was a forum for thinking about and discussing the breed.

I can't imagine what life in Poodles would have been if I had not had my close associations with all of these people through the years.

THE FAMILY

Who is family? Certainly, my wife, Sara, deserves first mention for all she's done and tolerated as my interests in Poodles and publishing a Poodle magazine dragged our family through a series of activities that above all served to complicate the business of five people being a "family." She has a wonderful ability to leave me alone and then haul me in just when I need it most. Her support and hours of involvement in the Poodle activities have been greater than anyone could possibly know. Our kids, Jeremy, Natalie and Cody, each deserve my appreciation. I'll always wonder if I should have spent more weekends fishing and playing ball with them and fewer going where the "judges are really great." But all three have been great about turning dogs out and covering bases when I wasn't there. And I guess in return I have to remember that Jer had his "Justine Poodle" and Cody still has Rodney as a bed warmer.

Our family includes two other special ladies—neither of whom we see very often these days. First, Josephine McCool. Without Josephine, there would have been no Fontella Kennels and no Fontella Poodles. She whelped all the puppies, grew all the coats, drove more than half of the miles we traveled together and has always been a terrific friend—from the days of "Chipper" to today. Then, the Kentucky woman, Carolyn Brown. If we get into unbearable fights as we discuss dogs, we just switch to horses until that topic gets too hot. Carolyn remains a vital part of the family and a really good friend.

Finally, I would like to thank those Poodle breeders instrumental in creating the Poodle Club of America and the legions of others who have nurtured its existence through the years and enabled it to grow and continue to serve and protect the breed.

PCA has provided a host of opportunities for me to learn and to teach others. I have always found that opportunities to teach resulted in tremendous opportunities to learn. The various seminars and programs conducted under PCA auspices throughout the years and now a focus of the PCA Foundation's work, have been most meaningful.

I am especially appreciative of the current board's willingness to allow the use of the Illustrated Breed Standard in its entirety. I find it a marvelous teaching tool and a welcome addition to this effort.

We are fortunate in our breed to have a parent club so closely attuned to the problems of breeders and willing to take risks in seeking solutions to problems. This book affords me the opportunity to publicly say think you, and I am grateful.

To all of those mentioned, and many others, thanks. This book is as much yours as it is mine.

Foreword

ANY DOG BREED is blessed when it has in its ranks people who are not only active breeders and participants in the sport, but also have the talent and dedication to write about what they have learned through their involvement.

That is the very set of ingredients that gives this book a freshness and practicality that will make it most useful to soon-to-be and relatively new participants in Poodle showing and breeding.

Del's background in animal breeding and judging and his long career in adult education at the University of Illinois give him a useful and unique background as a teacher.

Like so many of us, he has come through the ranks. Del's early and unsuccessful efforts (by his own account) are typical of so many during their earliest years. His years of work with a successful Poodle handler, and the people he met through that relationship, helped him become more successful.

During his nearly thirty years of involvement with Poodles he has developed a successful family of dogs that has gone on to produce for other breeders, he has managed the career of a notable stud dog, he has shown dogs that stood in the national ratings, he has handled his own dogs and those of others and, in general, has participated in nearly all aspects of Poodle husbandry.

In addition, he owned and edited *Poodle Review*, the national breed magazine. His many associations gained through the magazine put him in touch with breeders at all levels and with people who were only interested in owning a single Poodle as a companion or for the enjoyment that comes through Obedience work. Soon his column, "Catch Me Back at the Crates," was a tremendously popular feature of the magazine.

The column's acceptance was largely based on the fact that it focused on real breeder problems and questions, and that Del was able to deal with them in a practical, hands-on manner that was easy to understand.

A great deal of the strategy that was evident in the column is also evident in this book.

The first section deals with an overview of Poodle history, examines the concept of type and ends with a chapter designed to help the beginner get a start in the breed. The history is useful to any student of the Poodle, but by design is not an exhaustive look at Poodle history. That job is well done in Mackey J. Irick's book, *The New Poodle* (Howell Book House, 1986), and Del's strategy was to develop a book with features that complemented Mackey's.

The section on type is most useful and benefits greatly from the inclusion of the Illustrated Breed Standard developed by the Poodle Club of America. It is reproduced here in its entirety, and will be most useful to all readers. The chapter on purchasing a puppy is tied closely enough to type that breeders will find it useful, although it is primarily aimed at people who are seeking their first Poodle.

Next is a strong section that focuses entirely on conditioning the Poodle coat and getting it trimmed. Del's firsthand experience and abilities as a teacher bear him well, and many will be glad to have his thinking all in one place, as they approach the task of preparing their Poodles for the ring, or presenting them in pet trims that will enhance their appearance.

Following is the part of the book that helps newcomers develop strategies to get them started in a purposeful way rather than by accident as so many people have done. The practicality of this section and the cautions he offers should help new people see the need to seriously consider their interest and the extent to which they really want to get involved before they begin accumulating dogs.

The next part comes as close as I have seen in providing newcomers an inside look at how a handler approaches managing show dogs. However, the section is really written for the breeder-owner out on the road with his/her own string of dogs. The chapter on conditioning (muscle and weight) is a much-needed bit of thinking, and one that can benefit many of today's exhibitors at any level. The chapter on selecting a handler has the potential to benefit anyone who chooses to have their dogs presented in the ring by a professional.

The final section provides a philosophy for those interested in Obedience work, from the basic Obedience needed to have a manageable pet as part of the family, to advanced work in Obedience competition. Also included is a chapter that focuses on an unpleasant aspect of breeding dogs, heritable diseases. They are a part of the sport today, regardless of which breed you choose, and to an extent are problems in human lives as well.

As Del points out, many of the problems today are not totally solvable, and future success will depend on the combined efforts of breeders, practicing veterinarians and research scientists. But progress is being made.

Much of what this book offers is new to the written page. And much of it is practical and down-to-earth. In all, it is a valuable addition to the world of Poodles and an excellent complement to what exists.

It is a good read and a source that should be helpful to new breeders and to those who have their first Poodle and know in their hearts that they want to become more involved. All of these people are important to the future and well-being of the Poodle. One day they will be the ones to whom the breed's care is entrusted.

Anne Rogers Clark

Introduction

THE WORLD may or may not need another Poodle book. But if it needs this one, it will have to be because it offers information that others don't, it offers a different perspective on the material in other books or it provides a unique philosophical approach to particiaption in the sport of breeding and showing Poodles. The final function of a new Poodle reference might also be to pull together some agreed-upon thinking, now all in one place.

My intent is for this book to concentrate heavily on those four areas. The material is focused primarily at the maybe soon-to-be and new breeders, and at established breeders who are still learning. The final audience is the conscientious pet Poodle owner who is only vaguely aware that they might one day join the ranks of Poodle breeders.

Throughout our breed's history, so many of us have had our interest triggered by our first Poodle who was, as we said, "just a pet." There is nothing to suggest it won't be that way forever.

Here's how the book will unfold.

We will start by looking at the Poodle's "roots" and trying to establish a working and understandable definition of type. Some of you will be seeking just an overall understanding. You'll get it. For others of you, we'll be a bit more analytical—tying type to function and getting into the nitty-gritty definitions that result in a more thorough definition.

As I see it, we have to start with type. We trim to enhance type. We select matings to achieve a particular type. So it figures that we have to have a working appreciation for Poodle type before we can meaningfully deal with any aspect of breeding and showing Poodles.

To wrap up that section, there's a chapter on selecting your first Poodle puppy. It is intended for the absolute newcomer who is selecting a first Poodle. It focuses on finding a suitable source of puppies—and the pitfalls—and helps the newcomer more effectively communicate what they seek in the puppy they buy.

Next, a section on trimming. We'll deal with getting dogs ready to trim and then delve into each of the show trims—puppy, Continental, English Saddle and Sporting trim, which is acceptable in the show ring in some cases.

We'll also deal with what I call the "Convenience" trims: the retriever or kennel trim and a selection of other popular pet trims that retain the Poodle's dignity and that highlight and enhance Poodle type.

We will not, however, deal with the novelty or exotic trims.

Managing a small- to medium-size breeding kennel intended to produce show and breeding stock will be the next topic. We'll focus on the selection and management of broods through the whelping process and the first eight to twelve weeks of puppyhood. Then we'll move to the selection and management of stud dogs.

A fun section follows—managing show dogs. We'll talk about conditioning—coat, muscle and mental stability—from lead training through campaigning a top winner. We'll deal with baiting and helping dogs learn to sell themselves in the ring.

We'll think through a dog show weekend—from Monday night before the weekend until you arrive home from the shows and have everything unpacked. We'll develop a check list for the week's activities and develop an approach to scheduling all the work—even if you have an nine-to-five job and have to schedule show preparation around it.

We'll discuss strategies for getting your "great one" campaigned—by you, a handler, another owner or through a lease arrangement. And finally, we'll move to the wonderful world of Obedience where Poodle achievements have been legion.

The concluding section that deals with Poodle health-related topics and genetic concerns will follow.

That will about wrap it up. Along the way, we'll try to share some of the tricks of the trade that have been passed down one way or another—and never got put down in writing.

That's what the book is about, so let's get started.

1

Today's Poodle:

A Look at Its Roots

THE POODLE is one of the oldest breeds that American dog breeders work with today. Therein lies a problem. The absolute origin—if indeed there is a definable origin—is lost in antiquity. It seems likely that pinpointing a single point of origin is vastly more confusing because the Poodle comes in three different sizes, a wide range of colors and at least two coat types. So breed historians have had to construct a history, and in doing so have relied heavily on writings of the times and depictions of Poodle-like dogs in various art forms.

As early as 30 A.D., Poodle-like dogs appeared in carvings on Roman tombs and on Greek and Roman coins. While they might cite the origins of the breed, it is a sure bet that neither Anne Clark nor Frank Sabella trimmed them. They do seem Poodle-like, but in truth they might be any full-coated dog. By the fifteenth century, references to Poodles appeared in both writing and art, and the art of that time portrayed the Poodle in a facsimile of today's traditional trims.

COUNTRIES OF ORIGIN

Most breed historians agree that the Poodle as we know it in the United States today had its origins in Russia, France and Germany. But

CURLY POODLE CH. RUFUS M⁹ R. LONG OWNER .

the dogs of those countries were very different in type from one another, and we are left to wonder if those dogs did indeed have a common origin, or whether the resemblance among them was the effort of dog fanciers trying to develop a dog for a particular purpose—and in doing so, they independently came up with a similar, if not identical, type. The Russian Poodle was described as being somewhat Greyhound-like in body type.

In Germany, the Poodle was more thickset and had a wooly coat texture. And it was here that the two different coat types—curly and corded—were noted. The German word *pudel* means to splash in water.

In France, where this breed is the national dog, the Poodle was found in several forms. The **Petit Barbet**, a Toy-like dog, was evident, and periodically writers have suggested it might have resulted from the influence of dogs such as the Toy Spaniel and the Maltese. France's **Caniche** was a larger dog used extensively for duck hunting, and it is suggested that the size and sturdiness might have stemmed from the influence of the Spaniel. In fact, the similarity of today's Poodle and the Irish Water Spaniel remains evident. Still another type in existence was the **Truffle Dog** who found a niche in life ferreting out the tiny morsels so sought after for the unique flavors they provided French cooks.

A group of Labory Standard Poodles at play in the 1930s. Owned by Madame Lucienne Reichenbach, Switzerland.

But without question, in France, the Poodle's popularity (particularly the Petit Barbet) with the higher ranking members of society was such, that the breed was early on designated the National Dog, and much of the initial popularity and notoriety was associated with France.

That helps explain why you can walk down the street in any U.S. city today with an American champion Poodle whose pedigree reveals at least six generations of U.S. breeding and another six of English breeding, and almost be certain that somebody will ask you, "Is that a French Poodle?"

The Poodle's move to England is significant to American fanciers because so much of the foundations of our modern Poodles came from that country. But pinpointing that happening—or determining where the earliest Poodles came from—is another bit of information that cannot be documented. References suggest that Poodle-like dogs were there earlier, but the first documented reference dates from 1642. A Poodle-like dog appeared on the front of a Parliamentary broadsheet in that year, listed as "Prince Rupert's White Dog Called Boy." Neither Clark nor Sabella trimmed him either.

FORM FOLLOWING FUNCTION

The trims depicted in those early portrayals have always been of interest because they are the forerunners of the traditional trims we see in the ring at dog shows today. The Poodle was developed in a make and shape to accomplish the functions performed for man, so the trim is reminiscent of those functions.

A world of evidence suggests that throughout the formative years, the Poodle was a dog developed to work as a water retriever. This was also a full-coated dog, and the mass of coat offered some benefits, but also presented some problems.

The benefits focus on that blanket of hair keeping the chest and heart area protected from the cold and from objects that the dog might run into while working in the water. But working in the water in a full coat would be similar to teaching a young child to swim in baggy pajamas (with footies) while wearing diapers. Use of the hindquarters in either case would be hampered considerably. So the hindquarters were trimmed to make movement easier and the dog more functional in the water.

Now think about the Continental trim we see in the ring today, and today's trim is indeed reminiscent of that early trim—entirely based on the dog's function. You have only to realize that in the royal circles in France, where ruffles and powdered wigs were as much the rage as the

Poodle, the functional trim was plain and quite at odds with the fashion and decor of the times. So add the rosettes on the hips, the pompon on the tail and the puffs on each leg, and you have a trim that adds the panache that brings the functional trim into compatibility with the fashion of the times.

That's why dedicated breeders—those who appreciate the breed's history and tradition, and focus on protecting it—have willingly continued the traditional trims. Only the more recent aficionados are willing to sacrifice the tradition and history for their personal convenience.

THE POODLE IN THE UNITED STATES

Both Standard and Toy Poodles were shown before the beginning of World War I. But at that time, the two were considered separate breeds. As the Miniatures came on the scene, they were shown with the Standards, but the competition was divided into two coat types: curly and corded. The original Toys, almost always white, were really quite different from the Toys of today. The original Toys continued to be bred until 1943 when the Poodle Club of America recognized them as the third variety of Poodle. And at that point, Toy Poodle breeding took a decidedly different turn. While some remnants of the original Toys probably harbor a distant place in some of today's Toy pedigrees, the PCA action opened the way for the development of the modern Toy Poodle by breeding them down from small Miniatures and Toy-Miniature crosses. The accomplishments of the American Toy Poodle breeders in this brief fifty-year period is widely viewed as one of the breeding marvels in all canine history.

EARLY PROGRESS

While the U.S. Poodle population and the number of pioneer breeders continued to grow, it was not until the 1930s that the winds that blew life into the American public gave rise to an unmatched popularity of the breed that lasted twenty-three years, from 1960 to 1983.

The Poodle Club of America was founded in 1931, and one of their first tasks was that of developing a breed Standard to guide the work of American breeders. Permission was given by The Curley Poodle Club of England to use their Standard and rules. Approval came the following year, and at the same time, the plight of the Miniature was resolved by providing a separate variety. For several years thereafter the Standard and

Ch. Wilbur White Swan focused early attention on Toy Poodles with his 1956 Westminster Best In Show. Anne Rogers Clark handled him throughout his career. "Peanut" sired 38 champions.

Miniature variety winners had to compete to determine which *one* would represent the breed in the Non-Sporting Group.

The first Miniature to earn a title under the new system was Ch. Chieveley Chopstick, a black English import dog owned by Charles Price of Boston, Massachusetts. Another significant happening in 1932 was the importation of a group of Swiss Standard descendants of German stock. The best known was Eric Labory selected by Alice Lang Rogers from Mme. Reichenbach's Labory Kennel in Switzerland.

Ch. Whippendell Poli of Carillon, a black Standard dog, won the Westminster Non-Sporting Group in 1933, and in the same year Salmagundi Kennels completed a title on its first dog, and Mr. and Mrs. Sherman Hoyt entered the Westminster Kennel Club show for the first time.

While all of those events indicate the burst of interest developing in Poodles in America, the happening in 1933 that would ultimately have the greatest impact on the breed's popularity and rise to fame was the importation of a white Standard dog. The dog was the gift of Mrs. T. Whitney Blake to her daughter and son-in-law, the Hoyts, and the dog was none other than Tri. Int. Ch. Nunsoe Duc de la Terrace of Blakeen. The Duc was first shown at Westminster in 1934 where he won the Non-Sporting Group. A string of Best in Show wins followed, and in 1935 he returned to the Garden to win Best in Show. He was the first Poodle to win Best in Show at Westminster, and his handler, Mrs. Hoyt, was the first woman to stand in the Best in Show ring.

Few question the fact that the Duc and his Garden win contributed mightily to the rise in the Poodle's popularity, and the increased interest in breeding and showing Poodles that followed that launching point in the breed's development.

In 1936, the Poodle made its presence felt in California through the efforts of Col. Ernest E. Ferguson, Miss Lydia Hopkins and a small group of others.

With the 1940s came important Best in Show wins at Morris and Essex (a most prestigious event) with Mrs. Hoyt's Duc daughter, Ch. Blakeen Jung Frau. And in the same year, Ch. Monty of Gilltown became the first Miniature to go Best of Breed at Specialty show. He was owned by the Frelinghuysens and handled by Walter Morris. In 1942 the Miniature Ch. Ramoneur of Catawba became the first of his variety to win the Non-Sporting Group at the Garden. That win was followed by a Miniature earning the Best in Show award there in 1943: Ch. Pitter Patter of Piperscroft. Both were owned by the Frelinghuysens.

Eric Labory of Misty Isles

7

Int. Ch. Nunsoe Duc de La Terrace before coming to America from England. His 1938 Westminster Best In Show win with owner Hayes Blake Hoyt handling did much to popularize the Poodle in the U.S. He produced seven U.S. champions, providing a lasting impact on the breed.

Ch. Puttencove Promise scored a Westminster Best In Show in 1958 trimmed in the fashion of that time. He sired 27 champions and was bred and owned by Mrs. George Putnam, Puttencove Kennels. Her daughter, Helen Sokopp, breeds Standards today under the Syrena banner. (*Photo by Evelyn Shafer*)

Ch. Acadia Command Performance CD, the 1973 Westminster Best In Show winner for owners Edward Jenner and Jo Ann Sering, demonstrates how much the fashions had changed since Puttencove Promise's win in 1958. The tighter shaping of the mane and the raised placement of the upper band on the hind leg are most evident as is the overall shaping of the trim. "Bart" produced 38 champions.

World War II slowed the Poodle fancy for the next several years, but remember, it was 1943 when the Toy Poodle achieved its status within the Poodle Club of America and the American Kennel Club. That brought the introduction of colors other than white, and assigned to U.S. breeders the difficult task of breeding successfully within the ten-inch limit.

In California, Florence Orsie, Gladys Herbel, Lydia Hopkins and Hilda Miesenzahl were at the forefront. In the East Mrs. Hoyt, Mrs. Austin, Martha Jane Ablett and many others joined in. But the name that became a byword wherever Toy Poodles are discussed was that of Leicester Harrison who bred under the kennel name of Leicester. The family of dogs she produced won more Bests in Show than had been won by any other breeder at the time she was active, and yet today those dogs occupy important positions on the all-time Top Producers list and are behind a great many of the active breeding programs currently underway. She was a key force and lasting entity in the development of the modern Toy Poodle.

While this book was never conceived as a definitive book on Poodle history, it seemed impossible to approach the concerns of those interested in today's Poodle—particularly in thinking about type and breeding activities—without at least an overview. The Toy Poodle received more than its share of discussion because it is the most recent variety and less has been written about it, and because it is a distinctly American creation. Remember, the progress of American Toys is one of the great marvels in dog breeding history.

2

Type: What Is It?

W E'LL PROBABLY MAKE more progress learning about type if we don't deal with the concept of type as it applies to Poodles. And given that I'm the author, return with me to my childhood interests, and let's spend a little bit of time with—cows.

"A rose is a rose is a rose" may be true. But as the photographs of the dairy and beef cows show, one good cow may be very different from another. The trick to understanding the difference is to understand the function that each animal is designed to perform.

The dairy cow is intended to produce large quantities of milk—often one hundred pounds or more per day. While dairy beef can certainly be eaten, it isn't the highest quality, and most of the carcass does not go into the high-priced cuts. On the other hand, the beef cow is designed to produce offspring with a high percentage of high-priced cuts in the carcass. And so far as milk is concerned, the cow need only produce enough to raise her calf—and twenty pounds a day will more than do the job.

So there you have it: two very different-appearing cows. But still, two cows very correct in the type necessary to do the jobs they are designed to do.

And that kind of understanding should be helpful—especially to new breeders—as they strive to develop a concept of type that is meaningful and satisfying to them.

Gaining an appreciation and understanding of Poodle type is one of those good-news/bad-news situations. The good news is that under the

Illini Coronet Midge portrays the desired type of a high-producing dairy animal. She was classified Excellent–95 and produced a lifetime total of 154,710 pounds of milk. Her height, length of body and depth of ribbing assures she has the capacity for milk production, and her nearly ideal and capacious udder equips her well for that task. Her clean bone and correct feet and legs assure that she will last for many years, as, indeed, she did.

Hi Way Zara 475 typifies the desired type of young Angus female. She was Grand Champion of the Illinois Junior Angus Field Day. Her height and trimness (note her underline) and the heavy muscling over the loin and in the hind leg make her the type that wins and produces offspring who generate a high percentage of the most desired cuts of beef.

auspices of the Poodle Club of America, Poodle breeders have access to a very good breed Standard. And the breed Standard has historically been a piece of writing that describes what makes an ideal Poodle. Even more good news became available to Poodle breeders in June 1992 when the Poodle Club of America's Illustrated Breed Standard Committee produced a publication that not only presents the breed Standard but illustrates the various points to enhance understanding.

So what's the bad news? Well, compared to the two cows presented earlier—with different type because of their different functions—the issue of type is not nearly so closely related to function. If the Poodle had to "be" a particular way to "do" what it is designed to "do," it would be

It was "All in a Day's Work" for Dr. N. Boyd Hagen and his Standard Poodle hunting partner, Degana Acanthosis. "Can" enjoys his regular hunting outings in the fall as much as any other working retriever. He is sired by Ch. Neocles Enrico Sambo and out of Oikos Melody UD Can. CD. Individuals throughout the U.S. use their Poodles in the manner the breed was historically developed to work. From time to time small clubs have organized primarily for Poodle owners to enjoy the working Poodle together. At present no such club exists. "Can" was bred by Tom and Anne Dege.

a great deal easier for us to agree on what is and what isn't correct type. If we recall the breed's historical roots as a water dog, however, it is still possible to relate type to function. And if we don't make that relationship, what basis do we have to decide how a Poodle should look or what is correct type?

But today's Poodle—for all practical purposes—is a companion animal. So is a Bulldog. And they are very different. Our ability to relate type to function in the Poodle requires us to look to the history of the breed to learn what its function was at the time of development. And frankly, not all Poodle breeders—even those seasoned—really want to devote much mental energy to that task. So, as the preface of the "Illustrated Breed Standard" suggests, "just as individuals differ in their interpretations of the standard, artists will vary in their concept of the perfect Poodle according to the standard. It is impossible to please everyone, but that is an important part of our sport—comparing and criticizing and seeking an unobtainable ideal."

If your question is about type, this will define it. One of the classic Poodle pictures of all time is this portrayal of Ch. Rimskittle Ruffian's stellar performance at the Westminster Kennel Club Show with her handler Tim Brazier. She is totally collected with not one foot on the ground and the extension of forearm and hindquarter is exactly what the breed Standard prescribes. Ruffian was sired by Rimskittle Mugshot X Ch. Rimskittle Executant. Ruffian produced three champions—all Best In Show winners—including Ch. Rimskittle Roughneck who in turn produced 25 champions. She was bred by Mr. and Mrs. James E. Clark and owned by Margo Durney and Ed Jenner.

And who knows, one of us might just obtain it!

Let's get The Poodle Club of America's Illustrated Breed Standard before us in its entirety, because understanding it is essential to all discussion related to Poodle type. Once that is done, we'll dig into some of the issues within it that might benefit from greater discussion.

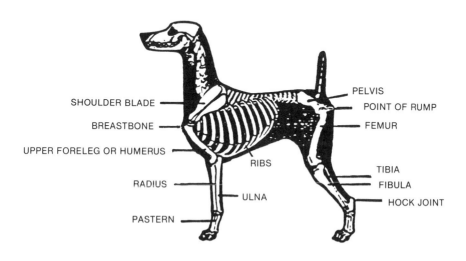

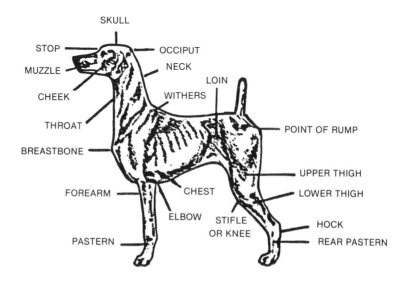

OFFICIAL AKC STANDARD
FOR THE POODLE

The Standard for the Poodle (Toy variety) is the same as for the Standard and the Miniature varieties except as regards height.

General Appearance, Carriage and Condition—That of a very active, intelligent and elegant-appearing dog, squarely built, well proportioned, moving soundly and carrying himself proudly. Properly clipped in the traditional fashion and carefully groomed, the Poodle has about him an air of distinction and dignity peculiar to himself.

Size, Proportion, Substance—Size: **The Standard Poodle** is over fifteen inches at the highest point of the shoulders. Any Poodle which is fifteen inches or less in height shall be disqualified from competition as a Standard Poodle. **The Miniature Poodle** is fifteen inches or under at the highest point of the shoulders, with a minimum height in excess of ten inches. Any Poodle which is over fifteen inches or is ten inches or less at the highest point of the shoulders shall be disqualified from competition as a Miniature Poodle. **The Toy Poodle** is ten inches or under at the highest point of the shoulders. Any Poodle which is more than ten inches at the highest point

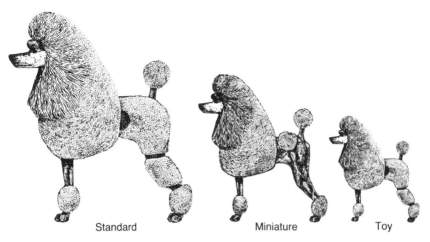

Standard Miniature Toy

of the shoulders shall be disqualified from competition as a Toy Poodle. As long as the Toy Poodle is definitely a Toy Poodle, and the Miniature Poodle a Miniature Poodle, both in balance and proportion for the Varieties, diminutiveness shall be the deciding factor when all other points are equal. **Proportion:** To insure the desirable squarely built appearance, the length of body measured from the breastbone to the point of the rump approximates the height from the highest point of the shoulders to the ground. **Substance:** Bone and muscle of both forelegs and hind legs are in proportion to the size of dog.

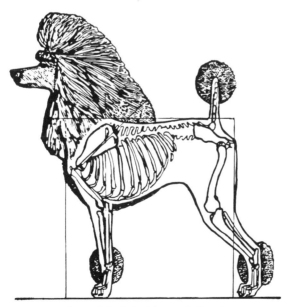

Squarely built: height equals length.

Head and Expression—a. *Eyes:* very dark, oval in shape and set far enough apart and positioned to create an alert intelligent expression. Major fault: eyes round, protruding, large or very light. b. *Ears*: hanging close to the head, set at or slightly below eye level.

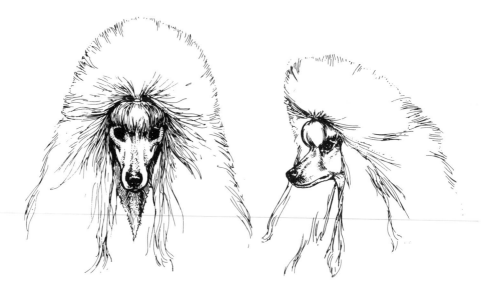

Round eyes, round
skull, snipey muzzle

Eyes: too large, too
round and too light. Cheeky.

Preferred

The ear leather is long, wide and thickly feathered; however, the ear fringe should not be of excessive length. c. *Skull*: moderately rounded, with a slight but definite stop. Cheekbones and muscles flat. Length from occiput to stop about the same as length of muzzle.

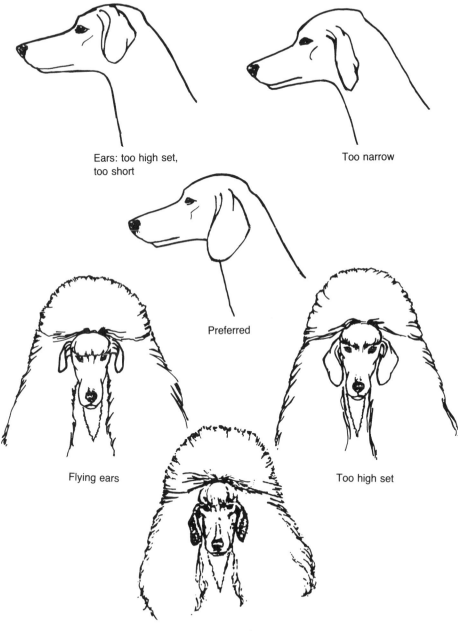

Ears: too high set, too short

Too narrow

Preferred

Flying ears

Too high set

Preferred

19

Correct side view

Correct front view

Broad, heavy
head, throaty

Too broad and heavy

Round skull,
short snipey muzzle

Round head, snipey muzzle

Lack of chin,
too narrow,
snipey muzzle

Too narrow

20

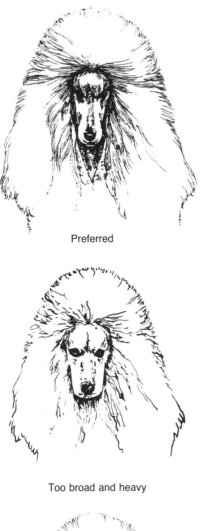

Preferred

Too broad and heavy

Round skull, snipey
muzzle, round eyes

d. *Muzzle*: long, straight and fine, with slight chiseling under the eyes. Strong without lippiness. The chin definite enough to preclude snipiness. *Major fault: lack of chin. Teeth* white, strong and with a scissors bite. *Major fault: undershot, overshot, wry mouth.*

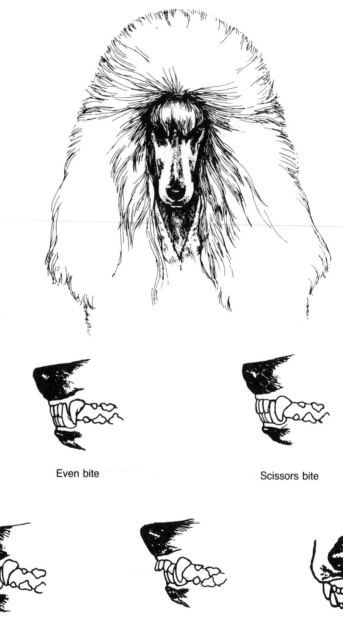

Even bite

Scissors bite

Undershot

Overshot

Wry mouth

Neck, Topline, Body—Neck well proportioned, strong and long enough to permit the head to be carried high and with dignity. Skin snug at throat. The neck rises from strong, smoothly muscled shoulders. *Major fault: ewe neck.* The **topline** is level, neither sloping nor roached from the highest point of the shoulder blade to the base of the tail, with the exception of a slight hollow just behind

Short neck,
steep shoulder

Ewe neck which sets
forward on shoulders

Preferred

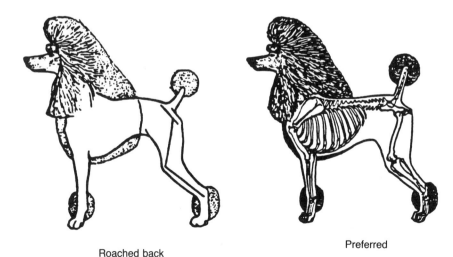

Roached back
low tailset

Preferred

the shoulder. **Body:** a. Chest deep and moderately wide with well-sprung ribs. b. The loin is short, broad and muscular. c. Tail straight, set on high and carried up, docked of sufficient length to insure a balanced outline. ***Major fault:*** *set low, curled or carried over the back.*

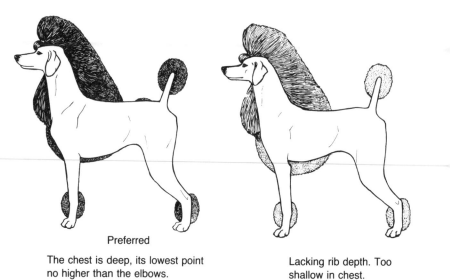

Preferred

The chest is deep, its lowest point no higher than the elbows.

Lacking rib depth. Too shallow in chest.

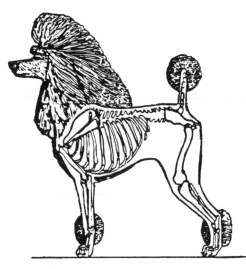

The loin is short, broad and muscular

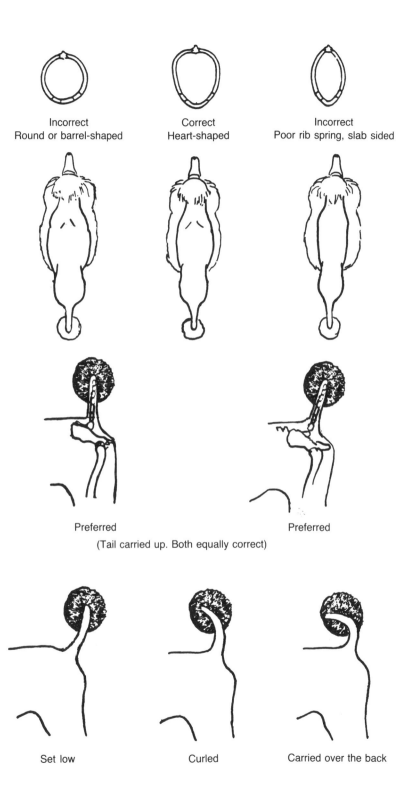

Incorrect
Round or barrel-shaped

Correct
Heart-shaped

Incorrect
Poor rib spring, slab sided

Preferred

Preferred

(Tail carried up. Both equally correct)

Set low

Curled

Carried over the back

25

Forequarters—Strong, smoothly muscled shoulders. The shoulder blade is well laid back and approximately the same length as the upper foreleg. *Major fault: steep shoulder.* a. Forelegs straight and parallel when viewed from the front. When viewed from the side, the elbow is directly below the highest point of the shoulder. The pasterns are strong. Dewclaws may be removed.

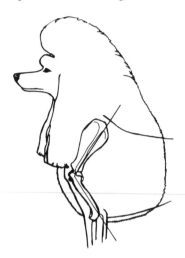 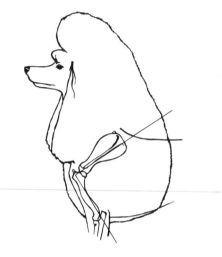

Upright shoulder blade combined with correctly angled upper foreleg—this does not allow the head to be held high while standing or carried correctly while moving.

Preferred
Proper layback of shoulder and upper foreleg gives correct forward reach with correct head carriage.

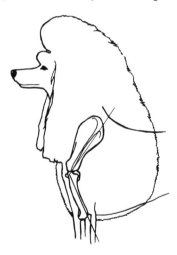 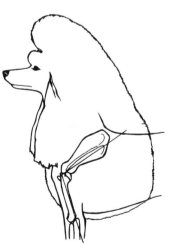

Upright shoulder blade and upright upper foreleg restricts smooth forward reach of front leg and allows for no forechest.

Correct shoulder blade combined with too steep upper foreleg restricts forward reach and allows for no forechest.

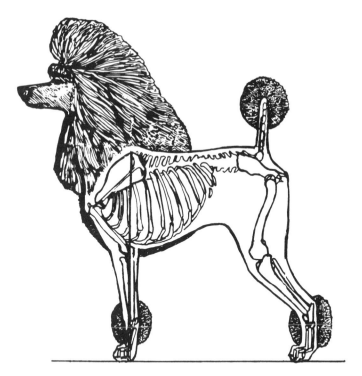

The elbow is directly below the highest point of the shoulder.

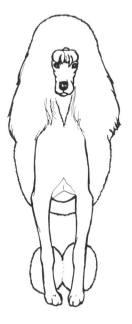

Out at elbows; toes in   Too narrow; toes out   Preferred

Feet—The feet are rather small, oval in shape with toes well arched and cushioned on thick firm pads. Nails short but not excessively shortened. The feet turn neither in nor out. *Major fault: paper or splay foot.*

 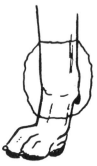

Correct foot
front view

Correct oval foot
side view

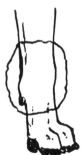  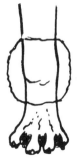 

Cat foot
side view

Cat foot
front view

Splay foot
front view

Paper foot
side view

Flat hind foot

Correct hind foot

Hindquarters—The angulation of the hindquarters balances that of the forequarters. Hind legs straight and parallel when viewed from the rear. Muscular with width in the region of the stifles which are well bent; femur and tibia are about equal in length; hock to heel short and perpendicular to the ground. When standing, the rear toes are only slightly behind the point of the rump. *Major fault: cow hocks*.

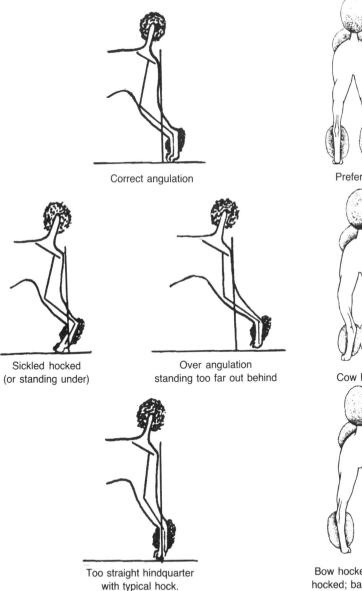

Correct angulation

Preferred

Sickled hocked
(or standing under)

Over angulation
standing too far out behind

Cow hocks

Too straight hindquarter
with typical hock.

Bow hocked or open
hocked; bandy legged

Coat—(a) *Quality.* Curly: Of naturally harsh texture, dense throughout. Corded: Hanging in tight, even cords of varying length; longer on mane or body coat, head and ears; shorter on puffs, bracelets and pompons. (b) *Clip.* A Poodle under twelve months may be shown in the puppy clip. In all regular classes, Poodles twelve months or over must be shown in the "English Saddle" or "Continental" clip. In the Stud Dog or Brood Bitch classes, and in a noncompetitive Parade of Champions, Poodles may be shown in the "Sporting" clip. A Poodle shown in any other type of clip shall be disqualified.

(1) *The Puppy Clip.* A Poodle under a year old may be shown in the Puppy clip with the coat long. The face, throat, feet and base of the tail are shaved. The entire shaven foot is visible. There is a pompon on the end of the tail. In order to give a neat appearance and a smooth unbroken line, shaping of the coat is permissible. (2) *The English Saddle.* In the English Saddle clip, the face, throat, feet forelegs and base of the tail are shaved, leaving puffs on the forelegs and a pompon on the end of the tail. The hindquarters are covered with a short blanket of hair except for a curved shaved area on each flank and two shaved bands on each hind leg. The entire shaven foot and a portion of the shaven leg above the puff are visible. The rest of the body is left in full coat but may be shaped in order to insure overall balance. (3) *The Continental Clip.* In the Continental clip, the face, throat, feet and base of the tail are shaved. The hindquarters are shaved with pompons (optional) on the hips. The legs are shaved, leaving bracelets on the hindlegs and puffs on

Puppy Clip

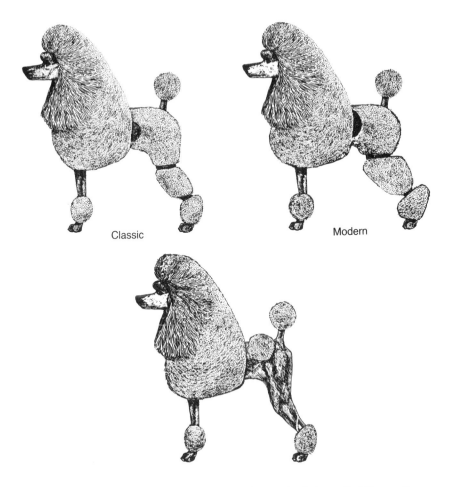

Classic

Modern

the forelegs. There is a pompon on the end of the tail. The entire shaven foot and a portion of the shaven foreleg above the puff are visible. The rest of the body is left in full coat but may be shaped to insure overall balance. (4) *The Sporting Clip.* In the Sporting clip, a Poodle shall be shown with face, feet, throat and base of the tail shaved, leaving a scissored cap on the top of the head and a pompon on the end of the tail. The rest of the body and legs are clipped or scissored to follow the outline of the dog, leaving a short blanket of coat no longer than one inch in length. The hair on the legs may be slightly longer than that on the body.

In all clips, the hair of the topknot may be left free or held in place by elastic bands. The hair is only of sufficient length to present a smooth outline. "Topknot" refers only to hair on the skull—from stop to occiput. This is the only area where elastic bands may be used.

Sporting Clip

Corded Coat

Color—The coat is an even and solid color at the skin. In blues, grays, silvers, browns, café-au-laits, apricots and creams, the coat may show varying shades of the same color. This is frequently present in the somewhat darker feathering of the ears and the tipping of the ruff. While clear colors are definitely preferred, such natural variation in the shading of the coat is not to be considered a fault. Brown and café-au-lait Poodles have liver-colored noses, eye-rims and lips, dark toenails and dark amber eyes. Black, blue, gray, silver, cream and white Poodles have black noses, eye-rims and lips, black or self-colored toenails and very dark eyes. In the apricots, while the foregoing coloring is preferred, liver-colored noses, eye-rims and lips, and amber eyes are permitted but are not desirable. *Major faults: color of nose, lips and eye-rims incomplete or of wrong color for color of dog.*

Parti-colored dogs shall be *disqualified*. The coat of a parti-colored dog is not an even, solid color at the skin, but is of two or more colors.

Gait—A straightforward trot with light springy action and strong hindquarters drive. Head and tail carried up. Sound effortless movement is essential.

| Straight normal | Single track As speed increases legs tend to move toward a single track. | Out at elbows. padding | Weaving, crossing over, plaiting, knitting. dishing or toeing in | Moving wide |

| Straight normal | Single track As speed increases legs tend to move toward a single track | Side-winding moving with body at an angle | Close behind | Cow-hocked | Bow-hocked, open-hocked, bandy, moving wide behind |

Correct. TROT: supported by legs on diagonal.

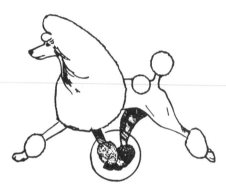

Incorrect. Over reaching

Incorrect. Hackney front, also lacks drive.

PACE: (incorrect) supported by legs on same side. The dog will rock from side to side when moving. A gait used by Poodles that do not have balanced angulation between forequarters and hindquarters.

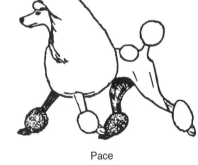

Pace

Temperament—Carrying himself proudly, very active, intelligent, the Poodle has about him an air of distinction and dignity peculiar to himself. *Major fault: Shyness or sharpness.*

Major Faults—Any distinct deviation from the desired characteristics described in the breed Standard.

DISQUALIFICATION

Size—*A dog over or under the height limits specified shall be disqualified.*

Clip—*A dog in any type of clip other than those listed under coat shall be disqualified.*

Parti-colors—*The coat of a parti-colored dog is not an even solid color at the skin, but of two or more colors. Parti-colored dogs shall be disqualified.*

VALUE OF POINTS

General appearance, temperament, carriage and conditions 30
Head, expression, ears, eyes and teeth 20
Body, neck, legs, feet and tail. 20
Gait. 20
Coat, color and texture 10

The current breed Standard was approved by the Poodle Club of America on August 14, 1984, and reformatted March 27, 1990. And it does the job of describing type, plus more. It describes in a limited number of words how the various pieces of parts of the Poodle should be. Many of those ''parts'' are elements of type. Some aren't.

The trick in defining type is to avoid getting too engrossed in how the pieces and parts should be, and, instead, focus on how the overall dog should look once the pieces and parts are assembled. And again, the breed Standard provides some very direct clues. Consider these lines from the sections on general appearance and proportion:

- General appearance: That of a very active, intelligent and elegant-appearing dog, squarely built, well proportioned, soundly moving and carrying himself proudly. Properly clipped in the traditional fashion and carefully groomed, the Poodle has about him an air of distinction and dignity peculiar to himself.
- Proportion: To insure the desirable squarely built appearance, the length of body measured from the breastbone to the point of the rump approximates the height from the highest point of the shoulders to the ground. Bone and muscle of both forelegs and hind legs are in proportion to size of dog.

Ch. Ale Kai Airy enjoyed a most successful ring career with her breeder-handler Wendell Sammet. In addition to an impressive list of all-breed and Specialty Best In Show wins, Airy won the Non-Sporting Group at Westminster Kennel Club in 1988. During her career she was owned by Tatiana Nagro.

When you read that, you gain an overall idea of how the Poodle should appear in an overall sense. Would those words describe a Maltese? An English Bulldog? A Dachshund? Of course not.

What about a Dalmatian or a Doberman Pinscher? It comes much closer, right? That isn't surprising. If you strip the hair from a Poodle, you have a dog that isn't identical but also isn't terribly dissimilar to good representatives of those two breeds.

The point is, the breed Standard provides you an overall picture of how the Poodle should look. It is a statement by the Poodle Club of America, and one of the Club's important roles is to serve as the protector of the breed. But in fulfilling that role, it is generally understood that each of us, both the stalwart breeder of many years and the new Poodle owner alike, will interpret those words in many ways. Still, the breed Standard gives us the thinking necessary to keep the Poodle from looking like a Bulldog or a Dachshund. That's important because type is the overall look; the picture; the outline.

Ch. BarKing's Scintilla stands as the all-time top winning Miniature Poodle in the U.S. When her ring career ended, she became one of the top-producing Miniature bitches in the nation with 14 champions so far. Scintilla was noted for her harsh, crisp coat, as well as her femininity, exquisite head and eye and her overall balance, which she maintained even as she moved around the ring. Bred by Kathy Poe and J. and S. Rowe, she was owned during her campaign by Dorothy Hageman, John Long and Chris Zaima.

The top-winning Toy Poodle in 1978 was Ch. Mari A Spring Storm, bred by Jaye Klein and owned by Patricia Averill. "Stormy," a multiple Best In Show winner was Best of Breed at PCA National in 1979 and won the PCA Regional in Chicago in 1978. She was sired by Ch. Syntifny Piece of the Rock X Grovenor-Jate's Tempest Storm.

Am. Jap. Ch. DeLorch's It's My turn provides the Toy example of correct carriage with reach and drive making up the picture desired when viewing side movement. "Winston" was the top-winning Toy Poodle in Japan in 1989 and 1990. He was sired by Ch. De-Lorch Love Me Tender, the sire of 40 champions throughout the world.

Ch. Hello Again of Sheleen demonstrates the reach, drive and collection desired in the Miniature Poodle on the move. She was bred and owned by Sheldon and Eileen Price. "Crystal" had a string of Best In Show and Best of Breed wins before beginning a successful producing career. To date she has produced three champions.

THE STARTING POINT

Getting a notion of the overall look of the Poodle is without question the starting point. In fact, many of our renowned Poodle judges counsel new Poodle judges to make their first ''cut'' on the basis of outline (again, that's general appearance or type) while the dogs are standing. Once that cut is made, judges are encouraged to move to the details: soundness,

Ch. Dassin Margarita demonstrates both the correct reach, drive and the carriage desired in a Standard poodle when moving. She was bred by Dassin Farms and owned by Mrs. Edward L. Solomon, Jr. She won multiple Best In Show and PCA Regionals in 1989 and 1990.

carriage, movement, shoulder structure, head and the rest of the pieces and parts that make up the Poodle.

Once you've sorted out the dogs in a class with the right outline, whatever follows will assure that you end up with a class winner that looks as much like a Poodle as the entries in the class permit. But if you don't make that selection first, you can easily end up making decisions on soundness, carriage, head and all the rest on a dog that doesn't look like a Poodle.

Remember the differences between the ideal beef cow and ideal dairy cow. Both are correct in type as their breed organizations define type. And so it is with the Poodle portrayed by the breed Standard. It defines through words and illustrations the ideal type for the Poodle.

The starting point for any Poodle owner intent on seriously developing a breeding program is to gain an appreciation of ideal type. Look at Poodles in all three varieties. Look at photographs. And keep in mind that type refers to the overall look—the outline.

A Poodle of exquisite type may have bad feet, a plain head, move incorrectly behind or be trimmed in an ineffective manner. It may be an eight- or ten-inch Toy; a twelve- or fifteen-inch Miniature; an eighteen- or twenty-six-inch Standard. A long-bodied, short-legged Poodle—trimmed to the nines—may move soundly, have an exquisite head and stand on impeccable feet. But it doesn't have type.

Evaluating animals—*for both the judge in the ring and the breeder outside the ring*—involves an entire world of compromises. The most typey dogs may not be the soundest or have the most correct movement. Those that are lacking in type may be very sound and move correctly.

The breed's most recent Best In Show winner at the Westminster Kennel Club is Ch. Whisperwind On A Carousel, bred by Linda Blackie and Penny Harney and owned by Dr. and Mrs. Frederick Hartsock. He is quickly joining the ranks of top-producing sires with 15 champions to date.

Judges and breeders alike must wrestle with those situations, compromise and make a choice. And until classes are filled with perfect Poodles, that is the way it will be.

The process begins to make a great deal more sense both in the ring and out when judges and breeders alike have as clear an appreciation of Poodle type as possible, then use it to make the first judgment as they sort or cut a class. But if you find yourself going to the ring and zeroing in on this head, those feet and the movement of that hindquarter, you are likely to keep yourself from formulating a concept of type as quickly as might otherwise be possible.

Type is the overall look . . . outline . . . general appearance . . . make and shape or whatever you want to call it.

It is also the essence of the Poodle.

3

Type: The Pieces
and Parts

HOPEFULLY, the previous chapter has helped you formulate an overall understanding of type. That is the starting point. But without question, once you've established an overall appreciation of Poodle type, you'll find there is still a world of variation that requires you to deal with the pieces and parts of an individual. Probably the place where most people focus efforts on evaluating the Poodle is the head, so let's start there.

THE HEAD

You'll find that all kinds of people prefer all kinds of heads on the Poodle. Some of the dear little Toys that dominate their owners and households are dearly loved because owners think the cute little stubby heads with those big, round eyes are just "so cute." On the other hand, some breeders get so carried away with the concept of breeding a long, lean head that they have created little pockets of Poodle populations with long, sharky heads and sinister expressions. Neither is correct, and both are offensive to studious breeders who have an eye on the description of head as provided by the Illustrated Breed Standard.

The illustrations provided by the Illustrated Breed Standard provide

This lovely headstudy of Ch. Wycliffe Virgil, by Gary H. Kokes, depicts the finish of chin and tremendous chiseling so desired in the Poodle head and dignity as called for in the breed Standard. Virgil, shown in the early sixties, was a multiple Best In Show winner, and the sire of 44 champions. He was important in establishing owner Joan Schilke's Koronet Kennel and was the sire of Ch. Jocelyne Marjorie, a foundation bitch in the Dassin breeding program.

excellent insight to the overall make and shape of the desired Poodle head—as well as showing some of the common problems or variations from desired type that frequently surface.

You may have already heard that the Poodle head should be "long and lean." And, indeed, the breed Standard does contain language that embraces that concept. But it does not say the head should be long or that the head should be lean.

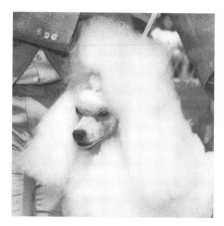

Ch. Syntifny Trinidad depicts a most attractive male Toy head with lovely expression, eye shape and color, pigmentation and finish of chin. He was bred by Pat McMullen and Jane Winne and owned by Halcyon Kennels.

Regarding *length*, the section on skull says, "length from occiput to stop about the same length of muzzle." And the section on muzzle calls for it to be "long, straight and fine." So yes, the muzzle should be "long," but only as long as the distance from the occiput to the stop. That's different from being "as long as possible." Regarding *lean*, the Standard says the skull should have cheekbones and muscles flat—rather than curved or bulging. It also asks for the muzzle to be fine. Both of those indications suggest a concept of leanness. But again, lean enough is lean enough, and just as the illustrations show the correct front and side view of the head, they also show heads too broad and heavy and those too narrow.

Most breeders agree that the longer and leaner the head, the greater the chance of losing the stop, the chiseling and the nice finish of chin that sets off the Poodle head. The muzzle that is too long and lean quickly becomes snipey. Breeders will also tell you that as you breed for long, lean heads—and are successful—you will find that the dogs those heads belong to will begin to take on a make and shape that may deviate more from what the breed Standard calls for than you are willing to accept.

The long, lean-headed Poodles often have a long neck *and* a longer back than most prefer. They also tend to be slabsided with shelly bodies, and frequently lack the ribbing that the Standard calls for. Frequently, they stand on thin feet with longer toes than most breeders can stand.

So the challenge to each breeder, old and new, is to interpret the breed Standard section on heads and to understand it as best they can. Based on what they think, they will logically select for that type of head as they develop their own breeding program.

While breeders often tend to discuss heads in terms of things you can see, stop, finish of chin, eye shape and color, for example, not one

Ch. Aizbel The Aristocrat, multiple Best In Show and a PCA National Best of Breed winner, depicts much that is sought after in the male Miniature head. Notice the slightly scissored effect on the topknot and how it is worn forward and carefully fashioned to frame the face. "Ari" was bred by Arlene McKernan and owned by Luis and Mary Jo Aizcorbe. He was sired by Ch. Aizbel The One and Only X Ch. Aizbel The Impetuous, a daughter of Ch. Aizbel All About Angels. He produced 28 champions.

of them would fail to mention the importance of "**expression**." To me, expression is the look a Poodle has resulting from the interrelationships of all the parts of the Poodle head. It is the Poodle's expression that communicates intelligence, warmth, love and devilishness. It is difficult to define—not unlike the print you want above your couch: "I don't know what I'm looking for, but I'll know it when I see it!"

Multiple Best In Show winner, Ch. Graphic Helvetica, depicts the lovely expression and finish of chin so desired.

The head is obviously an important part of the Poodle. But it is only a part worth twenty points on the scorecard. *A common mistake among less experienced Poodle breeders is to pay too much attention to the head.* Some even select individual dogs solely on the basis of heads. When you feel you're going overboard on one point or another, go back to the breed Standard and scale of points. You can find your way back to more acceptable lines of thinking every time.

THE FOREQUARTERS

If the head is the first part of the Poodle to which newer breeders turn, the forequarters are probably the last. In fact, some breeders frustrated by it all sometimes say, "if the toes point forward and it moves okay, the front is okay with me." Admittedly, in show trim, the Poodle wears the forequarters well covered by hair. For many, that makes the entire assembly difficult to understand.

If you are willing to get into the hair, the correct construction of the shoulder assembly (or forequarters) is fairly easy to assess. Just turn to the breed Standard and take it one point at a time.

1. "The shoulder blade is well laid back and approximately the same length as the upper foreleg."

If you know what the shoulder blade is—and the upper foreleg—you're well on the way to a good understanding. If you don't, look at the illustration on the Anatomy of the Poodle. Both parts are indicated.

What is meant by "well laid back"? Look at *the point of the shoulder*—the point where the shoulder blade and the upper foreleg come together. From that *point*, the shoulder blade should be "laid back" or slanted toward the back of the dog, so that a line extended from its tip through the point where the shoulder blade and upper foreleg touch and

Ch. Poco A Poco Uptown Girl won Best of Breed at the Poodle Club of the Lehigh Valley. Note the expressive head and eye, down to the straight front legs and tightly knit feet. Her well-constructed front assembly is placed well back so that her front legs are under her withers. She is sired by Ch. Wissfire Knock On Wood X Ch. Poco A Poco Girl Next Door. Gayle Roberson is her breeder-owner.

Ch. Campbell's Raz-Ma-Tazz remains the all-time leading brown Miniature sire with 39 champions. He was owned by Mrs. James Cutler and later co-owned by handler, Peggy Hogg. Raz was a multiple BIS and Specialty BOB winner, and founded several key families of dogs that remain vital in Miniature pedigrees today. His top-winning offspring was the black bitch, Ch. Cutler's Ebony Wysteria.

continuing on in a straight line to the ground, would make a 45-degree angle.

Look at the illustration on Anatomy from the Illustrated Breed Standard, and the 45-degree angle should make sense to you.

2. *"The elbow is directly below the highest point of the shoulder."*

You'll understand this best if you put a dog on the table and get a yardstick. Stand your Poodle in a normal show pose with the front legs

Ch. Fairview's No Nonsense was a top-winning Toy in the mid-eighties for owner Joan Hartsock. In addition to many Best In Show wins, "Nosey" won the Variety at the PCA National in 1985 and at the Regional in 1984, as well as the Toy Group at Westminster Kennel Club. She was sired by Ch. Hells A Blazen Carnival Fame X Syntifny Men Prefer Haynes. She was bred by Janie S. Conyers and has produced two champions.

perpendicular—not stretched out or scrunched together. Place the yardstick at the heel of the front foot and then against the point of the elbow. On a well-constructed Poodle, the yardstick should be perpendicular to the ground at this point, and you should find the highest point of the shoulder (the withers) also lines up with the yardstick.

When you can do that with a Poodle, you know that you are dealing with a dog that has a well-constructed shoulder—and that the shoulder is correctly placed on the dog.

Return with me to your high school geometry class, and we'll clarify the shoulder construction point. If you draw a line connecting the highest point of the shoulder down to the lower end of the upper foreleg, you have constructed a triangle—one where two sides are equal, and the three angles resulting are 90 degrees, 45 degrees and 45 degrees.

Ideally, the line you drew, extended to the ground, will run past the point of the elbow and past the heel of the foot to form a 90-degree angle when it meets the ground. And as indicated earlier, a line drawn from the *highest* point of the shoulder, that is, the *withers*, through the point of the shoulder and on to the ground should form a 45-degree angle. Enough geometry.

Understanding shoulder construction really is a fairly straightforward matter when viewed in those terms. However, more than structure is involved in having the shoulder function correctly. The shoulder is not tied bone-to-bone to the spinal column or rib cage. In fact, it is held in place by the network of muscles that tie the shoulder on to the body. So obviously, the extent to which those muscles are developed also helps determine how a correctly constructed shoulder will function.

Frequently you will find a sloppy, loose-moving front on a Poodle that seems to have a correctly constructed shoulder. That may be caused by the dog's lack of exercise. The race to grow hair on the Poodle—and keep it—has led many breeders to keep dogs confined, especially in inclement weather. That may help grow hair, but it does nothing to enhance the athletic ability of the Poodle and the development of muscle. And one of the negative side effects is loose and ineffective movement even when structure is correct.

THE HINDQUARTERS

Again, the Illustrated Breed Standard does an excellent job of helping us to understand how the hindquarters should be constructed. The only point that seems to need further discussion focuses on the difference between ''correct'' angulation and ''over'' angulation.

I suspect that if you asked thirty Poodle people, either well-established or just starting, to draw the correct hindquarters on a Poodle, more than twenty of them would draw a Poodle that is overangulated. Just as many breeders seek heads that are too long and too lean, there is also a tendency to select hindquarters that are too angulated. And if you watch Poodles in the ring, you will frequently find whoever is showing them

Am. Can. Bda. Ch. Dawin Banner Waver, owned by Linda Dawick Campbell. Even with many Bests in Show and Specialty Bests of Breed, his record was most impressive at the Poodle Club of America National. In 1988 he was Winners Dog and received an Award of Merit, which he repeated in 1989. In 1990 and 1991 he was Best of Opposite Sex to Best of Breed, and in his final appearance was again an Award of Merit winner. Banner was sired by Am. Can. Bda. Ch. Terima The Moor X Pamala's Darling Lil. He has sired 14 American champions.

stretching the hind legs back—just a touch farther than they really need to go.

The breed Standard makes it clear: "When standing, the rear toes are only slightly behind the point of the rump." It is as simple as that. You may personally prefer more angulation (or less), but it would then vary from what is asked for in the breed Standard

Ch. Aizbel The Knockout, from a full brother-sister breeding (Ch. Aizbel Headstudy In Black to Ch. Aizbel All About Angels) was an all-breed BIS and Specialty BOB winner with a Variety win at Westminster Kennel Club, all owner-handled. "K O" sired 13 champions. His trim is another model for students to study. Notice how, when correctly done and the front of the mane is correctly tailored, there is no reason for the English Saddle to make a dog look longer. The inset headstudy shows his lovely expression and finish of underjaw. Aizcorbe dogs have a reputation for producing attractive heads. He was bred and owned by Luis and Mary Jo Aizcorbe.

Strive for a Match of Angles.

The Standard asks for the femur and tibia to be about equal in length, and it also states that the angulation of the hindquarters balances that of the forequarters. That leads us to look at the angle formed by tracing a line from the point of the rump to the stifle and from the stifle to the hock joint.

In the forequarters, we asked for the angle formed by the line from the withers to the point of the shoulder and then to the elbow to form a 90-degree angle. And we asked that the line from the highest point of the shoulder blade to the point of the shoulder and extended on to the ground form a a 45-degree angle with the ground.

A match in the hindquarter, then, would ask that the angle from the point of the rump to the stifle and the stifle to the hock joint be 90 degrees. A line from the point of the rump to the stifle and extended on to the ground should form a 45-degree angle with the ground. That's a perfect match—but one difficult to obtain. And many breeders and handlers feel that the harder you work to achieve those 45-degree angles, the more difficulty you will have maintaining the balance and proportion you want: a squarely built Poodle.

Or put another way, get the angles right and the dog is a shade too long bodied; get the proportion correct, and the angles create a shoulder that is too steep and a hindquarter that is too straight. Once again, you are face-to-face with the kinds of compromises that judges face every time they enter the ring.

Once you have a good grasp of the breed Standard in mind, you are on secure ground, and you will establish your own priorities as you develop your own breeding program and select animals to be part of it.

While it is possible to delve into each section of the breed Standard, that isn't being done here. Instead, I have chosen to focus on the head, the forequarters and the hindquarters only because they are so important to the essence of the Poodle, and because they seem the three areas that are either most misunderstood, most overlooked or most subject to faddish thinking that frequently comes into play as breeders work at the continuing task of interpreting the breed Standard of this great breed.

4

I Only Want to
Buy a Puppy

I HAVE A HUNCH that somewhere in the book-reading public there are a number of people who have in one way or another had some association with a Poodle, and based largely on that association, have come to this book with the hope that they will get help in buying a puppy.

Don't worry about whether you want to raise a litter, become a breeder or join in the excitement of showing your dog in either conformation or Obedience competition. You are an important ingredient in the world of Poodle breeding. Far more Poodles are sold each year as pets than as breeding or show prospects. With a little study and homework—and a good dash of self-analysis—you can gather a considerable amount of information that will help you make your decision. Don't be embarrassed about your lack of knowledge. That is a correctable condition, and throughout the Poodle fancy—even among our most esteemed breeders—there are people who purchased their first Poodle with little or no knowledge. I'm one of them.

My first Poodle was a silver Toy bitch who enriched our lives for more than twelve years and triggered the interest in becoming a more active participant in the Poodle world. Even if that hadn't happened, she would still rank as one of the most satisfying dogs I've ever owned. She wasn't good enough to show, even I knew it.

She's been gone for more than fifteen years now, and I can still visualize the expression in her face . . . see her toss her head to tell me it was bedtime . . . see her come with her nose in the air for her special treat, a gentle chin-scratching.

I think I know the dog you are seeking.

WHICH VARIETY WILL SUIT YOU BEST?

If you live alone or if your living situation suggests an all-adult household for the next fifteen to eighteen years, base your choice on your personal preference. Any one of the three varieties can work for you. If you live with small children or see them in your future, it might be wise to choose other than the Toy. Children shouldn't be counted on to handle a Toy dog safely, and the two larger varieties are best able to withstand the roughhousing that children offer and survive the accidents that happen with less consequence. If you know the children involved, you may still have reasons to choose the Toy. Quiet, proven-responsible youngsters

Kids and puppies are good for each other. These white Toy puppies have had their first shots and enjoy a gentle play session. What looks like fun, as it happens, is often part of the socialization process that is important to all puppies whether they achieve success in the home as pets or in the ring.

really are capable of dealing with Toys. Toys aren't fragile. But the larger varieties can withstand the wide range of activities that children present.

If your household might include senior citizens who are somewhat unstable on their feet, the Standard might not be a wise choice. They are big dogs and everything they do (especially the puppies) they're apt to do in a big way. If you really prefer a Standard, consider looking for a young adult rather than a puppy. They pass through the raucous stage at twelve to eighteen months, and the Standard can be one of the most stable companions anyone could ever choose.

Your physical facilities may influence your variety of choice as well. Standards are big dogs. Some do well in an apartment situation, but it may require more effort on your part to provide the amount of exercise a Standard needs. So to a certain extent, your lifestyle is an influencing factor. If your house or apartment is vacant during the entire workday, and if you frequently have evening commitments, the Standard may need more time and exercise than you can provide.

Nobody can or should make the choice for you. But you'll need to balance your personal preference against the cautions mentioned. With a little extra effort, you can make any variety work with people of any age. But be aware of the cautions and make an informed, well-thought-out decision.

WHAT COLOR DO YOU PREFER?

I can lose my heart to any color. But what really happens is that as the dog and I begin to interact, color is no longer what is important. That doesn't mean that you shouldn't have a preference and seek to fulfill it. Generally, blacks and whites are the most available. Browns, apricots, reds, silvers and the others are more difficult to come by, but we'll talk about some strategies to locate those less frequently seen colors.

Personal preference should rate high. Availability may be a factor. But other than the fact that browns have a reputation as the clowns of the Poodle world, there is not a lot of counsel to consider.

One additional point related to color does need to be made. Browns, apricots and reds are born dark, rich colors, and, in general, they fade considerably as they age. Silvers are generally born black and their "fading" is called clearing to silver. If you are interested in a Poodle puppy of one of these colors, be aware that they only rarely stay the same color as they are at eight to twelve weeks. Ask to see an adult of the same color to learn what the dog is apt to look like during most of its adult life.

WILL IT BE MALE OR FEMALE?

Again, this is largely a personal choice. Some lifelong Poodle owners "only live with the boys." Others swear by the girls.

If it hasn't occurred to you yet, be aware that basic biology may be a factor worth considering in making your choice. Bitches will come in season at least twice a year unless they are spayed. For about a two-week period their cleanliness is totally dependent upon their willingness to clean themselves. Many are very good at it; others aren't. When the rush of hormones hits the boys, they will invariably develop a fondness for the leg of your most esteemed houseguest, and there's nothing more embarrassing. Discipline will be essential.

Neutering, like spaying, solves all these problems in a more lasting manner. Spaying and neutering are highly recommended practices for any dog that will not be bred or shown in conformation. Being responsible for members of an unwanted litter is not one of the joys of dog ownership.

YOUR POODLE'S PURPOSE

What do you want the dog to be? If your answer is without question a "pet," you need to follow one line of thinking. If you are looking for a dog to show in conformation or Obedience competition or to breed, you better dig into the other chapters of this book. You'll find help in gaining the answers, but it won't be compressed into one chapter.

If you can make the decisions we've talked about so far—variety, color and sex—you've simplified your information-gathering task considerably. You can now say, "I am looking for a brown Miniature female for a pet." And that's fairly specific.

One point needs clarification. Purchasers of pets and dog breeders don't always understand and agree on what the word "P-E-T" means. To the first-time buyer, a pet would be a dog they intend to live with and love. If they decide to breed or show her, that is fine, too. When the established and reputable breeder hears the word "pet" it means a dog that will not be bred *or* shown in conformation classes. It will be a companion dog and might be shown in obedience competition. Remember that when you get to the point where you talk with breeders. If you *might* show or you *might* breed her . . . say so.

That will cause the breeder to ask some questions and steer you toward another kind of animal with that potential. If you say "pet," the breeder will show you animals which in his or her opinion are not suitable for breeding stock and do not have show potential.

HOW WILL YOU FIND WHAT YOU ARE
LOOKING FOR?

Many people head for the want-ad section of their local newspaper or to a pet shop where they have watched cute puppies sleep and play in the windows. Those two options aren't the safest places to gather the information that you need to make knowledgeable decisions. You can do better.

If you turn to the newspapers, look for a "breeders referral" advertisement placed by the local kennel club. The purpose of such an advertisement is to help match up pet buyers and established breeders. If the kennel club does not have a Poodle breeder among its membership, they'll tell you. But they'll also begin their detective work to locate a source of brown Miniatures, for example, within the nearby area.

Why a breeder? Breeders by and large have a more responsible approach to breeding dogs than the run-of-the-mill want ad will produce. Because pet shops buy what they sell, rather than raise it, their information sources and breed specific knowledge are fairly limited as well. If you answer a want ad, you may discover that you're dealing with somebody who was in your exact position a year ago. They bought a puppy. They bred her to a dog in the neighborhood, and their entire knowledge base rests on that one dog and what they did to produce that litter. The pet shop salesperson may be no more than a young person who has always liked dogs. They can tell you what the paperwork says—details provided on the American Kennel Club (AKC) certificate and information provided on the health papers accompanying the dog when they received it. That will be the extent of the information they have.

A breeder will frequently know several generations of the pedigree. You should ask to see the dam and at least a picture of the sire, although they may own both. Breeders will volunteer information they have on heritable diseases affecting the Poodle. If that panics you, don't let it. Each breed has a set of health-related problems, but then so does the puppy you get from the pound. Breeders are more likely to know these and talk about them to help you understand.

In case they don't, ask. Acquaint yourself with the last chapter of this book. It focuses entirely on such factors, and you should certainly ask the status of the puppies you're considering and their immediate family members. As you delve into such matters, understand that you are dealing with probability, not absolute facts. Here's why. Consider canine hip dysplasia, a condition to guard against when considering Miniatures and Standards. Even preliminary tests aren't generally done until puppies are about ten months old. If you are looking at a ten-week-old puppy,

Hats and balloons and a special friend helped make the 15th birthday special for Ch. Bel Tor Blissful and a group of her children and grandchildren. The Poodles, Bliss's owners, Dr. Samuel and Mary Peacock, and the other owners had a marvelous time.

you can gather information about the sire, the dam and other ancestors, but there can be no guarantee. If the breeder doesn't volunteer such information, arm yourself with some notes from the last chapter here, and begin asking questions.

That approach won't work at many pet shops and it won't work for those people who only raise a litter now and then for whatever reason. They may be good, well-intentioned people. That doesn't make them knowledgeable.

MAKING A CHOICE

Breeders will also help you assess the temperament of the individual puppies you are considering, and seeing their sires and dams may help you judge which puppy will best fit into your living situation.

You typically will want to steer away from the shy, frightened puppy who doesn't quite seem to have a grasp on what life has to offer. And often, it is the most inquisitive and outgoing puppy that attracts attention. That's probably the puppy to choose if your living situation is such that you want an up-front, well-adjusted dog that can walk into a wide range of situations and deal with them in a straightforward manner.

If you are an older person—or if you have a shy, quiet child in the family—the up-front dog may not be the choice for you. Often, after the most inquisitive puppies have stepped forward and demanded their attention, you'll notice a quiet, more studious type of puppy who is not shy or fearful, but is just thinking through the new situation you represent. After the "up-front" group has had attention, the more studious puppy will come forward. Watch the play pattern. This pup is often far less demanding and rambunctious than its littermates and can be quite suited to people who are older or more quiet.

Sometimes, seeing the sire and dam is helpful, and it is always interesting. Breeders can most often show you the puppies' mother. Sometimes they also own the father, but chances are greater that he is owned by another breeder. Watch how they approach you and how quickly they settle down once you've been introduced. Watch how they play and interact with the litter. That can often provide some revealing clues about how the puppies will behave as adults.

HOW DO YOU FIND POODLE BREEDERS?

A local kennel club's breeder referral advertisement is often a good starting point. And the people who agree to take those calls are generally people who really are willing to go the extra mile to help you find what you want. So don't hesitate to rely on it if you find one in your local newspaper. But you have other options—if you don't need your puppy by the weekend.

Dog shows are a good place to start. You probably won't go to a dog show and come home with a puppy, but you will learn who in your geographic area is breeding dogs, and if you play your cards correctly you'll get to talk to some of them. Contact any of the organizations or the AKC to learn how to contact a local kennel club or Obedience club. Once you get that done, ask the clubs if they could provide you a list of dog shows scheduled in your area. This may take time. Most clubs host only one show a year. But if you're willing to drive a couple of hours, you'll probably find you have several choices within the next couple of months.

If a show is coming up in the near future, ask if they know anyone who will be exhibiting at that show. Then contact that person and confirm that they are entered. A week before the show, they will receive the schedule of judging. With that in hand, they can tell you exactly what time you will see each of the three varieties being judged, as well as providing you directions to the show site.

Get to the show an hour or so before the first judging is scheduled, and purchase a catalog. The dog show catalog is marvelous because it lists each dog's owner—with their address. A little detective work on the telephone will help you come up with telephone numbers if you need to follow up. Then locate the ring where Poodles will be judged, and the grooming area. Show Poodles require a lot of grooming, so you'll discover that their people spend a lot of time at the grooming area. But be aware, many exhibitors groom out of their motor homes or vans. That requires a bit more detective work.

If you find the Poodle people readying their entries in the grooming area, introduce yourself, tell them what you are looking for and ask when you might contact them later in the day. Don't try to talk about it on the spot unless they say you've chosen a good time. They're busy before judging. *Generally after judging is the best time.* If you find more breeders at ringside during judging, ask them when you might talk. During judging is usually the worst time. So, again ask when a ''good time'' might be.

Some of the dogs being exhibited will be seen in the ring with their professional handlers. The owners, sometimes not at the show, may live across the country from the show site. And some breeders travel to shows several hours from their homes. They may be too far away. But eventually, you'll find somebody within a reasonable range, or somebody will know somebody within a reasonable driving distance.

Be straightforward and honest. Tell them what you're looking for. If you want a pet, say so. *Don't say you ''might'' show a dog just to get a specific puppy.* Tell them how soon you must have it—or how long you are willing to wait. Ask them about the heritable problems related to the variety you are considering. Use them as a sounding board to assess what price you should expect to pay. If you do a bit of price shopping before you zero in on a specific puppy, you can establish a range of what breeders seem to be charging for your variety in your area, and you can do it in a positive, information-gathering manner. If you wait until a single puppy is in question, your questions may be taken in a more negative manner. You should try to gather information about prices, but you don't want to come across as cheap when you do it.

Don't be surprised if you are presented some opportunities to buy dogs a bit older than you might have expected. Many people want to buy an eight- to ten-week-old puppy. Breeders sometimes have puppies at that age, but often they want to hold them a bit longer to more carefully assess their show potential. And sometimes, they'll have a six- or eight-month-old puppy that they kept to show, but the puppy grew too large.

You'll have to assess how you feel about that. You'll miss the cute, ''fluffy puppy'' stage that makes Poodle puppies so attractive, but, at the

Almost any knowledgeable breeder would spot this as a most promising Standard puppy bitch. And indeed she was. She is now Ch. Dassin De La Rose, the dam of the Top Producing Ch. Dassin Delano and three other champions. Intensely Dassin-bred, she was bred and owned by Mrs. Edward L. Solomon.

same time, you'll be better able to visualize what your mature dog will look like for most of the rest of its life.

Many people prefer to have puppies at an early age so the puppy has the opportunity to bond with a new family, and the research suggests that really isn't a bad idea. But at the same time, puppies that have been adequately socialized at their first home and through the show routine often make the adjustment so quickly, that one month later the new puppy has totally adapted to a new living situation and works out beautifully.

It is all a matter of choice, but it may be helpful to be aware before you begin shopping that some of those opportunities may present themselves.

BRINGING THE NEW PUPPY HOME

Finally, be certain as you shop that you learn what inoculation program the breeder has followed and that the shot schedule is up-to-date. Inquire if further inoculations are needed and be certain you have a written record of what has been given and what remains. Most reputable breeders provide that information as part of their selling routine.

If you are a first-time dog owner, it might be wise to contact a veterinary hospital near your home and establish yourself as a potential client. Let them know that you are purchasing a puppy, and ask if they can provide any helpful information. Your veterinarian can advise you of the inoculation program recommended for your geographic area so you can see how breeders' programs compare. Many veterinarians provide pamphlets such as ''So You're Buying a Puppy,'' and ''Caring for Your New Puppy'' that will help you formulate your thinking during the purchasing process and will help assure that you are prepared to care for and manage the new puppy once you bring it home.

Also get your veterinarian's recommendations for the age to spay or neuter your pet. There is really no need to risk accidental breedings and having to decide how to deal with the resulting puppies. Neutering also eliminates the messiness that a female's season may present and the sexual interest that is part of any young male dog's makeup.

Once you have made your choice, you should expect the seller to provide you a registration application—either a litter registration form or the puppy's individual registration paper. Ask them to explain how it should be completed. The nominal registration fee is typically paid by the new owner. You should also ask for a pedigree. A pedigree is a graphic presentation of all of the puppy's ancestors. It is only a matter of interest if you are truly buying a pet. If you intend to breed, it is a storehouse of information that will help you make breeding decisions.

If you have purchased the puppy from a breeder, be certain you retain the name, address and telephone number. Most breeders will offer to counsel you as the transition takes place to the puppy's new home, and don't be surprised if you get a telephone call from the breeder a few days after the puppy moves in with you. Many breeders want to stay in touch just to be certain that all is going well and will want to answer your questions.

At the same time, don't be surprised if during the selection process, you find yourself answering a host of questions: Have you owned a pet before? Do you have a fenced yard or area? Do you have a crate for when the puppy travels? Have you established yourself with a veterinarian?

Reputable breeders want good homes for the puppies they sell. They are perfectly capable of turning down sales. It happens all the time. So in a sense, *as you are selecting a puppy, you are also being screened and chosen as well*. That's how it should be. As marvelous and intelligent as Poodles are, they are still dependent upon people to take care of them. Good breeders take care that the shifting of responsibility rests on shoulders of people who will care.

Typically, when we think of the Poodle in art, we think back to another era. But, in fact, the creativity with which modern photographers present current dogs relies heavily on an artistic approach. Here Ch. Valhalla's Jacquelyn stands out against the simple pattern created by the background of the photograph.

5

Grooming: Before You Pick Up the Scissors

WE ALL SWOON when we walk to the ring and see a group of Poodles of any size or color groomed to the nines and looking smart. And you can be at a park or a shopping mall and have exactly the same reaction when you spot a Poodle owner walking a pet in a smartly fashioned pet trim.

Somehow, we always assume that there is a bit of wizardry involved—something magic that we couldn't possibly accomplish. Granted, our top groomers—both those grooming for the ring and those grooming pets as their business—have a real talent. Grooming is a bit of an art, and some of us may never become as accomplished as the pacesetters.

All of the top trimmers and groomers have one thing in common. They know how to manage and work with *hair* so that they have it in the best possible condition when they pick up the scissors and begin to trim. Much of that procedure is such that you can be every bit as accomplished as those you envy. It starts with having hair to work with.

BUSHELS OF HAIR IS THE START OF IT ALL

Everyone who has ever presented a string of Poodles in good hair, no doubt has had beginner after beginner come up and ask, "How can I grow hair like that on my dog?'' I was always tempted to say "Keep it clean and keep it brushed, and your dog's hair will grow.'' That approach will work on about 80 percent of the dogs you work with—regardless of how you do it. But that answer really isn't helpful to new people or people having difficulty, so let's delve a little deeper into the topic.

Dirty hair generally mats more and breaks more easily than clean hair. That's the primary reason why most handlers and breeders today follow a fairly frequent bathing schedule, especially if dogs aren't kept in oil between shows or during the conditioning period.

There's another school of thought that exists in the minds of a select group of more seasoned exhibitors who really appreciate good quality hair—the harsh, good-textured coats that you see rather infrequently today. But again, the Poodle introduces each of us to a world of compromises. And most exhibitors today have opted to give up a bit of hair quality and have sought practices that help assure that hair grows as quickly as possible. That doesn't mean that they don't still appreciate a good coat when they see one—and certain stud dogs and families are incorporated into some breeding programs primarily because "we need that kind of hair.''

But in most camps, people don't worry about managing hair for the quality of texture. In some cases, excellent hair *quality* seems relatively unappreciated, by both breeders and judges.

So, let's get on with the more modern approach, but be prepared: If it's crisp, harsh, good-textured hair you're after, this approach probably *won't* get it.

THE BATH

Several years ago we moved, and as I began packing up the trimming and bathing room, I discarded far more than I kept. Most of what went was a hot tip that somebody had given me or a special potion that I discovered on my own. And all of them promised to make the task of bathing a dog so much easier. None of them worked like magic—and all of them worked.

As a matter of fact, there's only one product I've used consistently since 1965 when I started showing: Lux dishwashing liquid. It cleans, and it rinses out fairly easily if you use it rather sparingly. Now if I have a special problem—an itchy dog, fleas or a sensitive eye, for example— I turn to something else that might solve that problem. I'm not saying you have to use Lux. Use what you've had success with. But don't hold your breath waiting for any product to create miracles. It probably won't happen.

With Lux, I like to fill my tub with water—just deep enough to cover the dog when lying on its side. Stir in enough detergent or shampoo to get moderate suds. Put the dog in the tub, on its side with the head out of the water. Protect the eyes and ears (as your veterinarian suggests) and then gently pour the sudsy water through the coat.

Turn the dog over and do the same for the other side. And then work the sudsy water into the topknot and ears, taking care to keep water out of the eyes and ears.

When you're convinced the coat is really clean, *rinse, rinse, rinse and rinse some more* until you're convinced all of the suds are out of the coat. Now, just for good measure, repeat the process one more time.

THE CONDITIONING

If you're bathing for a show, use a conditioning creme rinse—one that isn't too heavy and doesn't leave the coat too oily. If what you use is too oily, either dilute the concentrate you use or switch to another product. Generally, the directions for use will tell you to rinse the dog thoroughly after using the conditioner. If you don't, the hair will be gummy or oily.

Some conditioners are designed to be left in the coat. If you're using one of that type, read the directions carefully and do what they say.

If you're bathing a dog that isn't headed toward the ring, follow the shampoo with a heavier conditioner or a light oil. If you're using a dog product, you can most often rely on the directions provided. If you're using human hair products, you can start with the directions, but you may have to do a bit of adjusting.

THE DRYING

Unfortunately, there's no single best way to do this job, either. But if you follow this procedure (and I'll point out some variables) you'll come fairly close to getting the results you want.

1. Towel-dry the dog, allow it to shake a few times, towel-dry again, and especially sop up the belly hair and the puffs. Remember, water tends to run downhill, so check legs and belly for water that runs to those spots.

   You may choose to cut your drying time by doing as many handlers and others who have full strings of dogs do: Put the dog out in a clean exercise pen where they can air-dry a bit as you get ready to use the dryer. That practice works, and it does save time. But you may find you have to dampen some parts of the coat as you go through the drying process because air-dried hair dries curly. That's generally the opposite of what you want to happen.

2. Set your dryer on medium heat and air. Hot or high dryer settings will speed the drying process. But again, you have less opportunity to brush the hair straight as you dry it when you operate your dryer on hot, high air-flow settings.

    If you choose to turn everything to the highest settings, you'll have to use a spritzer bottle to dampen the coat as it dries so you can get it brushed straight. You can also cover parts of the dog with a damp towel to prevent drying where you don't want the dog to dry.

3. Now, have the dog lie on the left side, the judge's side. I always dry that side last because that's the side the judge will spend the most time looking at.

You can start with any part of the coat you want—and we've all got different ways of doing it. But as the coat dries, you should be brushing it in the same direction—or in the same way—you will brush the dog just before it goes into the show ring.

I always start with the center neck hair and brush it up (toward the top of the dog) and forward. I dry a section and then move either down the side or back toward the tail—one section at a time.

Once I'm convinced the hair is dry and move to a new section, I check back on what I've finished. If it starts to curl near the skin—or if it has a different sheen than the tips of the hair—I assume it isn't dry and go back and do that section again.

If I've failed to get all the oil out of the coat, I spot the problem—and then it's back to the tub: detergent, shampoo, creme rinse, the whole bit. Leaving oil in a coat is one mistake I try never to make.

Puffs, rosettes and the pack have shorter hair than the body coat, so they dry quicker. I try not to let them get dry without a thorough brushing with a slicker brush. If that hair does get dry too early, use the spritzer brush and dampen it. Pay attention to the chest hair. It almost never wants to straighten. Frequently you will need to dampen that area before you begin drying it.

Always recheck that each section of the coat is totally dry. It will curl if it isn't totally dry. You can note a different sheen peculiar only to wet hair. Be particularly curious about the hard-to-dry places—under the front legs and inside the ear, right at the base. Get them totally dry. When you're 100 percent certain the dog is dry, again put it on its left side and begin brushing it as you would for a show. But use your eyes. You may find a damp spot here and there. If so, dry it.

If you use a texturizer, try misting just a small amount into the coat during the final brushing. It helps keep some coats from curling as the hours go by.

Keep your hands off the coat as much as possible until you're finished trimming and showing the dog. Your hands have oil on them and the coat will absorb those oils and begin to wave or curl. Also be careful not to subject the dog to weather conditions that will cause the coat to pick up moisture and curl. Obviously, if it is raining or snowing, you'll

Ch. Argosy Alucard Dracula, a Specialty Best of Breed and multiple Group winner is also the sire of seven champions. But Dracula is best known throughout the nation for his exuberant appearances in the Veterans classes at the National PCA show. He has made 12 *consecutive* PCA appearances. In his most recent at the 1993 show he earned an Award of Merit. He is sired by Ch. Penchant Pinkerton X Ch. Argosy Auspicious. He was bred by Charles Black and Hilayne Cavanaugh and is owned by his only handler, Patti Proctor.

do far better to set up an exercise pen inside. But the same is true on damp evenings when there is a heavy dew. Just a few minutes out in that kind of weather will cause many coats to begin curling.

Now you've got hair to work with. It's clean, freshly brushed and ready to trim. We'll get to that in the next chapter, but let's add a few thoughts about keeping that freshly bathed coat looking fresh through the entire show weekend.

REVITALIZING—ON THE SPOT

Most of us have resolved to carry a dryer with us to the shows. Some even carry generators to assure a power supply is always available. Whenever the coat begins to look a little worse for wear, just get the dryer going and use a spritzer bottle with either plain water or a weak dilution of a conditioner. Sometimes just blow-drying will refreshen a coat. Sometimes the spritzer is needed. The spritzer is especially effective on ears. Just wet them thoroughly, towel them dry and then use the dryer.

A number of professionals use the same practice to straighten the puffs and rosettes in a Continental trim—or the entire pack on an English Saddle. You can even work a bit of mousse into thin, stringy puffs to add fullness and make them easier to scissor.

But be prepared: Mousse attracts dirt, so you may have to bathe the areas where you use it at least once during the weekend. And dogs that are shown in the Groups as well as the Variety may need it more often.

If curly coats are a special problem for you, there's one final suggestion. Get acquainted with somebody who shows apricot Toys or Miniatures and does a good job of bringing dogs to the ring with straight, fresh-looking coats. Those coats tend to curl more than any others, so if you can find someone who is successful with them, you've found the right brain to pick about products used and procedures that may help you.

Part of the fun of showing the Poodle is exploring new products and creating your own. Don't be robbed of that fun. But at the same time, learning how someone successfully deals with a problem is also a good idea and it may save you time. As your experience grows, you'll probably find you do a little of both.

6

The Puppy Trim

WE'RE ABOUT READY to pick up the scissors and clippers, but before that happens, let's be certain we've got one thing clearly in mind. You need a picture of the ideal Poodle as you interpret the breed Standard, in puppy trim. It can be a mental picture or one from a magazine, but every step of the way, our trimming will focus on emphasizing the strong points *your* dog has—as *your* dog conforms to the breed Standard—and deemphasizing the weak points of your dog.

You also need an honest understanding of the strengths and weaknesses of your puppy. Unless you can come up with such an assessment, you are only fooling yourself and you'll never trim the dog to emphasize good points and compensate for problems.

It will also be helpful if you study puppies at shows and photographs of dogs in puppy trims. Both will help you formulate the overall picture that appeals most to you. And you will discover—if you haven't already—that there is considerable variation in the trims that puppies wear into the ring.

There's one additional element of the puppy trim that you should stay alert to. Puppies change a lot during the six months they are in puppy trim. They grow throughout that period and they grow a lot of hair. That means you really have to rethink your trim every two or three weeks. In fact, it is like trimming a different dog each time you do it.

But once you have an honest assessment of the strengths and weaknesses of your puppy and a clear idea of how you want your trim to look,

Few things are more appealing than a silver puppy in any variety. Generally born black, silvers retain the dark color on the ear tips and the topknot longer than on the rest of the body. This Miniature, Bayou Breeze Silver Plume, bred by Henry Cohen and owned by Dorothy Hageman, is in the clearing process with the legs already the clear, pale silver so highly desired. At maturity, Plume was the same clear color even on the topknot and ears.

you are about ready to start. There's just one additional point. If you are going to trim this puppy for the puppy classes, do it the way it needs to be done and forget about when the puppy will be a year old and wear an adult trim. *"Saving hair" for an adult trim almost always assures that the puppy trim will be wrong.*

It boils down to this. You can have it one way or the other—a puppy trim or an adult trim at twelve months. You almost can never have both. Don't even try.

LET'S START

Get a good feeling for how much hair you have to work with. Six-month-old babies simply don't have a lot of topknot and neck hair. So you aren't going to get a lot of "build" on the front of them to create neck and emphasize elegance as you can with a ten- to twelve-month-old puppy.

That means you are going to have to scale down the amount of hair on the sides, legs and ahead of the tail (forward over the loin area) so that the trim "fits" the amount of topknot and neck hair the puppy has. If you don't, you'll destroy the puppy's balance and overall picture. The puppy will appear to have less topknot and neck hair and less neck than she really has.

Learning this takes a practiced eye, but you really do need to learn to let the amount of topknot and neck hair "set the pace" for the amount of hair you'll leave in other places. And learn to do that on babies. That turns out to be the trick you need to beat the "new-dog-every-time-I-trim-it" syndrome. As the hair on the topknot and over the neck grows during the six-month period, you need to let the hair on the sides and legs "grow" with it.

The hair on the belly will probably stay about the same length during the entire period. If it doesn't, you'll find your puppy's legs are growing shorter as the months go by, and that's not the look we want.

Illustration A pinpoints the six points that I use to help me determine the shape. They may be helpful to you as guides to help you interpret the trim as you want to do it, while avoiding the problems we all run into trimming puppies.

Let's spend a bit of time considering how the six points are useful and what they cause the eye to see.

Points 1 and 2 are the starters in my book for two important reasons:

1. They tell the eye how long the legs are. And if you're looking for a short-high look, you've got to have length of leg to get it.
2. The line from Point 1 to Point 2 tells the eye how long-bodied—or short-coupled if you prefer—your puppy is. More about that later, but remember, the tilt of the line is important because horizontal lines look longer than tilted lines.

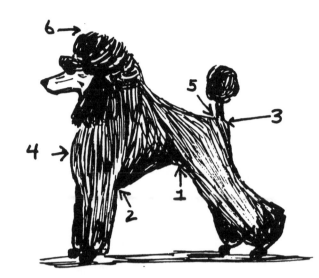

It takes a practiced eye and knowledge about how Poodles grow and how hair changes the picture. At first look, this is a short-legged Standard Poodle lacking the balance the breed Standard requires. *But*, he's only four months old.

By seven months of age, the same puppy has undergone several growth spurts and his balance has changed considerably. Stand by for more changes.

Points 3 and 4 also work to tell your eye how long the puppy is. Many people think those two points are the *ONLY* determinants. Maybe so. That leads many people into cutting everything off the back of the tailset and upper leg, and everything off the front.

I come close to agreeing with that approach on the rear, but at Point 4 I have trouble with the approach. And here's why. I want my puppy trim to communicate some things about structure. In this case, I want the overall shape to communicate that my puppy *has* a brisket and that the

At about 20 months, the puppy in the previous photograph became Ch. Nevermore Olivier at the 1986 PCA Regional. His correct balance is easily seen at this mature stage, wearing the Continental trim, and length of neck is particularly evident when enhanced by the topknot. Olivier is sired by Am. Can. Ch. Nevermore Newman CD X Ch. Nevermore Hepburn.

front legs are well set back *directly under* the withers (reread the breed Standard if this idea strikes you as a new and outrageous thought).

Too often, the "done-lop" approach (as in "I just done-lopped off all that hair") makes perfectly obvious a major structural problem: Some Poodles have next to no brisket, and their dear little front legs hang off the dogs' chins. That problem should never be made evident, and the trim should never create the impression the problem exists when, in fact, it doesn't.

Now let's move to Point 5. Admittedly, this seems strange, but if you are trying to communicate that your puppy has an adequate amount of neck, you've got two ways to do it:

At six years, Olivier was wearing the sporting trim. He earned his CD degree, and has produced four champions with several others nearing their titles. Olivier was bred and owned by Sue Henly. His series of photographs serves as an excellent reminder that you must consider both the age and stage of development as well as the trim and amount of hair when evaluating the overall picture of any Poodle.

1. Either starch every little hair she has on her head straight up at Point 6, or

2. Get Point 5 as close to her spinal cord as possible without drawing blood. Just as Points 1 and 2 work together to determine length of body, Points 5 and 6 work together to determine length of neck. Again, the "tilt" of the line between Points 5 and 6 isto some degree important in determining compactness or body length.

Ch. Cantif's Keeping Tradition provides a nice example of a Standard puppy in full puppy trim. He has a full topknot typical of a youngster at the end of a puppy career, but blended in to fit the rest of the trim is smartly tailored in a moderate manner—not too extreme—just right. "Tyler" is sired by Ch. Cotian Summerwind and his dam is Ch. Cantif's Keep On Glowing. Tyler is bred and owned by Carol Cargle.

BEYOND ALL POINTS

A puppy trim, neatly done, can indicate refinement. Bodacious amounts of hair hanging in all directions are more likely to communicate grossness.

Personally, the lines forming the sides of a puppy trim are important to me. I like the lines fairly flat and parallel. The rounder says the dumpier to my eye. And for some reason, flattening those sides always makes a puppy look a little leggier and sometimes taller. Keep that in mind if your puppy is pushing the size limit. From the front, I like the look in Illustration B. When puppies get overcoated and round, as in Illustration C, they get dumpy and top-heavy. They begin to lack balance and lose all their elegance. When viewed from the top, as in Illustration D, the sides are for the most part parallel, from the tailset forward with a bit of flaring out as you get as far forward as the shoulder.

The parallel lines forming the sides are important in communicating another concept, too: the strength, in some ways an indication of structure. The uniform width from front to rear suggests a wide (and consequently strong) loin and good spring of upper rib. Wide-made puppies have more heart and chest capacity and consequently have more endurance.

So straighten the sides, but as you do it, think about retaining enough width to communicate strength. Trim those lines too tightly, and you communicate weakness and slab-sidedness. Leave them too wide, and the puppy becomes too gross. Work until you get the width just the way you want it. Be particularly aware of the width over the loin at the point directly above Point 1 in Illustration A.

Many people get so engrossed with scissoring in the tuck-up that they end up with a tuck that goes all the way up to the topline. When that happens, you quickly get an "insect" look. The too-tucked tuck-up is a mistake to avoid. It looks bad on the day you do it, and the problem may remain evident throughout the puppy's career. That's another reason to keep the lines straight and parallel. You'll never enter the ring feeling you have a creature bred by the local termitarium on the lead.

Let's wrap this up by dealing with two final points: Point 1 and Point 3 in Illustration A. About Point 1. Before you decide where you'll put it, reach under your puppy and locate the webbing at the flank. Point 1 needs to be right at the webbing or a touch below it. It also needs to be well ahead of the leg. That helps shorten the distance between Points 1

Ⓑ   Ⓒ   Ⓓ

Dana Plonkey presented this Toy bitch in an immaculate puppy trim on a quick trip to her U.S. title. She is a daughter of the English Import Ch. Tuttlebee's Royal Knight, owned by Plonkey and Nancy Peerenboom.

and 2. If you set it too far forward, you can always move it back with your scissors. But if you put it too far back (welcome the insect look again) you'll be fighting it until a Continental trim finally solves the problem.

Now about Point 4. Let's rely on Illustration E. Somewhere in the mass of hair up front, you'll find the point of the withers (X), the point

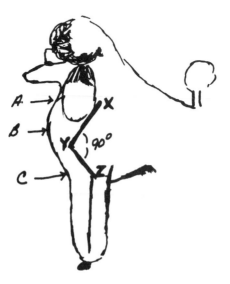

of the shoulder (Y) and the point of the elbow (Z). If you are lucky, X will be directly above Z, and you'll find the front leg right under both of them.

For that to be true, it is essential that the line from X to Y and the line from Y to X be equal in length, and that they form a 90-degree angle as shown. If you are really lucky, that little structural assemblage will be placed far enough back on your puppy that right beneath it you will find the brisket, the area below the chest between the forelegs.

The trick or challenge is to trim the front in such a manner that the brisket is evident (whether the dog has one or not). And you do that by

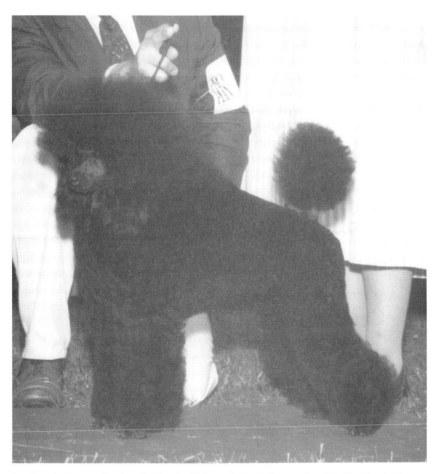

Ch. Dassin Dansarella, by Ch. Dassin Dickson (a Daniella grandson) X Ch. Dassin Dansa belle (a Ch. Dassin Deniella daughter) is shown here going Best of Winners and winning an Award of Merit at the 1990 PCA National Show. Her smartly tailored puppy trim reflects her overall balance and proportion and makes an attractive outline.

effectively creating a curve from A to C by going through B as shown in Illustration E.

Point A is a predetermined point: the base of the "v" where you trimmed the face and neck. The trick is getting Point B established without making your puppy look longer than necessary. What helps you do it is *your* placement of Point C. It is really Point C that tells the eye how well set back the front is, and, to some degree, how much length of leg your puppy has. If you get Point C established correctly, you can create the curved line from A to C without having Point B add a tremendous amount of length to the overall picture.

Several well-known handlers have been known to grab the scissors and cut a deep "hole" to establish where they want Point C. All that remains is to shape the curve to that point so that the hole eventually goes away. That is a drastic approach, but it works if you have a practiced eye.

Most people don't go to that extreme, but unfortunately many people never get Point C correctly established, and its placement is important. When placed correctly, it adds length to the front leg, avoids adding length to the overall picture and helps avoid the heavy ploddy look that we too often see in puppy trims.

Again, let me reemphasize that these are key points that help me interpret the puppy trim, as I want to interpret it. You may seek a totally different look and outline, but you will achieve it by dealing with the *same key points* as you interpret the puppy trim your way.

7

The Two Adult Trims—
The English Saddle
and Continental

ONCE A PUPPY REACHES twelve months, you have to make a choice. Adult Poodles (twelve months or over) wear either the English Saddle or the Continental trim. Deciding which trim to use is frequently difficult for people just starting.

Many beginners view the English Saddle as the most difficult trim to manage, and they're probably right. That trim also requires more grooming time, both at home and at the show. Sometimes you make the decision of which trim to use based on the talent you have to execute it or the amount of time you have available to work on it and keep it up, and sometimes those factors are a decent basis on which to decide. Frankly, some dogs can wear either trim. So decide based on your talent and time.

But sometimes one trim suits a dog better than the other because of the dog's physical attributes. Straight stifles, low flappy webbing, lack of muscle and coarse boning are all problems that the Continental trim makes perfectly evident. An English Saddle trim won't make those problems go away, but it does help camouflage them to some extent.

The Continental trim, however, makes a correct tailset, pretty bend of stifle, well-defined muscling, a clean tuck-up and strong driving move-

Ch. Vanart's Embattled Patriot, a Group winner owned by Kathy Catelain, provides a marvelous example of the English Saddle trim with a curly pack. The trim looks best on a high-stationed dog, and is particularly attractive here with the addition of curls on the top portion of the trims. The curls are easily achieved once the trim is finished by dampening the coat with water from a spray bottle and patting it with a pin brush. Repeated wetting and patting results in tight curls that add a touch of glamour to the trim.

ment all perfectly evident. And sometimes, the English Saddle trim seems to make dogs look a shade longer cast than they do in Continental. While it does hide coarse bone in some cases, it makes some coarse, plain dogs look even coarser.

If you don't decide to let your decision be based on your ability or

Multiple Specialty and BOB and all-breed BIS winner, Ch. Wavir Langcroft Jubilation, owned by Walt and Virginia Milroy, also ranks high on the list of all-time Top Producing Miniature sires with 51 champions. Handled by Dana Plonkey.

the time available, you'll have to use some judgment in deciding which trim you'll use. Sometimes a more experienced, objective pair of eyes can be helpful. But ask too many people what they think and you'll probably be more confused than you were when you started thinking about it.

One thing to keep in mind is this: Put a dog in English Saddle and look at the dog standing and moving. Then decide what you think of the trim. If you decide you've made the wrong choice, you can make the switch to Continental and have the dog in the ring within a couple of weeks. *But*, if you go to the Continental first and then change your mind, your dog will need several months before you have hair in all the places you need it. That may influence your decision.

Sooner or later, the dog has to be trimmed, and the decision will have to be yours.

THE ENGLISH SADDLE

Let's assume you have the face, feet and tail trimmed and that your puppy is freshly bathed and dried. Put a #15 blade in your clipper, and let's begin the English Saddle. Put your left thumb on the joint that is covered by the front puff. Line up the joint in your thumb with the joint on your puppy's leg, and then place your clipper at the tip of your thumb and begin clipping up the leg, clear to where it ends and the dog's body begins.

That rule of "thumb" works fine for both Toys and Miniatures.

Ch. Karalea Master Key of Alcala, owned by Karen and Phil Leabo, portrays a carefully sculpted English Saddle trim on a Miniature. The top band is placed on a line that passes over the stifle. The bottom band is a slanted line from the top of the hock slanted down to the front of the leg at the point where it bends. The English Saddle allows an illusion of more angulation, but carries the risk of making the dog look longer bodied than it really is if the trim is not carefully executed. Master Key, a white, is the sire of 19 champions and is a multiple Group winner.

You might slide up a bit higher on a Standard. Always err on the side of safety: You can always move the top of the front puff down if you want to. If you want to move it up, it may take months for the hair you removed to grow back.

Now take your scissors and get rid of any hair you are *certain* you won't need on the hind legs and entire area where the pack will ultimately be. Anything you can cut off at this point will be out of your way and will help you start to visualize the picture you're trying to make. Go slow, and err on the safe side.

Use your comb or a knitting needle to part the hair just behind where you think you will ultimately want the mane to start. The old rule of thumb used to be to put that line directly over the last rib. Today, that line is too far forward to suit most people's eyes. This is another situation where you err on the safe side. Set the line a bit farther back. You can always move it forward; it takes months to move it back.

This unusual pose of Ch. Aizbel Headstudy In Black offers students of the English Saddle trim an opportunity to see how Luis Aizcorbe fashioned the trim on "Junior." The Aizcorbe Miniatures were always fastidiously groomed. Junior sired 22 champions. He was a big-ribbed dog with an exquisite head and had a harsh, dense coat that is reasonably rare in the Miniature today. He was bred and owned by Luis and Mary Jo Aizcorbe.

Once you get the line about where you think it will ultimately be, use a bit of hair spray to hold the hair ahead of the line forward and out of your way. Then begin scissoring the top of the pack, removing all the long hair behind the line you created. Go slow and easy.

If your eye tells you the line is in about the right place, begin shortening the side, but work from the top down and the front backwards. Placing the point of the tuck-up that the eye sees (*it is actually hair, rather than skin*) is critical, and you'll be wise to leave that point until last, when you're absolutely able to pinpoint where you really want it. You may choose to put the crescents in with a #40 blade on your clippers at this point. The front of the crescent is on the same line as the beginning of the mane. They should be kept high on the dog's side, but not so high that they actually partially lie over the dog's topline.

You now have the trim "roughed out." And the trick is to work it over and over until you have created the shape that does the most for the dog you are working on. You may find that it helps to actually put up the topknot as you would for a show so that you can get a total picture of what you are working toward.

Refining the Trim

At this point, let's look at a series of illustrations that hopefully will help you think through the process of refining your trim and accentuating the strengths your animal has while minimizing its problems.

In Illustration A you see her—let's call her "Bitey"—as she was the last time you showed her and decided that the overall shape really didn't do the most for her. You're right; things about her trim make her appear longer than she needs to be, shorter in neck than she has to look, and bottom-heavy, a common problem for beginning groomers.

Some things are good about the trim. She's got plenty of hair to work with, nothing missing, and most of the problems can be solved by *removing* hair. That's better than having to change lines—a situation that may mean your dog has to sit out of the ring for a couple of months.

The challenge here is to give your dog some leg, shorten the overall appearance, find neck and give some cleanness that will add elegance and make her less heavy or "ploddy" looking.

Now let's look at Illustration B. Points A and C are generally what tell your eye how "visually" long your dog is. The trick is to shorten the distance between those two points. Or as some say, "cut off everything

(A)

(B)

that hangs off the front and off the back. They'll look shorter." That's going to work fairly well on Bitey because her shoulder assembly seems reasonably correct in placement so that the front legs are directly under the withers.

But that often isn't the case. If you're showing a *straight-fronted dog* (the kind whose front legs are *too far forward*) you'll make that fault all the more evident by cutting everything off the front. You have to leave a bit more hair out there because that's about all the "chest" a straight-fronted dog has. Without the hair, they don't have a chest and the entire world can tell.

Now look at Point B. That point is key in telling your eye how much leg a dog has, or how much daylight there is under your dog. Put your A, B and C together, and the distance between A and C makes your dog look "short"; the distance between B and the ground makes your dog look "high." If you're after the "short and high" look—and almost all of us are to some degree—you've got to deal with those three points as you create the general shape you want on your Poodle.

Now that brings us to Illustration C. It is essentially the same as Illustration A, with a "done-lop" treatment: We "done-lopped off" the front, lopped off the rear and lifted the underline a bit. This is beginning to work. Bitey definitely has more leg and daylight under her. Removing the "cheeks" of the saddle helps make her appear somewhat shorter. But more can be done. We haven't gained any length of neck, and the awkward curve, the line from the bottom of Bitey's "V" down to the point of her elbow, leaves her bottom-heavy and costs in elegance.

One nice thing about writing about trimming is that you can just go on to the next illustration. But at the shows, or at home in the trimming room, you just have to keep nibbling away at that hair with your shears.

©

Get away from Bitey and look for the line you want. Then keep working the hair with your scissors until the line finally begins to appear. A large mirror on the trimming room wall often helps.

The Overall Shape

In Illustration D, the overall shape we're after finally begins to appear. We've raised the trim a bit more, taking care that the curve from the "V" to the elbow is nice and smooth. Another key point in trimming underlines is having the lowest point of the underline right at the point of the elbow—nothing ahead of it and nothing behind it is *ever* any lower. Check that point several different ways—when you've stacked the dog both on the table and on the floor, when the dog is posing on its own and when it is moving. Sometimes you will have the underline trimmed to perfection when the dog is posed on the table, but when it is in any other position, it looks as if you've never even tried.

As a final check, pull the front leg forward and downward at the same time, as the dog would be in full stride. Any hair that hangs down and disrupts the underline should just be cut off. Even if it leaves a hole in the belly hair, no judge will ever see it.

Now, we've added a bit of lightness, elegance and refinement, but one other bit of trimming was done to make Illustration D different from Illustration C. That's what gives Bitey more neck than in the previous illustrations.

Not only is she cleaner or "tighter" at her tuck-up than before, we've changed the line from Point D to Point E. The changes have given that line a more vertical tilt than it had in previous illustrations. All it took to make that happen was removal of some of the garbage hair that

(D)

masked the neck that had been there all the time. There's an old saying that you have to cut off hair to make hair, and it is often true. But you often have to cut off hair to make a neck emerge and to give the overall appearance of cleanness that helps create an illusion of elegance that every Poodle must have.

A word of caution. You can do too much of a good thing. Cutting off too much from the front may remove the chest. Tightening the tuck-up too much will give a weak and wasplike appearance. Removing too much of the garbage hair (Points D to E) can give an unfinished look as if your dog isn't really quite ring-ready. Once you make one of those mistakes, you'll never forget it—and you probably won't do it again.

You might find it helpful to make several photocopies of the most recent photographs of a dog you have in the ring. Then simply trim the dog with a pen or a pencil. It may be a very useful way to help you see *where hair needs to go and where hair needs to grow.*

Shaping the Puffs—Front Legs

At this point, we've got the basic shape we want in an English Saddle, but we've completely ignored shaping the front puffs and the puffs on the hind legs. And they need attention. Done correctly, the hair on a dog's legs can add to the elegance and lightness of movement that is so much a part of the Poodle. Done cleverly, it can improve (not correct) movement problems. But when handled in an artless manner, the hair on a dog's legs can make them appear heavy and cloddy, can mask good movement and suggest incorrect movement. Legs need special attention, so let's start with the front legs first.

Think Toilet Paper Rolls. The thing that helped me most in approaching the task of trimming the front puffs was to find a shape most like what I needed to create. I think I started by trying to create apples. That didn't work and they generally ended up looking more like pears when they got in the ring. That taught me a never-ending truth. Hair falls down. Trim an apple shape, wait until the hair falls down, and right before your eyes you'll see a pear. Pears on the end of a Poodle's front leg always make the Poodle look plodding and lacking in elegance.

Finally, somebody said, "think toilet paper," and when they said it, I saw the trim Bud Dickey and Gary Wittmeier had on Ch. Dassin Blue Tango of Chalmar. From that point on, at least I knew what I was trying to do—whether or not I could do it.

Illustration I is the generic shape I strive for. It works best on Standards and Miniatures, but keep the shape in mind even when trimming Toys. The Toy puffs are really too small to pull off the total look, but

Ch. Dassin DeBussy, a Multiple Best In Show winner as well as winning Best of Variety winner at two Regional PCA shows (once as a puppy) and the PCA National, sired 30 champions. His sire, Ch. Dassin Broadway Joe (35 champions) is a son of Ch. Jocelyn Marjorie. His dam, Dassin Ruby Begonia, was a daughter of the other foundation dam at Dassin, Ch. Annveron Bacardi Peach. DeBussy was one of the rare Standards shown in the English Saddle trim. With the curly pack, the trim was deliberately done a bit old-fashioned for the late seventies and was reminiscent of an earlier time.

keep the shape in mind. Illustration II is the same basic shape with the dog's leg and foot added so you can begin to see the shape will work. But it looks wooden. It isn't elegant. The shape is beginning to look right, but it needs fixing.

Look at Illustration III. It shows the two basic areas that need to be fixed. At the top of the roll, that harsh line needs to be softened. You

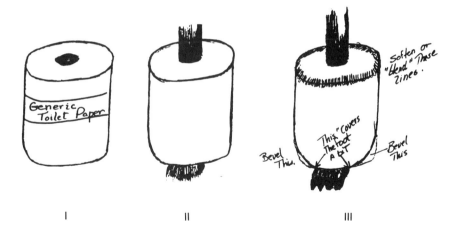

Generic Toilet Paper

Bevel This.

This "Covers The Foot A bit

Soften or "blend" These Zines.

Bevel This

I   II   III

eliminate the hard line and blend or bevel the two planes together. It won't take you long. Use a good pair of curved scissors, and five minutes later you can have the job done. Just play around over the top of the puff to eliminate that harsh line. You blend it . . . you soften it. You work that area, all the way around the leg until the line goes away and is totally blended for a soft, finished look.

Now, look at the bottom of Illustration III. Bevel it. Stand in front of the dog and begin nipping away—again with good curved scissors— at the areas shown, but stop at the sides of the foot. I like to work that part of the puff to that point, and then leave it awhile and see how it looks. Why stop? And why leave the hair longer over the foot? Because at this point I still have hair to work with to help camouflage whatever incorrectness exists with the dog's foot.

Despite whatever problem exists—long toes, flat feet or whatever— I clip the entire foot like the breed Standard says. If you don't, the bottom of the puff will always be heavy and suspicious. It will look like you're trying to cover a problem. So I clip the foot. But I use the hair above it—the area between the two beveled sides—to cover the long toes and mask the shallow foot. If you do that carefully, you can to some degree camouflage those problems and still keep the light-and-lifted look that adds elegance to the Poodle appearance.

Once you get the front puffs looking like you think you want them, put the dog on the ground and move it until the hair has had plenty of chance to "fall." And then, without lifting it with a comb, scissor it again. When you've done that two or three times, you can count on the puff looking like you want it to look—even at the end of the class.

Shaping the Puffs—The Hind Legs

Think Funny-Shaped Eggs. Trimming the hind puffs is a bit more intricate than the front puffs for most people, but let's have a go at it. First, look at Illustration IV—nothing but a funny-shaped egg that is probably little more than a painful experience for the dear hen. Think about it as the side view of the rear bottom puff. Illustration V will help when you see the leg and foot added.

Illustration V also shows the kinds of adjustment that are needed. You remove part of the roundness at the front to eliminate that heavy, floppy look and to give your dog a touch more angulation. You add just a bit of rounding to the back as shown. Take care that you keep your "funny-shaped" egg tilted as shown, because that tilt also helps to give an illusion of a bit more angulation.

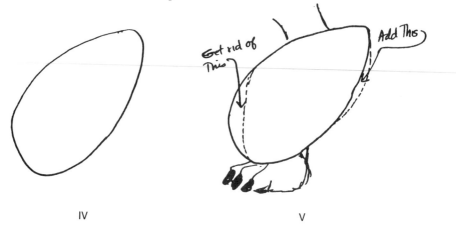

IV   V

Now, look at Illustrations VI and VII. They both show the egg shape I try to create when I view the hind puff from behind the dog—at eye level. That shape really doesn't need any modification if you're just going to look at it and not have the dog move. But often when a dog moves away from the judge, you find you'd like just a bit more width of rear movement. If you don't need it, leave the egg alone. If you do need more width, begin trimming away at the inside of both hind puffs as shown in Illustration VII. You'll end up with another funny-shaped egg, and this one is asymmetrical. And the shape will get you a bit more width of movement when viewed from behind.

The Moving Picture

Now you have the basic shapes you need, but you still aren't quite done. It is one thing to have a dog trimmed to stand—but quite another

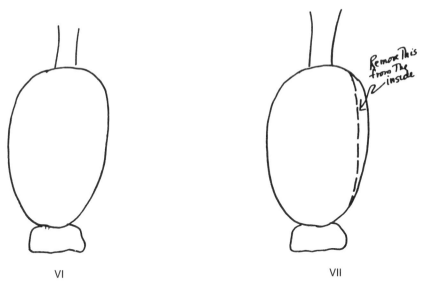

VI   VII

to trim a dog to move. Step 1 is accomplishing what we've already described in this chapter. Now we're going to move to Step 2, and that step begins when you have somebody move the dog on a lead so you can watch it move.

The idea is to carefully assess what the hair is doing and what you would like to improve about the dog's movement and total appearance when moving and standing on his own. This is also a time when you can do another check on the underline that looked correct on the table, but doesn't on the ground. Or you may find the underline picture is destroyed by tufts of hair that drop down from the elbow when your dog extends a foreleg.

These are both fixable problems. But to fix them, you've got to define them. To me that means you've got to *get down on your belly and watch the dog move away from you, toward you and around you*—moving fast and moving slow, on a loose lead and strung up.

Let's focus on the hind legs. Watch both the legs and the movement of hair as your dog takes each stride. No two dogs are alike, but I'd guess you'll find that dogs trimmed entirely on the table share a lot of problems, regardless of whether they're in puppy trim, English Saddle or Continental.

Look at the sketch of the dogs in the three trims in Illustration VIII. You'll notice that in all three of the trims represented, the outside lines create a fairly uniform width from top to bottom when the rear legs are placed as they are. And especially notice the lines that form an inverted V, with the top of the V being the crotch, and the bottom being the hair above the foot on the inside of the leg. Most of us know to create the two

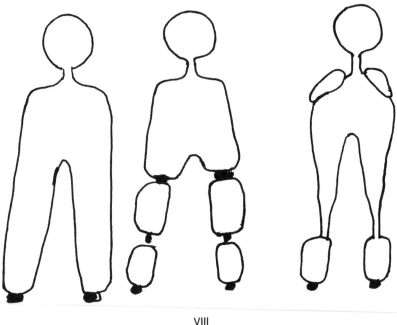

VIII

lines that form that V. And we know that the closer a dog moves, the more hair we need to take off the inside of the legs.

But you can only go so far. If you cut that hair too short, your efforts will be obvious to judges—even those judges who have never thought about scissoring a hindquarter, much less done it.

Again, let's think about how your dog's hindquarter moves. The hind legs do not move parallel to one another (and they shouldn't). Dogs tend to single-track. As the leg goes forward, it reaches toward the center of the dog's body. As that happens, the foot and the entire leg turn in. If you lie on your belly . . . observe . . . and think . . . you will see it happen.

When it happens, the nice straight lines you created on the table will be lost in the swoosh of hair on the front of the leg that flops to the center as your dog moves. Another thing happens: the visual "width of movement" you created on the table is lost.

Now, pretend we cut off the legs and could look directly down at the cross section of the bottom puffs in a still-standing position. We would probably see something like the two blocks in Illustration IX. The blocks are in the position they would be as the dog stands, and notice how the two inside lines are parallel.

But in movement—at the point of greatest reach—those front inside corners would turn to the center as in Illustration X. The line you saw in

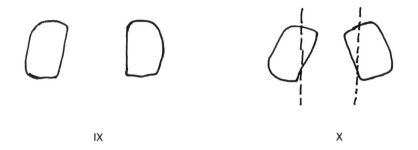

IX   X

the previous illustration is lost to the eye, and the line you want is represented by the dotted line in Illustration X. You must have that dotted line to maintain the width of movement you want when the dog is moving. How you get that line is up to you. Some experienced handlers who have done it for years just add it to their on-table trimming routine, and they do it while the dog stands.

I use a different approach. I pick up the hind leg by the foot and extend it by pulling back. As I pull, I gently twist the foot so the toes turn in and the hock rolls out. As I do that, I can (1) see the line I created when the dog was standing, (2) see it disappear as I twist the leg and (3) scissor the front inside of the leg until the new line (dotted line on Illustration X) and the standing lines (Illustration IX) are both evident when the foot is twisted and held in a standing position.

To double-check myself, I sometimes put the dog on a lead and watch him move to make certain that there's nothing left flopping.

If you're dealing with a really quirky movement problem, you may find you have to trim one leg a little differently from the other. With some dogs, you'll have to trim and move, trim and move, and trim some more and move until you get the movement straightened out and the width you want.

In most cases, if you get down and observe and think, you can define the problem and then set about solving it. If you only trim on the table, however, you may never get the width and directness of movement you want.

THE CONTINENTAL

Everything we've talked about in trimming the front puffs, the bottom puffs of the hind leg and the mane or body coat of the English Saddle will apply to the Continental trim as well. In fact, to convert an English Saddle to the Continental trim, you'll rely primarily on your clippers, using your scissors only to shape the rosettes.

Ultimately, you'll probably do all of your show clipping with a #40 blade. But until the skin is used to having the hair clipped closely, I always use a #15 blade to avoid clipper burn. Even then, I like to use a lotion over the clipped areas to further avoid irritating the skin.

You start on either leg right at the top of the bottom puff by clipping upwards. And you can remove all of the hair behind the mane—except for the areas where the rosettes will be placed. This is another of those situations where you err on the side of safety. You can instantly make the rosettes smaller. Making them larger will require waiting for hair to grow.

Let's think about the placement of the rosettes. Here are the guidelines I use to think about placing them.

1. The entire rosette should be far enough forward to avoid the hair covering the side view of the tailset. When set too far back, they really do look as if they are falling off the dog. The *only* exception to that rule would be made when you have a dog with a tailset so low that the risk of having the rosette look peculiar is preferred to having the poor tailset left evident.
2. The rosettes should be placed well up or fairly high on the side. In fact, they not only are on the dog's side; they are also on the top surface.

Ch. Wavir Hit Parade is the only Poodle to win Best of Breed at four Poodle Club of America shows—two June Specialties and two regionals. She was the top-winning Miniature in 1983 and is the dam of eight U.S. champions and one Swedish champion. Handled by Harold Langseth.

3. On Toys, only about a half-inch clipped area separates the two rosettes. On Miniatures not more than an inch separates them; and on Standards, probably not more than one and one-half inches separates the two.
4. When viewed from behind, and when the dog is standing in a normally posed position, the rosettes should not extend to the side (that means be wider) than the widest part of the dog's body when in that pose.

Rosettes are round, but they are not on a flat surface. Consequently, it takes a bit of experience to get that shape and to make one rosette match the other. Leave the hair a bit longer than you really want it when you first trim them. They can always be shortened.

Ultimately, you will want to keep them short enough that they do not distract from the dog's exposed topline. Because they do visually add height to the topline, you want to watch that they do not make the dog's neck appear shorter than it might. If that seems to be happening, you shorten the rosettes until you have the look you want.

Ch. Lynn's Valcopy Pipe-dream was a multiple Best In Show winner as was her dam, Ch. Valcopy Dream Walkin'. She is sired by Ch. Camelot Rocky Reflections. She traces back through both her sire and dam to the Top Producing Ch. Syntifny On The Move. Her impeccable feet, expressive but moderate head and her carriage when moving made her a strong contender for Groups and Best In Show. Bred by Margo Durney and Linda Kofmehl and owned by Dana L. Plonkey.

Can the rosettes be too short? Certainly. If you finish trimming them and they look like sausage patties, you've gone too far. Do it once and you never will again. It really boils down to this: Keep them forward . . . keep them high . . . start with them bigger than you think they should be and you've avoided the most serious mistakes you can make in placing the rosettes. The more you trim them, the easier it gets.

For some, the three show trims accepted in breed competition are an albatross about the neck. But for many others, the Poodle trim is the icing on the cake. It makes the Poodle a Poodle. And it is amusing to many people that the trims we work on so diligently today really can be traced back to their functional roots when the Poodle was viewed and used as a water retriever.

Those elegant trims are work and they require time. But the satisfaction of making progress in learning to do them—and to finally have your abilities recognized—is a real high.

8

The Convenience Trims

ALTHOUGH THE SHOW TRIMS define the Poodle for most people, even those who feel that way often find themselves at the point where there are too many show trims to keep up, and it just doesn't seem practical when dogs are no longer being shown.

If you arrive at that point, or if you want to maintain a good-looking pet, you will be looking for a trim that is more convenient for you. Exploring the alternatives that are convenient but also retain the dignity of the Poodle, is the focus of this chapter.

As you probably know, professional dog groomers offer their clientele a wide range of choices about how their pets can be trimmed. Some are convenient to maintain, some are amusing, creative or artistic, and some are unique. But only some of them retain the integrity or the dignity of the Poodle. The scope of trims offered here will be far more narrow than that offered by professional groomers. The focus will be on convenience and retaining the essence of what the Poodle is about.

THE SPORTING TRIM

This trim is the convenience trim most highly endorsed by the Poodle Club of America. In fact, it is described in the PCA's Illustrated Breed Standard and is the accepted trim for showing Stud Dogs and Brood Bitches and for exhibiting in the parade of champions at Specialty shows.

Ch. Magicstar Voyager finished his U.S. championship in Continental trim, but now wears the sporting trim popular with breeders and pet owners because it is much easier to maintain. Dedicated breeders appreciate the convenience of the shorter trims once a ring career is over. Voyager is sired by Ch. Syrena Commodore CDX X Ch. Marens n Pepsi's Magic Marker. He is bred and owned by Roberta (Pepsi) Gilson.

The breed Standard describes the Sporting trim this way:

> In the Sporting clip a Poodle shall be shown with face, feet, throat and base of the tail shaved, leaving a scissored cap on the top of the head and a pompon on the end of the tail. The rest of the body and legs are clipped or scissored to follow the outline of the dog, leaving a short blanket of coat no longer than one inch in length. The hair on the legs may be slightly longer than that on the body.

Within those parameters, there is still considerable opportunity for individual interpretation—especially to adapt the trim to enhance the overall picture of an individual dog. Once again, your interpretation of the breed Standard and your concept of desirable type will be important in determining how the Sporting trim will look when you execute it. Many of the concepts and techniques described when executing the puppy and two adult trims will apply to the Sporting trim as well, and it may be helpful to highlight them again so that it isn't necessary to repeat them.

First, the approach to trimming the hind legs, to clean up rear movement and to enhance the width of rear movement, is exactly the same as that described earlier. Those approaches work across the board on all the trims discussed.

Second, the illustrations in Chapter 5 that highlight the key points in achieving a "short-and-high" look are also the same. And so are the cautions noted for when you are trimming a dog with a relatively straight front and a shoulder placement ahead of where it ought to be.

Third, the concern about locating the dog's visual tuck-up applies when doing the Sporting trim as well, and the efforts described to use hair above the front feet to lessen the impact of less-than-desirable feet are equally apt to the Sporting trim.

Illustration A shows the Sporting trim as it is portrayed in the Illustrated Breed Standard. And on a dog of that correct proportion and shape, the trim seems perfectly suited. But not all Poodles—even champions—carry that perfectly balanced look about them. With a bit of fine-tuning, the Sporting trim can be adjusted to enhance the proportion and balance that the eye sees. It doesn't change the dog; it only changes how you see it.

Illustration B shows the minor adjustments that could be made on the initial portrayal to create an illusion that the dog is even shorter and higher than seen in the untampered-with illustration from the Illustrated Breed Standard.

By adding just a bit of height to the "scissored cap," you seem to have added length of neck (Point A). By leaving the hair at the back of the neck just a touch longer (Point B) than the illustration, you give a

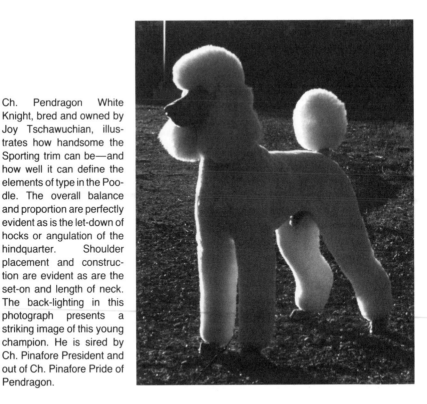

Ch. Pendragon White Knight, bred and owned by Joy Tschawuchian, illustrates how handsome the Sporting trim can be—and how well it can define the elements of type in the Poodle. The overall balance and proportion are perfectly evident as is the let-down of hocks or angulation of the hindquarter. Shoulder placement and construction are evident as are the set-on and length of neck. The back-lighting in this photograph presents a striking image of this young champion. He is sired by Ch. Pinafore President and out of Ch. Pinafore Pride of Pendragon.

somewhat "stallionlike" look that many people like, particularly on males. The other advantage is that the neck hair shortens the distance between where the neck visually comes out of the body (C) and the tailset (D). So the dog seems somewhat shorter coupled.

By tightening the trim just a touch on the backside, from the tail (E) down to Point F, you further create an illusion of shortness. Moving the tuck-up a touch further forward (Point H) and letting the hair fill in just a little behind the elbow (Point I) shortens the underline a bit. If the dog has enough leg you can drop Point I just a bit to give the line from I to H a tilt. Extending the hair on the top of the hock (Point G) creates an illusion of increased rear angulation.

So you can do some problem solving with the Sporting trim, but use of those approaches should be just that: problem solving. Each individual needs to realize that not all the enhancements that can be done should be done. *If you don't have a particular problem, don't trim to fix it.* Adding the appearance of angulation to a correctly angulated dog results in an overangulated appearance. Overangulation is not a desired attribute. It is a problem. Adding neck to an already necky dog doesn't add value. Making a balance dog look too short or too high isn't an advantage either.

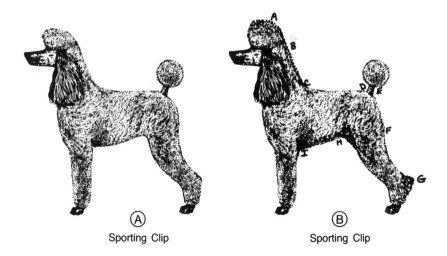

(A)
Sporting Clip

(B)
Sporting Clip

That's why having a firm personal definition and concept of Poodle type is so essential. If you have that concept in mind, you'll avoid "cheating with scissors" when it doesn't contribute to your concept, and when you do "cheat," you'll recognize when enough is enough.

RETRIEVER TRIM

The Retriever trim is really quite similar to the Sporting trim. Except for the scissored topknot and the tail, the hair is much shorter both on the body and the legs. *The beauty of this trim is that it presents the dog so honestly.* And when you see dedicated breeders with their companion dogs wearing a close Retriever trim, you know you're seeing a good dog.

Another attractive aspect of the Retriever trim is that if you prefer, the entire body and legs can be done with the clipper, either using a #04 or #07 blade, depending on the length of hair you want. Scissoring can be limited to the topknot and tail with only a little touch-up needed where the clipper doesn't leave a smooth finish.

Unlike the Sporting trim, there are no guidelines, so you are really left to do the trim as you like. But when we say "retriever," we're really talking about dogs working in the water. And putting a dog in the water wearing a lot of hair is like making a child wear baggy pajamas when learning to swim. It just doesn't make sense. However, in all honesty, a little extra hair left on the back of the neck to give the cresty, stallionlike look, probably wouldn't cause a dog working in the water a lot of trouble.

To my mind, the Retriever trim is a short-all-over trim. If you add

Although his trim is less extreme than his son and kennel mate's, Ch. Wycliffe Martin was another who wore only a short blanket of hair in the manner commonly called the "retriever" trim. Certainly his coat would cause little problems when he went to the water. Martin sired 19 champions for owners John and Elizabeth Campbell. He was bred by Jean Lyle. His sire was Ch. Wycliffe Ian, and his dam was Wycliffe Theresa.

Ch. Dhubhne Robert The Bruce at 11 years wore one of the most convenient trims imaginable. Face, feet and tail were trimmed with an Oster #40 blade, and the balance of the coat was trimmed with a #10 blade that left just a soft cover of hair after a few days. Not only is such a trim easy to do and maintain, it can serve as a constant reminder of how the pieces and parts of a Poodle work together when the dog is in motion. Breeders are most apt to use this trim on a dog that is respected for his type and correctness. He was bred by M. A. Graybill and owned by John and Elizabeth Campbell. His sire was Ch. Wycliffe Martin X Acadia Fleur de Lis.

a little here and a little there, you're only kidding yourself, and you may end up doing a Sporting trim in spite of your best intentions.

CLOWN TRIM

This trim suits may breeder-owners and pet owners, perhaps because it retains some decorative elements of the show trims, but at the same time offers the convenience of the short hair. Most people leave only a short cover of hair, and some make that cover even as short as they get with a #10 blade. The topknot and tail are scissored, as are the puffs on each leg, and they can be done in the same manner described in the chapter on the English Saddle and Continental.

Frequently, the puffs are scissored somewhat tighter than in the traditional show trims. You have the opportunity, again, to please your eye, and the more tightly trimmed puffs don't require retrimming quite as often. Of course, the trim can be used on any dog, but it really does seem to best suit those dogs that have that clownish element that you so often see in the Poodle.

MODIFIED CONTINENTAL

This is probably the least convenient of the convenience trims and the most reminiscent of the show trims. To understand how to do it, assume you're starting with a dog in Continental trim. Remove the rosettes on the hips with the clippers, and do the face, feet and tail and the entire hindquarters as you would for the Continental.

Then the scissor work begins. Your challenge is to shorten the mane as much as it pleases your eye. Scissor the topknot to a manageable length with the front of it quite similar to what you would do in any of the trims described so far.

Continue scissoring back above the ears and behind the back of the topknot into the neck. Again, suit yourself regarding the length. But take care in shaping the topknot and the rest of the mane so that you manage to highlight your dog's neck.

The scissored topknot really does give a nice effect, although some people accustomed to the show trim require a bit of time to get used to it.

Perhaps the greatest difficulty in executing this trim lies in shaping the mane in a manner that still gives the "necky" look and that maintains the balance and proportion essential to the Poodle.

Others may disagree, but I really like the hair left long enough to give a feeling of robustness. Sometimes when the sides are trimmed quite tight, the lack of width communicates a degree of weakness that isn't offset by seeing the width of loin.

The convenience trims have their place in most kennel operations and many homes. In truth, whoever feeds and loves the Poodle, and, in fact, pays the bills, has the right to trim the Poodle in any manner he or she finds pleasing.

9

Developing a Breeding and Show Kennel

$\mathbf{F}$OR MOST OF US who have bred Poodles throughout the years, it just happened. We found ourselves acquainted with people and Poodles associated with the show ring, and we finally admitted that we wanted to do it, too.

For many, an existing pet got ''converted,'' often into a less-than-satisfying show animal. And soon, that dearly loved pet began to share the limelight with the new dog—''one we can show.'' I doubt that the percentage of successful ''first show dogs'' is much different from the percentage of successful ''converted'' dogs. And somewhere along the way, ''something to breed'' became a part of our jargon. Without fully recognizing it, we were breeding Poodles and hoping for success in the show ring.

In this chapter, we're going to focus on the process of getting started, and we'll begin by dealing with the ''bug''—just before it bites you.

In almost all species of livestock breeding—horses, cattle, sheep, for example—there is fairly clear evidence that the life cycle of breeders is about seven to ten years. What this means is that seven years from now, a lot of the people you see at shows, who advertise in breed magazines and seem so much a part of the sport of breeding and showing Poodles, won't be involved anymore. Look back. How many of the people you watch and admire today started fewer than ten years ago? You may be surprised.

The lovely headed Ch. Bel Tor Cause Scandale, owned by Wilmont Eaton Salisbury, Eaton Kennels, was the foundation dam for a most successful family of Standards, used extensively by Standard breeders. Chief among the Eatons is Ch. Eaton Affirmed, the all-time Top Producing Standard sire. His count of champions is well over 100 now, and though Snapper is no longer living, several offspring remain to be finished.

Now, of course, there are those who do continue: Anne Rogers Clark, Sam and Mary Peacock, Dan and Betty Jo Gallas, Betty Yerington, Frances Rubinich, Dana Plonkey, Sharon Isgro, Bud Dickey, Wendell Sammet—and the list goes on. But the fact remains: Somewhere along the line probably three-quarters of the people who breed Poodles quit before they reach the ten-year mark.

SETTING GOALS AND LEARNING

You want to begin breeding Poodles? For how long? Forever? Or just until you get tired of it? If you can get a feel for the answer to that

Ch. Jocelyn Marjorie, by Ch. Wycliffe Virgle and out of Mogene's Beauzeaux, is one of two foundation dams for the Dassin Farm Standard breeding program. "Yo Yo," shown in the tremendous coat popular in the sixties was a multiple Specialty and all-breed Best In Show winner and won the PCA National in 1968. She is the dam of 17 champions. Her offspring, combined with those of the other Dassin foundation bitch, Ch. Annveron Bacardi Peach, have generated a family for nearly 30 years.

question, it can be terribly helpful information as you make your start and as you choose from among alternatives during your formative years. Let's consider some suggestions from established breeders who have "stayed the course" well beyond that ten-year mark.

1. **Know Yourself.** Glenna Carlson, Ascot Standards, sees that piece of advice as the starting point for every person about to be bitten by the proverbial bug. She stresses that showing and breeding Poodles takes an enormous amount of time and a true commitment if it is to be done well. *If you don't have both time and the desire, there might not be adequate reason to begin.*

2. **Get Set for Frustration.** In Glenna's view, the start-up period

for a new breeder is often fraught with an entire set of frustrations that result from being new and not being able to accomplish all that you want to do. Success is often measured against long-term breeders who are successfully producing generation after generation of puppies that make important contributions in the ring and in the breeding program. And in that context, it is hard to measure up.

3. **Is It Ignorance or Politics?** Most beginners deal with those frustrations fairly unaware of all that they *don't* know. Because of what they don't know and understand, they rather quickly advance to the point where they conclude that what they don't know is political. Just as politics is a part of life, it is also a part of the sport of breeding and showing Poodles. *But*, with experience comes knowledge, and with knowledge, politics tends to fall into perspective. Nobody is as quick to turn to the answer, "politics," as a newcomer. It's been that way for years. To many seasoned breeders, deeming something "political" really means "I don't understand."

4. **Become a Student.** Once a new or soon-to-be breeder reaches the point that politics explains away all their problems, one of two tracks is apt to be followed. Some quit. Others dig in and begin to learn.

   Merle Marsh, Marais Miniatures, stresses that the obvious starting point is attending shows. *New people need to sit at ringside and watch.* Watch all Varieties—not just the one in which you are interested. Make it a part of your routine the rest of your life. "And while they're watching," she adds, "they should ask questions and listen to the answers."

   Merle encourages potential breeders to begin developing a Poodle library. Subscribe to every Poodle publication you can get your hands on and give yourself a set of *Poodles in America*. If you are going to be a student of the breed, you need at least a nodding acquaintance with the pedigrees of top-winning and top-producing animals in your Variety as quickly as possible. There's no better source.

   Nelson Radcliffe, a long-time handler and judge, used to tell people to go to dog shows for at least a year—before they buy their first show dog. That way they can observe and learn without the emotional biases that come from having a dog entered.

5. **Narrow Your Focus.** Your study of pedigrees and top-producing families within your Variety, combined with watching dogs that appeal to you at shows, may ultimately help you begin narrowing

Often Poodle breeders bring entire litters of puppies to shows to provide "cultural enrichment" for the puppies and to gather opinions of fellow breeders as they evaluate puppies.

your focus. For many, a certain family, line or offspring of a particular sire or dam may rather frequently be the object of your attention. If that happens, you can begin getting acquainted with dogs from that family—both inside the ring and out—and the people who own them.

6. **Now Add People.** During the many years that I traveled with Peggy Hogg, I was constantly reminded that a major part of showing Poodles centered around dealing with people. Frankly, when things went especially well or especially bad; people, not Poodles, played a major role in those outcomes.

MENTORS

Most dedicated breeders with established reputations (of the positive kind) are quick to point out that their greatest satisfactions stem from the people with whom they are associated. Pat Deshler, Deshler Miniatures, puts it this way: "The neatest part about the sport of dogs is the lovely friends you make, most often through working and sharing the pains and pleasures of the sport. It has really been fun to watch a particular dog or person and know that you have been part of their development."

Merle Marsh offers: "The personal satisfactions from helping others

Ch. Surrey Sweet Cecily, a Best In Show winner and the dam of seven champions, spearheads a family that traces its roots to the great Ch. Fontclair Festoon, Best In Show at Westminster. Sired by Ch. Bevanton's Mischief Maker, X Surrey Sweet Grass (who produced seven champions) a granddaughter of Festoon. She was bred by Mr. and Mrs. James E. Clark and owned by the Clarks and Barbara Furbush.

are probably the most addictive thing about the entire process.'' And she adds that just as there are satisfactions from watching a new generation of a dog family come along, satisfactions also exist because among those you help, you see the new generation of teachers or mentors emerging. As she puts it, ''Graduation comes eventually for all students, and those of us who play the role of teacher or mentor must accept this with pride

A top producing son of Ch. Surrey Sweet Cecily is Ch. Surrey Sweet Timothy, the sire of eight champions. He is sired by Ch. Cherwilene Skylark. He is a dog of lovely proportion and type with deliberate movement and an appealing head and eye. He was bred by Mr. and Mrs. James E. Clark and Barbara Furbush and is owned by Cheryl Geurds.

in our students' achievements and accept with grace the knowledge that as we have done our job, we have made ourselves obsolete.''

Doris Cozart, Cotian Toys, cites two situations that produce super feelings from the mentoring role. The first is when she sees someone she helped helping others. The second is when someone she has worked with brings a litter of puppies to evaluate. ''I try to get them to tell me what they think first. When they reach the point where they can see what is there rather than what they want to be there, I really get a special feeling of real satisfaction.''

Ch. Surrey Bevanton Sweet Talk is another Top Producing offspring of Ch. Surrey Sweet Cecily with eight champions to her credit. She is sired by Ch. Surrey Sequoia (11 champions) who traces three times back to Ch. Fontclair Festoon. Her litter brother, Ch. Surrey Samurai is the sire of 14 champions. Sweet Talk was bred by Mr. and Mrs. James E. Clark and Barbara Furbush and was owned by Mrs. Furbush.

Ch. Surrey In Clover was a multiple Best In Show winner and the dam of five champions. She is from the breeding of Ch. Surrey Sweet Cecily to Ch.Cherwilene Skylark. One of her daughters, Ch Whitefarm Cosmos was Best of Winners at the 1989 PCA National. She was bred by Mr. and Mrs. James E. Clark and Barbara Furbush and is now owned by Anne Clark, Kaz Hosaka and Barbara Furbush.

LEARNING—A GIVE AND TAKE PROCESS

So one conclusion is obvious: Your search for a family of dogs includes the people associated with that dog family. Therein lies a problem. Just as you are searching for a foundation animal and evaluating the people who own it, so are the current owners evaluating you—as a potential owner of a family member and as a person with whom they would like to associate. Frankly, those who have preceded you as newcomers to the breed have not always set the stage for you in a positive manner. And as a result, you may find that the people with whom you would most like to associate seem a bit slow to take you to their bosoms with open arms.

Any relationship features a host of trade-offs. It seems logical that as new breeders look to established breeders for help and guidance, they too should feel some responsibility to those who helped them. In many ways, the process of an established breeder becoming a mentor—and the newcomer becoming a student—is similar to courtship patterns of yesteryear. It is a slow process accomplished one step at a time.

Anything that raises the tremendously important issue of trust has the potential to set back the relationship, and, in some cases, destroy it. Some key factors to help assure the relationship develops and blooms would include these:

1. *Be honest about your knowledge level.* Suggesting a knowledge level that you don't have will soon become evident to people established in the breed. They didn't get off the turnip truck yesterday, and you aren't the first newcomer they've associated with.
2. *Be honest about your intent.* Are you showing the dog yourself or using a handler? Are you starting a small breeding program or just buying a dog to show? Do you have an understanding of what breeding and showing dogs costs?
3. *Listen more than you talk.* If you ask a question, don't answer it. If you already have all the answers, asking questions really isn't essential. And answering the questions you ask sends some really important signals to many breeders.
4. *Treat the information and help you get as relatively confidential.* That doesn't mean that every breeder has a world of juicy secrets and hot new inside information to share with you. It simply means that until you've had the opportunity to internalize and think through the various kinds of help you get, you really aren't in a position to be an effective teacher.

Nothing turns me off to helping a newcomer more than having somebody tell me what the person I've just started working with claims *I* said. Somehow, something always changes in the telling, or the situation in which it is applied isn't the same as the case where I said it. But when I hear it, the trust level begins to slide. In short, established breeders look for some degree of loyalty as they begin working with new people. They're hopeful that early efforts will lead to lasting friendships. And as that process unfolds, they don't have an aversion to hearing the words "thank you."

FINALLY . . . LET'S BUY SOMETHING

Let's assume that you've spent enough time at ringside and talking to established breeders, and you've read everything you can get your hands on. You've pinpointed a family of dogs in which you are interested, and established some contacts among the people associated with that family. Now you know you're ready to get started.

Three words will tell you what your next step should be. And while breeders rarely agree on anything, I'd bet that 90 percent of the Poodle breeders in the U.S. would agree on what those three words should be: *Buy a bitch.* Most of them would probably add, the best you can afford.

What does that mean? When it comes to buying a bitch, you can start with anything from a puppy to show and or breed, to a proven matron, maybe even a champion or champion-producer. In between there are young broods, young bitches to show, both in hair and those not quite ready.

When it comes to "what you can afford," that may require a bit of interpreting as well. Some breeders sell cash-on-delivery while others take checks and credit cards, and still others sell on Breeder's Terms or offer payments over time. Any of those possibilities can be considered, of course, but of key importance are the people with whom you are dealing and the terms that are agreed upon. Some caution is needed, but with the right people and the right contract, you may very well be able to afford more than you originally thought.

Contracts

Purchases on Breeder's Terms may cost you fewer out-of-pocket dollars, but some of the other nondollar costs may make your purchase seem like a headache with no apparent end. You need to look carefully

Ch. Dassin Rita La Rose was another multiple Best In Show winner who won the PCA Regional in 1979 and the PCA National in 1980. Rita, the dam of two champions, was sired by Ch. Dassin DeBussy, X Ch. Dassin Six Pac, by Ch. de-Russy Necromancer and out of Ch. Jocelyn Marjorie. Six Pac produced 12 champions, and many Dassin dogs trace back to her. Rita was bred by Dassin and owned by Mrs. Edward L. Solomon, Jr.

at the contract offered you—both for what it includes and what it doesn't. For example, does it provide a clear understanding of how many puppies are required for payback? From how many litters? If you are splitting litters, how are the choices made—and at what age? Who pays stud fees, whelping costs, shots, worming and other veterinary costs? What happens if breeding or whelping problems emerge? Is the contract too specific about when the bitch will be bred? Who is responsible for sire selection and shipping costs associated? When will you own the bitch outright? Can you sell the bitch once she is yours?

Your contract should answer those questions and any others that you have. And if it doesn't, you may find some hidden costs coming out of hiding, and in many cases friendship circles have turned to enemy camps almost overnight.

But let's not assume the worst will happen. If you've planned your "beginnings" wisely and thoroughly, you have the opportunity to begin your venture in breeding Poodles with a lot of things going for you.

119

Ch. Jocelyn Marjorie returned to the PCA National in 1973 when her daughter, Ch. Dassin Blue Tango of Chalmar, was named Best of Breed. There she teamed up with Blue Tango and her son, Ch. Dassin Sum Buddy, a multiple Best In Show winner and sire of 24 champions, to win Best Brood Bitch in Show. She showed like she had during her youth and drew resounding applause.

Ch. Dassin Delano and three other champions resulted from breeding Ch. Eaton Affirmed to Ch. Dassin De La Rose. Franklin struck his mark as a multiple Best In Show winner as well as the sire Dassin Farms hoped to obtain. He produced 28 champions by the time he was seven years old. Bred by Mrs. Edward L. Solomon, Jr., and F.C. "Bud" Dickey, he is owned by Mrs. Solomon.

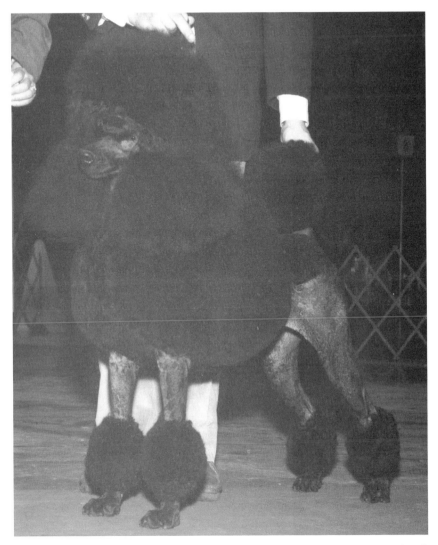

Ch. Dassin De La Rose completed her title as a young bitch and was never campaigned. Instead, she was chosen as the dam of an outcross litter sired by the all-time top producing Standard sire, Ch. Eaton Affirmed. She was sired by Ch. Dassin Broadway Joe and out of Ch. Dassin Rita La Rose, so her pedigree reflected an excellent example of line breeding that focused on the two foundation dams and the trust placed in her sire. She has produced four champions. Bred and owned by Mrs. Edward L. Solomon, Jr.

LONG-TERM GOALS

You have an overall vision of what you want to do as a breeder of Poodles. That vision can really be the basis of formulating your long-

Am. Can. Ch. Shamrock Disco Sue stands alone as the top-producing Toy Poodle dam with 14 champions. She has been Best Toy Brood Bitch at the PCA National three times and Best Brood Bitch in Show in 1989.

Disco Sue's son, Am. Jap. Ch. Broad Bay Hells A Blazen Revue, by Ch. Hells A Blazen Kinda Kostly, is a top producer and multiple Best In Show winner. He is now owned in Japan.

Am. Can. Bda. Ch. Broad Bay Just In Time, a littermate to Revue, is also a multiple Best In Show winner and top producer. He won both the 1986 and 1987 PCA Regional shows.

term goals as a breeder. A lack of long-term goals may be the underlying reason such a high percentage of breeders lasts only ten years or less. Once the short-term goals are accomplished, there's nothing left to sustain the long-term interest.

But short-term goals are important, too. And that's another area where you're ahead of the game. You've gone through the fact-finding process as a potential breeder, you've aligned yourself with people who are interested and supportive of what you are trying to do and you have selected one or more animals that will hopefully emerge as the foundation of the breeding program you are ready to begin.

The Veterinarian

You will also need to do some searching for another member of your team: your veterinarian. If you've owned dogs before as family pets, for example, you may already have an alliance and comfortable working relationship with a veterinarian in your area. If your associations have been pleasant through the years, that person may be the team member you have been looking for.

But as you move from the ranks of pet owner to breeder, you may find that your needs are different, that you are willing to take a more active part in health-related activities and that you need specialized assistance because you are breeding dogs to show. You will want a veterinarian who is attuned to the needs of show dogs and is willing to accommodate those needs.

The business of docking tails is a perfect example. Most veterinarians seem to think that in docking puppies' tails, you should remove one-half and leave one-half. And as far as most pet owners are concerned, that is fine. However, most of us who show Poodles believe that only about one-third of the tail should be removed. Hopefully, after you've discussed your wishes and reasons, your veterinarian will do what you ask.

As breeding programs grow, some veterinarians go to their clients' kennels to administer shots, worm dogs, assist with whelpings and to provide other specific needs. Some veterinarians offer professional discounts or breeder rates.

Those extra services are a good assurance that just as you treat your veterinarian as a professional, he or she also views you as a professional and is willing to go the extra mile as a part of your team. That's the kind of team member you value as the years go by.

Keeping Goals in Sight

So, while you are still a newcomer, you are no longer alone as your beginning effort gets underway. You have support and concern from people who are interested in seeing you succeed.

One word of caution. Don't lose sight of your long-term goals. On a day-to-day basis, breeding Poodles will have ups and downs. As a newcomer—with hopes as high as an elephant's eye—you won't be terribly good at putting the ups and downs in perspective. You'll be over the moon with a nice win one day and convinced that judges are crooked when the same dog stands fifth in a class of five, twenty-four hours later.

You have to remember that in terms of your long-term goals, that dog was what it was before the weekend, was the same dog after the big win and, amazingly, was still the same dog after standing fifth in a class of five. Your dog didn't get better when winning and didn't get worse when losing.

Keeping your long-term goals foremost in your mind will help you believe that.

10

So You're in Poodles —Now What?

WHEN THE FIRST DOG ARRIVES, you scrunch things around a bit in the utility room or den so you have room for the crate. A gate across the kitchen door keeps the new dog off the carpet. Add a grooming table, an exercise pen or a fenced-in area, and you've got Wondersabouttohappen Kennels. But getting an etching for the holiday card is going to be difficult.

Actually, thinking about adding one show Poodle to a family dwelling is a fairly good way to think about kennel planning. And it is realistic as well because today the bulk of the "kennels" exist as part of the home or an attachment to it. And because of the labor required to maintain a Poodle kennel—the difficulty of finding it and the costs associated—most Poodle kennels are fairly small-scale compared to the great kennels that were important during the breed's formative years and its rise to popularity.

At any scale, certain activities are essential in any kennel operation, and space for them must be provided—either by adapting existing space or by adding it to existing facilities.

HOUSING

In the ideal setting, the show Poodle would be a house dog, free to be totally involved in the family's activities. But in the real world, with dual earners in many families, houses are vacant during much of the day. If you have more than one dog, especially an exuberant puppy, you can quickly understand why most people seek ways to provide confined housing for certain periods of each day. And generally, the larger the kennel, the greater the reliance on confined housing.

Two points need to be made. First, one of the most serious problems facing all breeder-owners is too many dogs. Space isn't the only problem. As your labor demands increase, you're apt to find that what you once thought was fun has quietly become an albatross around your neck.

And, those gutsy, confident puppies you brought to the ring get more difficult to find as the kennel grows because they don't get the individual attention and socialization that you were able to manage when you had fewer dogs in your care. At the same time, your dog's strong, forceful movement that you always enjoyed may quietly disappear as the months pass, because dogs who are crate bound for a great deal of time tend to lose muscle tone. Unless you implement an alternative exercise program (another demand on time and labor), the combined problems of too many dogs and not enough space can provide some unpleasant surprises.

So for a variety of reasons, space being one of them, set some limits. The more you confine dogs the more you have to rely on management to offset the problems likely to result.

If your kennel setting is in a relatively rural area—or one where zoning ordinances permit the operation of a kennel and the accompanying noise that dogs are apt to make—you have more freedom to make use of outdoor kennel runs and open forms of outdoor housing. Don't be afraid of it. While many Poodles are kept under almost ''hothouse'' conditions, there are several breeders who house dogs outdoors year-round even where weather conditions are fairly extreme. When shade is provided and the area is open to permit air movement, young, healthy dogs can be kept outside during all but the hottest of days. Heat stress is particularly harmful to young puppies, pregnant bitches and older dogs.

The Poodle is really a great deal better able to withstand the rigors of winter weather than most people expect. John Suter's Poodle sled dog team lives outside in Alaska in all but the most severe winter weather. And I know of a champion Toy that was accidentally left outside in below zero weather overnight. He was found the next morning up against the house deep in a hole he had burrowed in the snow, and never developed even a sniffle.

So if you exercise some caution and acclimate them gradually, except for the problems of managing the show coats, the Poodle is really adequately hardy and capable of withstanding all but the most severe

Must the Poodle be pampered? John Suter, Alaska, would answer a resounding "No" as he drives his Poodle team through an Alaskan winter setting. The team competed in the Iditarod, and several members are closely related to top winners in breed competition.

weather. If you live in town and have nearby neighbors, your opportunities for outdoor facilities will be much more restricted. But you will have to provide space to confine dogs at times, and you will also have to have facilities to exercise them.

Exercise Areas

The term "exercise" needs some explanation. Many Poodle breeders and handlers use the term to mean provide a space where dogs can relieve themselves. With that definition, an exercise pen will do. But there are others who view the term as an important element in the process of conditioning dogs—particularly in developing muscle tone.

I've known kennels numbering as many as twenty-five dogs that were really comprised of crates in a single room with exercise pens in the center of the room and no more than a fifteen-by-fifteen-foot concrete area where dogs could be turned out to relieve themselves.

Minnesota winters meant nothing to Ch. Wycliffe Excellente of Shamlot who regularly enjoyed his time out on bright winter days. Excellente sired 20 champions for owner Glenna Carlson. He was sired by Ch. Wycliffe Thomas Too, CD X Ch. Wycliffe Genevieve. He was the wheelhorse dog in the half-sister, half-brother mating that produced Ch. Ascot Olivia, the dam of 1990 PCA National Best of Breed winner, Ch. Ascot Easy Does It.

But some of those kennels had their problems. Dogs periodically chewed their ear wraps or puffs—seemingly out of boredom. Managing sanitation problems was a daily battle. Everything had to be moved, scrubbed and mopped on a daily basis. And despite those excellent efforts, the odor from stored newspapers and dog food frequently gave hints that a kennel was a part of the house. Some of the outdoor areas had drains and could be picked up and hosed out. Other gravel areas could only be picked up, and keeping odors down was a problem during warm, humid periods.

Ideally, each dog should have an indoor stall, large enough for it to comfortably stretch out full length, and tall enough for it to stand up with head raised. In addition, a dog needs a turn-out area, and a series of long, narrow kennel runs is preferable. With such an arrangement—and the careful scheduling of when the dogs are out—you can get dogs to run the fences against each other. A square paddock arrangement just doesn't work as well.

Indoor Housing

If indoor stalls aren't realistic, you are probably going to turn to the use of crates or built-in boxes. So many choices exist in the market place, and the talents of local builders expand the choices even more. Three factors demand priority attention.

128

First, the crate or box should be large enough to assure the dog's comfort. Raised four-by-four-foot exercise pens can be used for puppies and Toys to provide a bit more freedom than individual crates. *If space is limited, have fewer dogs* rather than providing smaller crates. The dogs' comfort is paramount.

Second, assure that the choices you select can be cleaned easily and thoroughly. In my experience, crates that are difficult to clean invariably will last forever—or longer. Seek the opinion of breeders in your area with kennel arrangements similar to yours.

Third, consider how open or enclosed you want the housing units to be during the various seasons of the year. Is the housing area cool and breezy enough during the warm periods for the dogs to remain comfortable during hot summer afternoons? And will open crates subject the dogs to drafts during cold periods?

Unless your dog numbers increase too much too fast, you can *lessen the impact of crate living by providing groups of dogs that get along well together opportunities to come into the house and be members of the family*. Not only does that lessen the time they're restricted, it also provides continuing opportunities for socialization.

Housing for Special Circumstances

As far as housing is concerned, you'll also need to provide a place apart from the rest of the dogs where your brood bitches can whelp their litters and bring their litters along until they've been protected by inoculations. That is particularly important when new dogs are being introduced to the kennel and when show dogs are out on the road and exposed to everything the dog show scene might introduce.

Almost any veterinarian will also suggest having a place where ill dogs and new additions to the kennel can be isolated. Isolation is a key factor in reducing the spread of various kinds of disease problems.

THE FEEDING AREA

Ideally, your kennel operation will have some representation of a kitchen where you can soak, mix and store dog food. Ideally you'll have a refrigerator and a sink where you can wash feeding bowls and other utensils you use during the feeding process.

You can get by using the family kitchen facilities, but if you're really serious about this dog breeding business, you owe it to yourself to have a modest kitchen adjacent to the kennel where it is convenient. And while you're at it, provide yourself with all the cabinets and storage space you can. You can never have too much. In fact, regardless of what you do, you will probably wish you had more in a matter of time.

THE GROOMING AREA

My first trip to Sealark Farms, the Clarks' kennel in Cecilton, Maryland, I was surprised to learn that the grooming room—complete with bathtub—was on the second floor of the grand old plantation house, adjacent to an upstairs utility room. It seemed peculiar, but before the first afternoon ended, it made marvelous sense. The windows on the east let in a lovely natural light, and you could look out the window and see the puppy pens, keep an eye on the driveway and follow whatever activity was going on outside.

It made me remember what Nancy Cutler, Cutler Miniatures and Toys, had written about years earlier. Nancy contended that grooming, trimming and coat care were all so much more tolerable when done in a pleasant setting where friends could visit, where you could watch favorite television programs and where coffee or cool drinks were readily available. She was right. Too often a poorly lighted, crowded and "leftover" space is defined as the grooming area. And it is a miserable place to be. You hate being there, regardless of what you're doing. Mundane coat care activities seem all the more mundane because of the surroundings.

As far as possible, establish your grooming area in a light and airy room that provides a view. That assures you have light to work by and something to look at while you're working. At a minimum it needs to be large enough for several crates and grooming table, a bathtub and storage for grooming supplies and equipment.

A good water supply is essential. But even more important is adequate electricity. You'll be running one or more dryers, operating clippers and relying on good lighting to help you see what you're doing. And your friends, handler or fellow breeders may be stopping by to visit—and perhaps join in bathing and drying some of your dogs.

Get assistance planning how you will provide adequate wiring to handle all your needs, and put it on a separate circuit so you're not forever blowing fuses or having to reset the breaker switches. Put in an unbelievable number of electrical outlets, and if at all possible consider installing a lighting system that lights a major part of the ceiling. No trimming room has ever had too much light. You'll also need a telephone in the trimming room or you'll forever be missing calls as you put dogs away before you run to answer the phone.

This Scintilla granddaughter, Ch. Whitefarm Ms PB of Wildways, bred and owned by John Long, Chris Zaima and Dorothy Hageman, is out of "Riva," sired by the white, Ch. Karelea Barking Bachelor. Her June 1993 Best of Variety win at the Poodle Club of America marks the first time three consecutive generations of bitches have been PCA Variety winners.

Finally, find a large expanse of wall where you can place a big mirror. Later you'll be able to trim, check what you've done in the mirror and then refine your trim again and again until you get it exactly as you want it.

On the simplest scale, that's it. Your kennel must consist of a place to house and confine dogs inside. They need an exercise area. You need to plan some arrangement for whelping space and a way to isolate dogs from time to time. You need a kitchen area and a trimming area. If you have those things and access to laundry facilities, you have the elements necessary for a modest beginning. But above all, make your place a pleasant place to work. You'll probably spend more time there than you ever imagined.

Don't miss opportunities to learn how fellow breeders have provided the kinds of space and facilities essential to a successful kennel operation. They'll know product lines, suppliers, carpenters and at the same time be willing to share alternatives they considered in making their plans and choices. Every breeder has their list of "I wish I hads," and by learning from them, you can make your "wish I had" list fairly short.

Go for it!

This is every breeder's treasure once you have it. It is also a photographer's nightmare when you get the assignment: A portrait of a Poodle and her litter of six. Using a good share of his tricks of the trade, photographer John Ashby managed this memorable shot of Ch. Bel Tor Blissful with her young litter. She is owned by Dr. Samuel and Mary Peacock.

11

Managing the Brood Bitches and the Litters

WHETHER YOU HAVE one bitch that you consider your breeding stock—or more—pointing them toward the time they are the dams of your litters has to be one of your highest priority jobs. Not doing so is a little like losing a nation—"all for the want of a horseshoe nail," as the adage goes. The responsibility for seeing that all management practices are carried out in a timely manner is *yours*, whether you do the kennel work or manage a staff that does it. The responsibility is yours. That's the focus of this chapter.

If you're wise, you'll draw on the experience of fellow breeders whom you respect and you'll develop a relationship with your veterinarian so that you are confident he or she is very much a full-fledged partner and squarely in your corner.

As a breeder (and that is a coveted term which in full meaning is not ascribed to everyone who owns a bitch in whelp), your responsibilities rest in several directions: to the bitch and the litter she produces, to the future owners of the puppies you produce, to the breeders who played a part in helping you get started and to the breed itself.

BEFORE YOU BREED

But enough preaching, let's start thinking about managing the bitches you've acquired. Before you even begin thinking about selecting a sire for a litter, you need to do your homework. An appointment with an ophthalmologist is the starting point to determine that all heritable eye diseases are as much out of the question as possible. If you can gain access to an ERG (electroretinogram) you should do that as well. Your veterinarian and fellow breeders will keep you well counseled on the need and procedure for obtaining the information you need on canine hip dysplasia, von Willebrand's disease, sebaceous adenitis and other heritable diseases in your variety. Stay alert to new developments. It is not unlikely for new problems to surface within the next five years or so. *It is senseless to get three or five years into a breeding program without any knowledge about the status of your foundation animals in terms of heritable diseases affecting the Poodle.* Do all you can to know the possibilities before you start.

Consult with your veterinarian for recommendations on controlling internal and external parasites. Many veterinarians can recommend a year-long program that is as effective as possible in controlling such problems. Each internal parasite has its own life cycle, and the trick is to determine if your bitches have parasites—and then treat at the life cycle stage when the parasite is most vulnerable. You can't treat once (or even periodically) and control internal parasites. Treatment must be repeated and timeliness is the key to success.

Once you have obtained all of the information possible about heritable diseases, and if you have the parasite problems well in hand, you're now at a point to begin thinking toward the actual breeding.

Bitches ready to breed should be of moderate weight—not thin and not fat. Thin bitches will lack cover over the backbone and ribs. They will stay a little too tucked up at the flank and have a ''Whippet'' look in that area. The real problem, however, is that they will have little or no reserve to draw on as their bodies take on the responsibilities of developing the litter.

Think about how a brood bitch uses the nutrients you provide her from the time *she* is born until she is a retired matron. Initially, it is important that she be fed enough nutrients to maintain her essential body functions as well as the nutrients necessary for growth. Once she is full grown, her nutrient intake can be shifted somewhat because maintaining herself is all that she is doing. When she enters the ring, you may opt to increase her intake a bit—not because she needs it, but rather because many judges like the full-bodied feeling that a little extra weight gives a dog when it is being examined.

In moderation, the extra weight doesn't hurt. But watch it. Toys especially develop little fat rolls ahead of their tailset, and sometimes fatty deposits around the head and neck can make the head far less attractive than it could be.

Ch. Rimskittle Rampant, a multiple Best In Show winner and the dam of five champions, was the foundation of Rimskittle Standards, bred by Mr. and Mrs. James E. Clark.

Once the dog matures or is retired, there's no need to strive for that modest covering of fat. It isn't needed. And in fact, when dogs gain too much weight, it often interferes with their reliability as breeding animals. In dogs, as in all livestock, too much weight (really fat, remember) leads to reduced reproductive efficiency. Don't let it happen.

Most of the artful livestock breeders like to bring their breeding animals into the breeding season gaining weight. And once conception occurs, they continue gaining weight until the demands of the developing embryos bring it to an end. At this point in the pregnancy, your bitch needs to be fed enough to maintain herself and needs an allowance for the reproductive process that is going on.

That process will continue until whelping. Then your feeding program should focus on providing nutrients for maintenance and lactation, the business of producing milk. Once the litter is weaned, you again shift your intentions to continue maintenance feeding—and just a bit more to rebuild the bitch to a more moderate condition than when she finished nursing.

What to Feed?

We could have fun with this, and some people feed dogs in a manner far more complicated than dieticians plan for hospital patients in critical condition. But all of my background and course work in animal nutrition tells me that the U.S. dog food industry has made it very difficult for U.S. Poodle breeders to do an *in*adequate job of meeting the nutritional needs of the kennel charges. Admittedly some products are better than others, but a number of brand name product lines are really quite comparable. They are not identical, but they do approach developing the product line with a keen eye for the nutritional needs of dogs during the various stages of their life cycle.

What about all those supplements—those for minerals, vitamins, coat condition and the list goes on. They won't hurt a thing. But unless your attentive eye has told you you're dealing with a nutritional problem—and your veterinarian has confirmed it and made a recommendation—don't expect any of them to do any good. Try some of them anyway. It is kind of fun to watch day after day to see if your great discovery really does what it promises. (The same is true of grooming products.) And one day, you'll decide to clean your cupboards and you'll laugh at what you've accumulated but never use. I always tear the price tag off when I buy a product so that it is impossible for me to remember what I spent.

I'm reasonably convinced that the formulated product lines offer a stand-alone feeding program unless I've detected a particular problem and have a veterinarian's recommendation. I like the puppy formulations because they provide a higher level of digestible protein, and protein is essential for growth.

The experience of fellow breeders suggests that providing a mineral and vitamin supplement during a puppy's first year probably does provide some benefit in bone development and increases your chances of getting the kind of feet you hoped would develop. Either the breeders or your veterinarian can direct you to a specific product with which they have had experience. Once the puppy reaches maturity, it makes sense to switch to the adult formulation—usually with a somewhat lower protein level. That level is adequate for pregnant and lactating bitches, especially if you increase the amount you feed them. Many breeders routinely supplement the diets of the in-whelp broods with dicalcium phosphate, a mineral compound that protects bitches from eclampsia. Eclampsia is a condition that occurs shortly after whelping and is caused by the sudden drain of calcium that occurs when bitches begin producing milk.

As soon as a bitch finishes her reproductive career, it just makes sense to switch to a mature dog formulation—primarily because it contains an even lower level of protein. As the dog ages and moves beyond the processes (growth, reproduction and lactation) that require higher levels of protein, you can reduce stress on the kidneys by lowering the level of protein.

Two final points on feeding. If you absolutely can't stand having a research-based feed company formulate what you feed your dogs, there are a couple of sensible additions you can make to the basic diet.

1. Most feed companies recommend soaking their meals with hot water. You can solve some recycling problems by keeping a stew pot on the stove and using the stew to soak the meal. Start with a pot of water and add both meat and vegetable trimmings, leftovers and even egg shells (an excellent source of calcium). The stew can't be harmful. It soaks the meal and it may also increase the palatability of the feed. If that idea doesn't appeal, but you're concerned about palatability of the formulated feeds, add just enough canned meat to the soaked meal to entice the dogs to eat it.

2. If you have a dog you'd like to gain a bit of weight fairly rapidly, try adding fat to its diet by adding either ground beef (raw) or a small amount of corn oil. Fat tends to soften dog stools, and, if overfed, results in stools too loose for polite company. Start by adding only a small amount, and anytime you see stools softening, hold at that level or cut back a bit.

But remember, dogs aren't humans. Rather than striving for variety in their diets, they benefit from consistency. They are not bored by eating the same thing day after day. So once you begin a feeding program, stick with it. Switching from one product line to another, and constantly toying with this supplementation and then another is most often a nonproductive and cost-adding approach to feeding a kennel.

IT'S TIME TO BREED HER

Timing is everything in getting a successful breeding. Consequently, it's wise to have your planning nearly complete by the time your bitch

Ch. Rimskittle Romp, winner of the first Veterans Sweepstakes at the 1992 PCA National show, is one of the modern Rimskittles. Her pedigree reveals seven crosses back to Rampant, the foundation dam, and the influence of two key outcross sires used by the Clarks. She is by the Top Producer Ch. Rimskittle Roughneck and out of the Top Producer Ch. Syrena On Course. (*Photo by Tauskey*)

comes in season. Hopefully, you and your mentors have arrived at a decision about how she will be bred. And if the plan involves shipping your bitch by air, you've got a special planning cycle to work through, so let's start there.

Check the bitch's record to see when you anticipate she will come in season. Alert the owner of the sire or the dog's agent, and see if they have any preferences about shipping arrangements and timing. Also check to be certain that all immunizations and routine examinations for heritable diseases are current. You'll need a set of health papers before shipping, so arrange for them with your veterinarian. But check the period covered. Be certain the examination will remain current even at the time the bitch is shipped back.

Preparations for Shipping

As the time approaches, do some detective work with your airline offices to determine what alternative shipping plans you have available. You'll probably delay making shipping arrangements until she comes in season, but you can save time at the last minute by planning ahead. You can also involve the sire's owner or agent to see what would be most convenient to them, if you know your alternatives early.

At the first hint of a season coming, get the bitch ready to ship. Remember, your attention to teeth, ears and nails will communicate a great deal about your management ability as a breeder. Have the bitch freshly trimmed and bathed when you ship her, and if the bitch is in coat or growing it for a future ring career, you should be certain the hair is in whatever oil or conditioning agent you use so she doesn't need constant attention to her coat while in the stud owner's care.

Also, put together a little verbal care-package if you have any specific instructions about the bitch. That may seem a strange suggestion, but I've had bitches sent for breeding and I didn't even know their names. One sheet of paper is all that's needed to provide the name and call name, a pedigree (if you haven't already sent one), the date she came in season (and an assessment of your confidence) and any other instructions or cautions on feeding and coat care. You might also note telephone numbers where you can be reached, even hotel numbers if you'll be out of town or at shows. And if you've explored alternative ways to get the bitch shipped back or returned, indicate what you've learned, including the names and telephone numbers of people who you have contacted to bring her back from a show.

Put the information in an envelope and tape it to the crate. Also put a note on the outside of the envelope that says "Read This." Often you pick up a dog at the airport, and all you see is an envelope that says, "Health Papers." Since they will go back with the bitch when she has been bred, I never opened them. I did that until one time I discovered I had returned the breeding fee which the bitch owner tucked in with the health papers. So don't assume anyone will read the health papers.

With this out of the way, you're ready to move when the bitch comes in season. First contact the people associated with the sire to learn what will work best for them. You'll often have to work around dog shows and dog show travel, so don't assume they're sitting at home by the telephone waiting with the same level of excitement you are experiencing.

Then confirm and book whatever air travel seems most suitable. Be prepared to learn of weather-related shipping instructions. It is my experience that bitches always come in season when it is either too hot or too cold to ship them.

I always liked to ship at least two days before the day I thought the first breeding should take place. That gave the bitch a bit of time to settle in and recover from the stress of shipping. I usually didn't put a totally clean towel in the shipping crate. I preferred to send them off with something that smelled familiar—particularly when shipping bitches that hadn't had to withstand the rigors of the show routine.

I either fed bitches very lightly or not at all on the days I bred them. If the bitch is under stress to start with, a heavy feeding just adds to it, and they can get by comfortably for twenty-four hours with no problems.

Finally, always remember that bitches have not read the textbooks on when bitches should be bred. The tenth and twelfth days are good rules of thumb, but they don't all play by the rules. Some bitches will be ready to breed as early as the seventh day. I knew one who finally was successfully bred (the first day she would accept the dog) on her twenty-second day.

The more breeding you do, the more you will be convinced that in breeding dogs, anything is possible.

12

The Whelping

GETTING READY for your first whelping is about like doing any household repair job. It is a lot easier if you have a plan and have the right tools to do the job. So before whelping begins, let's think through what you will need to have on hand to do the job—and to cope with any of the unexpected happenings that might occur.

THE WHELPING BOX

The most time-consuming task will be providing a place for the bitch to have her litter. Breeders talk about the "whelping box," and that's what we're going to need. Follow this rule: Regardless of the variety you have, the box should be large enough for the bitch to stretch out comfortably with room left over to place a heating pad if you need it and a stack of towels and washcloths. Standards will require about a four-foot-square box; Miniatures, a three-foot-square; and Toys can get by with a two-foot-square box, and really always did nicely in my Miniature box. Boxes of those approximate sizes are not only large enough for the bitch during whelping, but will also accommodate the litter for several weeks after whelping. Each breeder has a favorite design, so in your early associations and visits to kennels, you might ask to see what they use.

My box had a raised floor that was covered with remnants of kitchen flooring. It could be removed for cleaning and cleaned easily with any of several kitchen cleaners. The four sides were of quarter-inch hardware cloth that I draped with towels during winter whelpings. But the open sides allowed air circulation when it was needed. One side was hinged about halfway down. During whelping, the hinged side made it easy to reach in and work with the bitch and litter. When the side was raised, the bitch was confined with her puppies. And for a while after the birth, letting the side down enabled the bitch to leave the box—but confined the puppies. I generally leave the side down until the first puppy begins exploring ways to get out. At that point, the side went up and the bitch would have to be lifted in and out of the box until the litter was weaned.

Keep it big enough, be certain it is easy to clean and consider a hinged side for the variety of reasons listed. Have it ready for use when whelping seems close at hand.

SUPPLIES

Other supplies you should have on hand include a huge supply of **towels**. You'll use them to dry the puppies and get them started and to clean up the area and keep it dry. Don't use good towels. They frequently come through the whelping fairly stained. You'll also need a **hemostat (clamps), Scissors** and some **white cotton thread** to clamp, cut and tie-off the umbilical cord. Some use dental floss and like it better because it handles easier when wet. A baby **ear syringe** is a useful tool to remove fluids from inside the puppies' mouths, and a **hot box** (a small cardboard box with a heating pad) is also a near necessity.

Many breeders keep detailed notes on the arrival of each puppy in the litter. The note includes birth sequence, color, sex, weight and any other details they want to remember such as whether the placenta was expelled.

Think through where you want the litter to be born. All of the litters I whelped were born near a coffeepot, telephone and television set. When I consider creature comforts, I include my own! But you really might as well make yourself comfortable. Some whelpings go on for hours, and there's no reason to be more miserable than necessary.

So find a quiet place that suits your interests and begin to set up shop at least a couple of weeks before you expect the litter. The more comfortable the bitch is with the whelping box, the less traumatic her adjustment will be at whelping—just in case she has a more preferable location for the whelping.

The first puppy I whelped was born under the Christmas tree—without assistance; the second in the whelping box. The third was born under the tree, and the final puppy in the litter was born during the process of putting the dam back in the box. It was several days after whelping before that bitch gave up her choice spot and finally accepted mine. Experienced bitches usually understand the plan and go along with it readily. Maiden bitches (those having their first litter) are frequently uncertain about what is happening and they require more time for adjustment.

THE WATCHFUL EYE

Remain attentive to your bitch's behavior during the last week or so. This may be the easiest task you ever assumed, because some bitches stay so close to their owners it is like having a third leg. Don't be surprised if she sleeps a lot, but then, don't be surprised if she is restless and nervous. The whelping process teaches many of us just how individual our bitches really are.

Once again, read everything you have seen on whelping a litter. Just remember one point: Those references are designed to help you with anything and everything that might go wrong. Few, if any, of those problems will surface. So don't get paranoid. Remember, you are there to assist in a process that dogs in the wild routinely handle. This is not an insurmountable task.

If you're really concerned, call one of your mentors and ask them to be on telephone standby, just in case. If *you're* a mentor, don't offer

"Give us three more days and we'll be outta here." With eyes wide open, these three-week-old Miniature puppies are ready to venture away from their whelping box.

assistance too quickly, but if distance isn't too much of a problem, be willing to do the telephone routine, and have a plan in mind to make a late-night trip if it is necessary.

I THINK IT IS GOING TO HAPPEN!

You know when the sixty-third day will arrive, but keep an eye on your bitch and particularly note when she has milk. Several days before the anticipated whelping, expose the entire breast area with a #10 blade, being careful not to nick or clipper-burn her. Also either clip around or expose the vulva and the inside of the rear legs. The point is to eliminate any hair that will interfere with the birth and nursing process.

At about the fifty-ninth day from the first breeding, begin taking the bitch's temperature morning and evening. Write the readings on a handy calendar because the temperatures will be an important reference. Most bitches will read between 99 and 100 degrees during the period before labor begins. About twenty-four hours before the start, the temperature will drop to about 98 degrees. Here's a surefire bet: You will have puppies within twenty-four hours. At least you should prepare to have puppies within twenty-four hours.

Your bitch will likely be disinterested in her food, may be increasingly restless and may have an increased amount of clear vaginal discharge. The nipples will also become more pink or reddish. If it is during office hours or your veterinary clinic has an answering service, you might advise the office that the whelping seems imminent. There's no reason to speak to the veterinarian. Just inform the office.

If you have examined your bitch's abdomen periodically throughout the pregnancy (and every person does, even long past the first litter), you may notice that the placement of her "pouch" has shifted sharply to the rear. That simply means the puppies are getting in line as they prepare to be born.

LABOR DAY!

Nervousness, a rippling of the stomach muscles and a slight straining motion will probably be the first signs that your bitch is officially in labor. As soon as you see those signs, take the bitch to the place where she normally relieves herself and offer her that opportunity. Her litter will not be born there while you're watching. But you do need to offer her that opportunity periodically during whelping.

144

As her litter nurses, this brown Miniature bitch keeps an eye on all strangers who come near. Most bitches are protective by nature, probably because such a stance was a necessity in the wild when dogs faced predators.

As the contractions continue, just be on hand. Read a book. Watch television. Polish silver or do any of those other jobs you've been putting off. And periodically, scratch her chin and tell her "good girl." You can also call the veterinary clinic and advise that labor has started. Again, you need not speak to the veterinarian unless you have some specific questions or concerns.

Be prepared. This process may last anywhere from two to eighteen hours, but most actual whelpings will get underway in a matter of two to four hours. Expect your bitch to be a touch restless at times. You'll notice that her determination increases as the time goes by. But then she'll drop her head between her front paws and rest a bit. Even then you'll notice gentle rippling action across her abdomen. Soon you'll notice that she's working a great deal more diligently. And she may brace herself against the wall of the whelping box. Those are certain signs that she's trying to expel the first puppy.

So fill your coffee cup, make a last check of supplies and get prepared for action. Soon you'll see a bubble appear from the vulva. All is well. Just give it time. The bubble may disappear for a while and them come back again, and that process may be repeated several times before the bubble breaks and the fluid is released. Your bitch will notice it immediately and will begin licking her vulva.

How long should you stay patient as this process unfolds? Longer than you want to. But note your bitch's behavior. If she labors awhile and then rests a half hour, don't worry. But if she seems rather determined and really works at it for a two-hour period, it is now time to speak to the veterinarian directly. From that point on, you should simply follow the doctor's counsel. Most often, however, you won't need to call the veterinarian, and you'll be working on your own. Once the bubble ruptures you can expect hard labor to follow and if you feel the skin between the anus and the vulva, you'll see the bulge the puppy creates and know that it is well on its way.

The first puppy in a bitch's first litter may require considerable time to pass through the cervical opening. And that process is the time when she will likely indicate pain. Reassure her, and get set to deal with the puppy. Puppies are most often born headfirst, but breech births are really of little consequence. Expect the entire puppy to be expelled rather quickly, with the entire puppy in its sac and the placenta attached.

At this point, you need to focus on the **A, B, C,** approach I learned from Jean Lazarus, Torchlight Standards. **"A" is for airway, "B" is for breathing, and "C" is for circulation.** Jean explains it this way.

"**Airway.** The puppy cannot survive without a clear airway. Rupture both membranes with your fingernail near the puppy's head and quickly peel them back over the body. Fluid will rush from inside the membrane.

"Now place the puppy, cord, placenta and all, in a towel (the puppy will be slippery) and hold the puppy with its head downward as you wipe the face with another piece of towel. Use the ear syringe to remove fluids from the oral cavity and upper respiratory passage to get the puppy breathing as quickly as possible.

"Now start rubbing and drying the puppy with another dry towel— paying attention to the rib cage to stimulate respiration and to the face to keep the nose and mouth clear. Some puppies breathe and cry spontaneously as soon as the membranes rupture. I like viable puppies like that, but even with those I still use the syringe and towels.

"**B is for breathing**, and let's face it: No puppy can grow up unless it breathes quickly following birth.

"Once the puppy is breathing fairly well and is fairly fluid free, you can go to **"C" for circulation.** Remember in this case the puppy was a classic delivery and the placenta is still attached. The entire time you work on A and B you must be careful not to let the cord and placenta dangle or pull at the puppy's belly. You'll cause a hernia. That's why you keep the entire package wrapped in a towel.

"During this period the blood has been draining into the puppy where it certainly is more useful than when thrown in the trash. Once the puppy is breathing well on its own, it doesn't need the placenta anymore. At this point, carefully place a clamp around the cord about one and a half inches from the belly and lock it. You might practice a one-handed locking a few times before the delivery so you feel adept at it.

"Next, cut the cord with dull scissors—but remember to keep the clamp between the scissors and puppy. Otherwise you may subject the puppy to excessive bleeding from the cord. Puppies are small and can't sustain a large blood loss and stay in good viable condition. All that is left is to tie the cord with the cotton thread and release the clamp. Now the puppy is finally living totally on its own."

This entire procedure really takes longer to describe than to happen. But once it is complete, your bitch's attitude will determine whether you place the puppy in a position to nurse or first put it between her front legs where she can give it a thorough look-over and licking.

Experienced broods are usually totally attentive to the new puppy and anxious to care for it. First-time whelpers are often confused and frightened by all that has happened. Most often however, you'll have the experience of watching the new mother move from the confused state into the throes of motherhood, and it happens before your eyes. As Jean Lazarus observes, "It never fails to amaze me that bitches perform so well on instinct what some humans never achieve even with education and guidance."

But one puppy doesn't make a litter. And you will have some decisions to make following the birth of the first puppy. If all is going well and the mother is at work producing subsequent puppies, some breeders prefer to follow a natural approach and leave each puppy nursing as the process goes on. So do I—but only if the bitch remains quiet and the puppy is nursing successfully.

Sometimes, however, the bitch wants to move positions or gets so involved in her contractions that she totally ignores her new whelp. In those cases, she generally won't mind if you remove the puppy from the nest and place it in the "hot box" on a heating pad. You must be careful that the heating pad is not too warm. Let the pad heat up and then place it on its lowest setting. You can partially cover the box with a towel to contain the heat generated.

Obviously, if the bitch has an anxiety attack when you remove the puppy, your choices are more limited, and you may have to forego use of the box. This is really a decision that needs to be made on a litter-by-litter basis, and how you handle your alternatives will be based on the actions and reactions of your bitch.

DEALING WITH SOME UNCOMMON PROBLEMS

The problems we'll highlight here can't really be called "frequent," but they are the kind most breeders are likely to experience during their first few years.

First there's the puppy who is half born when mother takes a break. The whelp is still in the membrane, but seems "stuck" in a location where he'd rather not be. And sometimes puppies get stuck after the membrane is ruptured. Don't panic—but do deal with the problem. Grasp the puppy firmly with a section of towel in your hand so you can get a good grip. Then wait until the dam produces another contraction. Grasp firmly and pull downward and outward at about a 30-degree angle. When the contraction ends, stop pulling and wait for the next one. Repeat that cycle until the pup is totally expelled.

Remove the membrane as quickly as possible and go through the standard routine. If the puppy was born breach (rear legs first) pay particular attention to getting the fluids out of the mouth. If the membrane is ruptured on a "stuck" puppy, you can actually use the syringe to get the puppy breathing even before the birth is complete.

Sometimes a puppy will get born without your assistance. And when you find it, it seems chilled. Work quickly to assure that you have taken care of the routine that you follow typically, and then offer the pup a chance to nurse. Don't be surprised if it refuses. A brief stint in the hot box to get it warmed will often make all the difference in the willingness to nurse.

Throughout the whelping process, remember that you have several unseen partners with you. Your veterinarian and fellow breeders are only a telephone call away. If you encounter something you don't know how to handle, use the telephone. With your veterinarian alerted, you can always make a quick trip to the clinic if necessary.

Once the process is over, let both the mother and litter rest. Offer the bitch a chance to relieve herself, provide water and then take a break. If it is a reasonable hour, you might report your success to the clinic and see when your veterinarian wants to see the dam and her litter. Some veterinarians do; others don't unless there is a problem. Talk about when tail-docking will take place and whether your veterinarian wants a post-whelping look at the bitch.

When your second litter is born, you will begin to develop an understanding that each whelping is different. That will remain true for as long as you continue to breed Poodles. But one thing will not change. With each litter's arrival, you will find a certain excitement and anticipation as you wonder whether each of those tiny puppy lumps will be your next key breeding animal, your next big winner, the next guide dog or the next adored pet that teaches its young family members the responsibilities of caring for others. And you'll never know the potential that exists in that puppy lump until long after your work at the whelping box is done.

Poodle bitches often encourage the weaning process as puppies get too rough in the nursing process. But many of them enjoy their puppies even after weaning. This cream Standard bitch illustrates a pigment condition referred to as "winter nose." The black seems to fade away leaving a lighter color in its place. A few days in the bright sun restores the pigment—just as it does on white or cream Poodles wearing a Continental trim.

13

The Weeks that Follow

BORING. That's how I've always felt about the days and weeks that follow the birth of a litter. Actually, unless something goes wrong, there's very little to do, and the puppy lumps that held such hope and promise at whelping time, now seem again like what they are: puppy lumps. They nurse, perform bodily functions and sleep. And except for yawning and providing the most marvelous smelling puppy breath, they do nothing else.

Your task is simply that of monitoring basic biology. A key part of doing that is recording puppies' weights on at least every other day. That will assure puppies are gaining weight and will give you a double-check on what your eyes see. You can be fooled.

Pay attention to your bitch. She is so much the center of everything. A couple of lighter-than-usual feedings generally follow the whelping, but as soon as you get signals that her stools are normal (always an indicator that something is wrong or that things have returned to normal), she can be eased back toward full feeding. *Remember, when you feed her, you are also feeding the litter* and assuring that she will be able to meet their demands as they grow.

Also, keep an eye on vaginal discharge from the dam. For a period following whelping, you'll see signs of bleeding and the discharge may well have a cloudy, yellow tinge to it. That is normal following whelping, but after a week or ten days, those signs should be reported to your veterinarian. You really want to see a clear discharge or none at all to indicate that all has returned to normal.

THE NEWBORNS

You can learn from the new puppies as well. If they stay busy doing the normal boring things described, all is well. If they sleep a lot, that is another good sign. And usually a litter will sleep in a pile with one puppy crawling away from the rest if it gets a bit warm.

A crying puppy is a warning sign. Is it hungry? Hurt? Does it have a bellyache? I also worry about the puppy that seems always isolated from the rest of the litter. When I see those signs—or if the dam seems to reject a puppy—I worry. I call the veterinarian or a fellow breeder.

Watch for eye infections *before the eyes open*, or while they are in the process of opening. They are usually accompanied by a swelling which is most obvious. Don't treat this problem yourself. A wrong guess could result in blindness, so take the puppy to your veterinarian as soon as you notice it.

The old rule of thumb suggests that puppies begin opening their eyes at about ten days. And that's usually a good rule of thumb. But don't expect the eyes to pop open on the morning of the tenth day. You'll see the line between the upper and lower lids begin widening day by day until the eye is indeed open.

Don't be surprised if the eye has a grayish blue cast to it. They often do during the opening process, but they will change to a bright black color fairly quickly.

As the days pass, you'll find the puppies gradually become more mobile as they drag themselves from here to there. How they feel changes, too. They feel firm and respond to being touched, now more reaction than resistance. When you pick them up, they grab out with their legs in an action that seems to be the beginnings of that you see later on when you begin trimming them and placing them on the grooming table.

Don't miss the chance to handle each puppy as frequently as you can. Just pick them up and hold them. Run your fingers over their legs. To my mind, all of these experiences, starting right after whelping, communicate that people are a part of their world, too. As you handle them, pay particular attention to their toenails. And check their dam's breasts as well. Baby puppies need their nails clipped at a remarkably early age, primarily to keep them from injuring their dam as they nurse.

Somewhere along the line, usually between three to seven days, you will want the tails docked. Many experienced breeders do that themselves and also remove the dewclaws. You may decide to do it at some point, but at the start, let your veterinarian handle that work. Just be certain that tails are docked long enough to provide the look you want. Talk with a breeder who has your variety—and it is ideal if you share the same veterinarian. My rule of thumb is to leave two-thirds and remove one-third on Miniatures and Toys. Leave a little less on Standards. Or as both of the Beaumont brothers said when they docked my litters, "I know. Just tip them."

WHEN FEEDING BEGINS

I always have mixed feelings about when to start accepting the responsibility for feeding a new litter. It is so nice when the dam provides everything, because when she is totally responsible for feeding, she also accepts total responsibility for cleaning up after the litters. Because she uses her tongue and the licking motion to stimulate both urination and defecation, she has total control, and her system seems so much more efficient than any we as humans can design. But soon after the eyes open—usually at about the third week—you can begin to relieve the stress nursing is placing on the dam and can begin the puppies' transition to eating on their own.

So far, their diet has been entirely liquid. Let's start by keeping it that way. Esbilac is a product that many breeders rely on when the dam doesn't produce milk or for some other reason is not able to nurse her litter. Diluted as indicated in package directions, Esbilac is a near-perfect transition food. But since we're also beginning the transition from liquid to solid food, use Esbilac to make a really soupy mixture with packaged baby cereal commonly called Pablum.

Frankly, don't be surprised if your first few attempts at feeding are less than fruitful. But you will see some progress. Try offering them the mixture—at about body temperature—in a tiny bowl or the lid of a jar. Steady the puppy enough to keep it in one place and pass the lid under the puppy's mouth. Your goal is to get the mouth into the lid just enough that the hair on the face picks up the soupy mixture. And then watch. Soon the licking will begin, and that's the first step to having your puppies eat on their own.

I like to feed the puppies one at a time initially to see how they respond and to get a reading on their willingness to eat. But I switch to group feeding as soon as I feel everyone is comfortable with the process.

Put down lots of paper. That's important, because the early forays into eating generally consist of the puppies walking back and forth through their feed pans. So use plenty of paper and keep a supply of damp towels available to wipe off the food on their faces, feet and belly. They'll get it everywhere.

Many breeders add pureed meat baby food to the mix and then

gradually switch them to ground meat. The development of the home blender makes creating the early puppy food mixtures for puppies far easier than it used to be. Ground beef can be reduced to its most digestible forms quickly. And we had excellent success switching from the baby food to the first prepared dog food meal by using one of the puppy food formulations with powdered milk coverings. We would simply run it through the blender until it had a coarse flour consistency. We mixed that with baby food initially, and gradually switched them to all prepared food. Later we were able to eliminate the blender step and the process was complete.

WHEN DO YOU WEAN THEM?

Not until they are capable of sustaining themselves on their own. Listen to the dam. She'll let you know when she needs time away—and when she thinks it is time. If she seems quite milked-out, you may force the time ahead a little bit, but really, she'll let you know when she's ready, and when they're eating, they're ready.

Be certain you and your veterinarian have a clear understanding of what inoculations are being recommended and the schedule you need to follow. Most veterinarians will give you a shot record log that you can keep for each puppy and provide to those who purchase the puppies later.

ONCE THEY CAN WALK

Once the puppies get past the one-step-forward, two-steps-backward stage—a stage I liked most of all—you're ready to help them start thinking about being show dogs and outgoing companions. Get the puppies used to expecting to find bits of meat in your hand and give the puppies little nibbles from time to time. I always tried to convince puppies that I had a magic hand that always had something good to eat. Those who believed ultimately became those that would bait in the ring.

Take a puppy from the whelping box and loosely put a soft, narrow lead on it. Just let the puppy stand around while you talk to it and periodically give bits of meat. Do lots of "good boys" and "good girls" to keep the pup responding to you. Then try calling and letting the puppy follow you. Never tighten the lead. We're in the forerunner of lead training now, and if the puppy never discovers he's being trained, so much the better.

Many puppies respond to the individual attention—especially with

Children who are gentle can have a marvelous effect on the development of Poodle puppies. In fact, some breeders have "rented" carefully selected children to play with puppies and take them for walks. Socialization of puppies should remain a high priority for all breeders, regardless of how pressing the day-to-day schedule of work may be.

their littermates watching. Soon, they'll be tagging along with you—often forgetting that they are wearing a lead.

Each puppy should have a turn for a few minutes at most. In a few short sessions, you'll begin to get the feeling that lead training has begun. *Keep it fun.* Go where they go. *Don't tighten the lead and don't force anything.* If a tail goes down, it is always because *you* made a mistake.

As the puppies become more reliable on the lead, you can increase the frequency of the sessions. Change the location. Take them away from their whelping box or playpen—away from the littermates. Once the puppies have had their first shots, you can take them outside to the patio or out on the sidewalk where they will meet strangers. Shopping malls and parks are other places to continue such outings and they offer the opportunities to meet new people.

In addition to the prebaiting training and the prelead training, one other activity can be of tremendous benefit to every puppy in the litter, whether or not they make it to the ring. Get down on the floor and play with them. Squeak their squeak toys, tug on their sock, let them walk on your chest and chew your hair and do anything else that they think is fun.

I once taught a handling class for a Poodle club and discovered that the people who brought puppies were so engrossed with making the babies become show dogs that they had never taken the time to play with the puppies. The puppies and the owners really had no relationship other than that of caregiver and recipient of the care. That's really sad. It also lessens the chance that the puppies will enter the ring with that "I-am-the-star" attitude that is so essential to the Poodle. Don't downplay the importance of play time, and start it early.

Poodle puppies aren't hothouse flowers. Don't treat them that way. They dish out a good deal of roughhousing to each other, and they'll do the same with you. Tweak their noses. Pull the hair on their chests. Stiff arm them away from you, and see how tough and determined they become to get back in the middle of the action. That kind of attitude developed in play will be a tremendous benefit when they enter the ring.

DECISIONS, DECISIONS

By the time the eyes are open, most breeders (headhunters that they are) are ready to clip faces and trim feet. Get the puppies accustomed to the noise of the clippers a couple of times before you use it. And forget about doing a good job. Nobody cares. Just clip the easy parts and forget about getting between the toes and getting every last hair. Try to make the first several clippings nontraumatic happenings.

As this process begins, you'll probably begin getting the puppy accustomed to the grooming table and being stacked. My rule was that during the first sessions if they were on the table and their tails were up, everything was perfect. Keep it fun. We can teach them to have their squirrley fronts twisted into place much later. All they have to do in the beginning is stand with their tail up.

As the eight-week point draws near, you'll no doubt be considering which puppies you'll keep and which you will sell. And of those being sold, you'll have to decide which will represent you best by becoming good family pets—and which shall represent you in the ring under the banner of your or another person's ownership.

What can be more appealing than a litter of Standard Poodle puppies at five weeks? While this age is too young to let go, many breeders introduce potential pet buyers to the litter once they've had their first shots.

In the horse world, people who sell horses frequently sell them with a veterinarian's certificate. It is simply a statement of the horse's health and detectable soundness. It wouldn't be a bad idea for dog people to explore with their veterinarians. The certificate could do those things and summarize the state on inoculations and the current status on internal parasites and any treatments that had been given.

Whether a puppy goes to a pet home or a show home is a decision that has to be made. If you can rely on a fellow breeder, you could benefit from their thinking, especially if they have had experience with the family you are developing. If you have aligned yourself with a professional handler, they, too, might have valuable insight. Some handlers are willing to evaluate litters at an early age. Others who may have limited breeding experience of their own, are less willing. But if you are picking a puppy from the litter and know who will be handling it, it would be a real mistake not to have that person's opinion as you make your decision.

The hucksters of the dog world, those moving pets into the market place as early as possible, are always willing to sell puppies at seven or eight weeks of age. Respected breeders tend to want to hang onto puppies a bit longer. Your personal situation will be an important determinant. And frankly, it is generally a lot easier to hang onto a litter of three Toy puppies than it is a litter of eleven Standards.

But without question, inoculations should be at a point where it is safe to sell, and internal parasite problems should be dealt with. Be certain that problems such as fleas, ear mites and the like are nonexistent, and if they are problems, you should seriously question whether your level of management is such that you should continue in this endeavor. Such problems generally create one-time sale opportunities only, lots of return puppies and even more bad will. You face a no-win situation over the long haul.

14

Choosing a Stud Dog for Your Kennel

NEARLY EVERYONE will agree that a kennel's beginning should focus on a bitch—the best you can afford. And many successful breeders have stayed with that theory. *They've bred dogs for many years without owning a stud dog.* Unless you have a sizeable battery of bitches suited to a single dog, you'll probably find you can send bitches to your optimum choice sire for a cost less than that of maintaining your own stud dog.

But there seems a certain fascination with owning stud dogs, using them to develop your own program, and then offering their services to other breeders. And it is probably understandable, as so much of the history and development of our breed seems to hinge on the contributions of benchmark sires. Without question, dogs are capable of producing a far greater number of puppies than bitches, and in that respect have the potential to exert a more far-reaching impact on the breed. Probably not more than one stud dog in ten ever reaches that potential. And remember, many stud dogs have a negative impact on their breed.

The decision to retain or purchase a male breeding animal is usually accompanied with unlimited hope in the heart. But it will be many years before the breeder and the Fancy in general will be able to determine whether that decision resulted in hopes fulfilled, heartbreaks unlimited or just another dog in the kennel that left little or no lasting impact.

Ch. Penchant Paladin is the top all-time Top Producing Miniature sire with 83 U.S. champions. A Specialty Best of Breed and multiple Group winner, Danny was bred by Betsy Leedy and later co-owned with Margo Durney. Danny seemed to work well with a variety of bitches and he was widely used by both established breeders and beginners. He is sired by Ch. Aizbel The Imperialist X Ch. Fontella's Penchant Laurel, both Top Producers. His two grandsires are the littermates Ch. Campbell's Raz-Ma-Tazz and Ch. Campbell's Clansman.

This chapter will focus on factors to consider in acquiring such a dog, his care and management throughout a breeding career and the need to promote such a dog to get his potential recognized.

Norman A. Austin, Baliwick Toys, wrote an article long ago that last appeared in the April–May 1979 issue of *Poodle Review*. He made this observation about dogs who left a lasting imprint on the breed:

> You will find that they all had in common five virtues: type, balance, personality, soundness and glamour. These are the essentials to the greatness of any dog, most certainly in his show career, and without them, all the promotion in the world will not make him great.

Norman observed further that

Ch. Kirsch's Rodeo of Halo, a multiple Best in Show and PCA Regional Best of Breed winner is sired by Ch. Langcroft Country Pride X Ch. Kirsch's Delphi Moonstone. Rodeo sired 20 champions. He was bred by M. Mattox and D. Levaque and was owned by Dr. and Mrs. Hartford Hamilton. Robert N. Peebles handled him throughout his career.

Great dogs don't belong to any one individual. Success comes in the fact that a little bit of them is shared and loved by admirers in various regions, in all walks of life, and each one having in common the admiration of a beautiful animal. The secret in the success of these dogs lies in the fact that for the most part, their owners are sincere in their humbleness, and have shared with Poodle lovers the wonderful experience of having a great one.

Great dogs don't come along every day. Even today, it is difficult to come up with long lists of sires in any of the three varieties that have had massive, lasting impact on the breed. And yet, all breeders have the hope—and truly have the right to hope—that the young dog they have taken on will become another Souvenir or Sparkle among Toy breeders; a Square Dancer or Richard among Miniature breeders; a Thomas or Debauchery among Standard breeders.

The odds aren't great. But it is part of the package of hopes and dreams that make breeders continue as breeders.

WHAT TO LOOK FOR

In selecting a future stud dog, two factors in making a choice seem imperative. First, the dog must be a representative of a family that makes

Ch. Syntifny On The Move has been an important Top Producing sire with 46 U. S. champions. He is a multiple Best In Show winner and has sired a number of Top Producers including the breed's current all-time Top Producing sire, Ch. Darrette's Das Es All. He was bred by Lee Paul and owned throughout his life by Dana L. Plonkey.

sense to you. He might be at the heart of the family you are attempting to perpetuate through your foundation animals, or might be the result of a key member of that family having been bred to a carefully selected outcross animal. Either way, the young stud dog hopeful needs to make sense in terms of your own breeding program. In the beginning, his greatest use will be within your own breeding efforts.

Second, *the dog must be added only after the most thorough search possible to determine that he and his family are completely tested and believed to be as free from heritable diseases as possible.*

Ideally, the dog would be a perfect Poodle. That is impossible. He would also be guaranteed free of heritable diseases and the potential to produce them. That is equally impossible. In fact, there is nothing to assure that the dog you select today will not produce a condition that has not yet been observed.

Owning a stud dog can open an all new world of hope. Owning a stud dog can lead you directly into heartbreak. The risk of heartbreak is so great that it really isn't worth involving yourself with a dog unless he offers considerable value to your own breeding program and unless you have made every effort possible to determine his genetic soundness. You can be absolutely certain of one thing: Every problem that surfaces in the

162

puppies your dog sires will be without question his fault. Seemingly, outside bitches bred to your dog are incapable of producing anything that falls short of perfection.

TAKE A DEEP BREATH

When you decide to acquire a stud dog that meets those two exhaustive criteria, it is time to develop an overall management plan that will help you provide the dog with the opportunities to fulfill your hopes and

The black Miniature, Ch. Wilhoit Whoodeni, owned by Dorothy Hageman and bred by Marcia Lawson, sired 29 champions, and was the sire for Ch. Barking's Scintilla's early matings. He stood a shade over 14 inches, was a balanced, big-ribbed dog free from exaggeration.

expectations and his promise. Hopefully, in making your choice, other people associated with the family you are developing had a hand in the decision and share a level of enthusiasm similar to yours. The more support a young dog has, the better.

Most often, a dog selected for such an awesome task is not chosen as a young puppy, but rather is old enough that your confidence in his type and soundness is relatively high. That means he is almost old enough to show and can be bred on a limited basis in the near future. Sometimes the dog chosen is fully mature, ring ready and old enough to begin breeding. Obviously, you can rush into the ring career and the breeding career too soon. But for good reason you will feel somewhat pushed to get started on both fronts as soon as possible.

Knowledgeable breeders don't rush to use a new dog the first time they see him, see an advertisement about him or see one of his puppies, even if it is a good one. They are not looking for "flash-in-the-pan" stud dogs. They are looking for a dog that sires consistent quality and offers a safe pedigree. Waiting for something negative to surface is as important to them as watching for something positive.

THINK ABOUT THE RING CAREER FIRST

If you are showing the dog yourself, you'll have to accept the responsibility for your strategy even though you may get considerable input from breeders who share your interest in the dog. If you are using a handler, you need to clearly communicate your hopes and intentions for the dog. It would be an excellent idea to involve the handler in the selection process.

Either way, when the dog walks in the ring the first time, he should be totally ring ready, that is, in coat, totally table-trained and capable of making an attractive picture while circling the ring. To have him any other way is less than his best. That's no way to begin a career for a young stud dog.

The first show or two can really be almost anywhere, as long as the judges are generally good for you and for the new dog. But once you've seen the dog in the ring and you or the handler have a feel for what he's like, look at the shows coming up over the next several months. What Specialty shows and prestigious shows are coming up during that period with judges that seem likely to do well for this dog-handler team?

Is their any reason to have an instant trip to the title? Or is there a particular show that would make a perfect debut for the Specials career? The point is, your dog's start will benefit if he is seen doing well in a lot

Ch. Yerbrier Lovem 'N' Leavem is the sire of 18 champions for breeder-owner Betty Yerington. He was sired by Ch. Arundel A Lovin' Spoonful X Yerbrier Rippling Rhythm. Students of pedigrees will notice the lasting influence this dog has had on the Yerbrier family.

Ch. Yerbrier Standing Room Only earned a spot on the Top Producing Sires list with 19 champions. His sire is Yerbrier Sellout of Valcopy (a full brother to Ch. Yerbrier Done To Perfection), and his dam is Ch. Yerbrier Dancin 'N' Romancin' (a daughter of Ch. Yerbrier Lovem 'N' Leavem). This cream dog was whelped in 1976 and is still a significant factor in Yerbrier pedigrees.

of respected places. And you're going to get him introduced to more of the right kind of people if you pick and choose those prestigious shows. Do you want to point him toward earning his title in time to go to PCA as a new Special? Or do you want to forever be able to say he completed his title at the Poodle Club of America?

The new stud dog should be photographed initially until you have a really nice collection of photographs that represent him well in the ring. The posed ring shots are easy to get, so continue having him photographed at shows until you get several good ones. Also ask photographers to shoot candids of the dog at work: posing, baiting, moving. Despite your best efforts to get the dog seen, many people will meet and know him best through photographs in your ads. A professionally produced portrait is also a near must in the album of photographs you can use to promote your dog.

GETTING THE BREEDING CAREER STARTED

Let's start by assuming that this young stud dog is in good health, free of parasites and as up-to-date as possible on his situation with heritable diseases. Even if he is too young for the tests to be totally meaningful, have preliminary readings done to protect yourself by learning all that they can tell you.

Consider turning first to what *you* have in the kennel that you intended to breed to him. I'd start there or with a proven bitch owned by a fellow breeder who has been supportive and helpful to you in the past. The bitch should be right for your dog, but in addition, the more reputation she has the better. Norman Austin explains the benefit this way:

> I am a firm believer in getting champion bitches or dams of champions bred to young dogs prior to any spectacular rise to fame. Beg, borrow or donate, but here again timing is of the essence. These children should be old enough to make their show debuts prior to any spectacular Specials career of their sire, and consequently could make a wonderful impression on the minds of serious breeders. Frankly, these early days are the time to dedicate yourself to intelligent planning for the future and hard work. Be constantly on the alert for those bitches that will help your great one find his place in the gold circle. I am one who does not believe that every bitch is made for every dog, but I do feel that there is a proper bitch for every dog. No mating should be made for the mere acceptance of a fee. No profit comes from this.

I have personally been involved with one stud dog—a dog who would be twenty years old in September 1994—that approached being one of the sires who made a lasting impact on the breed. He was Ch. Surrey Postmarc, and ultimately sired thirty-six U.S. champions and three more in Canada. A look at current pedigrees in the ring show that his influence is behind many individuals and families that seem to be accomplishing what their owners want.

166

Ch. Surrey Postmarc, and owner Del Dahl, twice won the Stud Dog competition at the Poodle Club of America National. With Surrey are his daughters Ch. Esar Penchant Pzazz and Ch. Penchant Poison Ivy. Both were Group winners; Ivy was a Best In Show winner. Postmarc was bred by Mr. and Mrs. James Edward Clark.

I always felt that much of Marc's success as a sire stemmed from some lucky breaks he got early in his career. Through luck rather than planning, he ended up getting the kind of start Norman Austin advocates. Three champion bitches were the first he bred. One was a Poodle Club of America Best of Variety winner, one was a Top Producer and one was from a respected kennel that had purchased her from an even more established kennel.

Those three bitches produced his first five champions and made him a Top Producer. The first to finish was a daughter that I finished. And rather than campaigning Postmarc, I chose to give the opportunity to the daughter, Ch. Lin-Ed Del's Doll. She completed her puppy career with a Specialty Best of Breed, multiple Group wins and placings and was the No. 6 Miniature Poodle that year as a puppy.

From that point on Postmarc was never campaigned. But throughout his breeding career, he always had an offspring as a Special in the ring with me or others. These Specials were seen at National, Regional and Midwest Specialty shows. He came to the ring at every opportunity when there were Stud Dog competitions and Parades of Champions. Each year he was at the June PCA show as a Stud Dog if I could see a competitive entry possibility. If not, he went for the Parade of Champions. One year he would be in the Sporting trim. The next year he would return in Continental trim.

After each ring appearance, he would go back to the setup and take his place on a grooming table. When the people came by to see him— and they did—he was theirs to go over. I tried not to put a hand on him or set him up unless someone asked me to. He was a good-tempered dog with no holes to hide, and he sold more stud services on himself than I ever did. Early on in that process—with less advertising than he should have had—people called. And many of those calls started with, "I saw a Postmarc son at one of our shows, and . . ."

I'm convinced that in the long haul, it was the family he represented, the offspring that represented him, and his appearance at as many of the "right" places as possible, that helped him achieve his level of success. And in looking back at the stud dog careers that I have seen emerge, mature and sustain themselves, I'm more convinced than ever that Norman Austin's thinking is very sound. Advertising plays a part, but mostly it is a reminder to people once the reputation is established.

YOUR OBLIGATIONS AS STUD DOG OWNER

One other factor is important. If you intend to develop a stud dog's career, you need to be certain that you have a high level of commitment to the following two areas:

1. People skills. You will spend a considerable amount of time at dog shows and on the telephone helping people who are in the process of deciding to use your dog and arranging to get the bitch shipped to you and returned home. At dog shows, those conversations will always take place when you are at your busiest. At home, the telephone will always ring when it is least convenient. Your people skills will be tested. More than half of the callers will describe their bitches in a manner that suggests she should have easily defeated the most recent PCA Best of Breed winner.

Somehow, you have to accommodate all those inquiries, get a grasp of what the bitch is really like, negotiate your right to approve the bitch, and endure the shipping arrangements that are planned—whether you want to or not. If you aren't up to it day after day, the entire effort will suffer, and so will your reputation.

2. Visiting bitch management skills. You will be expected to pick up the bitch as soon as she arrives at your airport. Once you have her, you will be expected to provide care in the manner to which her owner is accustomed—or better. You will be expected to monitor the heat season, attend to two or more timely breedings, arrange return shipping, and confirm that the bitch arrived home as planned. In doing those things, you will be subjected to numerous telephone calls to see "how things are going," at times that are frequently inconvenient. All of these things you will handle in a perfectly pleasant manner.

You will find that some bitches shipped to you will test your patience. Some will arrive matted and dirty. Some will have fleas. Some

Ch. Tuttlebee's Royal Knight is an English import and fast moving up the list of Top Producing Toy sires. He currently has 20 champions and is highly valued because he has produced blacks, whites, browns, silvers and apricots and seems most color-safe. He is sired by Eng. Ch. Seabrook Don't Bug Me X Tuttlebee's Royal Style. Godfrey is owned by Dana L. Plonkey and Nancy Peerenboom and was bred by Norman Butcher.

will bite. Some will bark and whine enough to disrupt your entire kennel and household. Some won't be in season. Some will refuse to accept the dog. Some will arrive appearing so different from their description that you question whether the bitch should ever be bred. And you will find a quiet, professional manner to deal with all of those situations.

Accidents will happen in your kennel. Some will be beyond your control. Some will be your fault. You will find an up-front, direct manner to deal with those situations and the veterinary bills that will result.

A key factor in handling all of this is open and frank communication. When something goes wrong—your fault or not—make certain the bitch

Ch. Aizbel The Heir Apparent was the last in a line of six important Miniature sires from the Aizbel Kennels. During a 20-year period, those six dogs produced 146 champions, and "Regan" stood highest on the list of Top-Producing Sires with 60 champions. Bred by A. Granner, he was sired by Ch. Aizbel The Aristocrat X Aizbel Junior's Achievement, a daughter of Ch. Aizbel Headstudy In Black. He was owned by Luis and Mary Jo Aizcorbe.

owner knows the problem, has your assessment of what needs to be done and opportunities to suggest alternatives, agrees to a plan of action and then gets periodic reports on developments.

The worst possible course of action is to keep the bitch owner uninformed. If the situation worsens, you will be faced with reporting a graver problem at a point where no good alternatives exist.

This previous section paints a fairly dismal picture of stud dog ownership. Any one or all of the dismal aspects mentioned might happen to you during your stud dog's career. But the negative situations need to be put in perspective. Many of your contacts regarding your dog will be from people who you know and respect, or who you get acquainted with and respect. Many of the bitches that arrive will be all you hoped they would be, and some will be even better than you had hoped.

Some telephone calls will be at convenient times, and you will learn a new litter has been born, the litter looks marvelous, a puppy earned points the first time out, a puppy finished, a puppy won a Group and a host of other satisfying bits of information that will instantly help you remember why you wanted to be part of the team developing your dog's career.

It is imperative going into stud dog ownership that you understand the negatives that might emerge and have a basis to deal with them from the start in as positive a manner as possible. Only a few ventures into stud dog ownership end up positive, but the experience of owning a dog that makes a lasting impression on the breed is a very special experience and one that is certain to enrich your involvement in the sport of dogs.

After generations of studied breeding, families of dogs begin to take on a recognizable "look" that becomes the trademark for the kennel they represent. Ch. Parade Presentation and Ch. Parade The Right Decision are from the Parade Kennels of the late Nancy Kinowski and her daughter, Katherine. These litter sisters by Ch. Penchant Paladin X Ch. Parade Precipitation were bred by Nancy Kinowski and Ruth Ann Campbell. Presentation was an all-breed Best In Show winner and multiple Specialty and Group winner. She also won the Miniature variety at the National PCA show.

15

Wrapping Up on Breeding Strategies

THE SECTIONS ON DEVELOPING your own concept of type, choosing a bitch as your foundation breeding animal and selecting a stud dog have each, in one way or another, focused on helping you select an animal that is sound for breeding purposes, is the basic type of Poodle you want to develop and is part of a family of dogs that you believe capable of reproducing itself.

In a rather loose sort of way, those sections have laid a foundation for thinking about developing breeding strategies. The intent of this chapter is to build on that thinking, while helping you develop a concept of how breedings work and how you should select sires of your next litters—or additional females to use with a sire you are developing.

CONCEPTS AND IDEALS

If you have not developed your personal concept of Poodle type, do not pass "go." **Do not start.** There is no point in starting if you do not know where you are trying to go. Everything hinges on having an understanding of what you want to produce, and you can't do that without a personal concept of Poodle type. Without it, you are making a difficult task even more difficult, and you greatly increase your chances of frustration and disappointment.

You must have a concept of type that makes sense to you.

Let's assume you do. Now, let's add three other components to the mix, because I feel they are elements we breed for at one level or another. So when we talk breeding strategies, in addition to breeding and selecting for type, we need to select for the other three as well. They are soundness, correctness and temperament. And we'd better define our terms.

Soundness. Anna Katherine Nicholas, in her book *The Book of the Poodle*, defines the term as "mental and physical stability," and those two attributes certainly are important attributes of the Poodle. But my sense is that mental stability is a concept Poodle breeders most often deal with through the notions of temperament and personality. When we use the term "soundness," I think we are most often talking about movement. "That dog moves soundly." "That bitch isn't sound at either end." Those expressions are fairly common alongside any Poodle ring, and clearly they refer to how a dog moves.

If that's what we mean when we talk soundness, and we delegate mental soundness to our discussions of temperament and personality, I keep coming up with one other term that is essential for me to consider when I am participating in those discussions. I want to talk about "correctness."

Correctness. It works like this for me. I can eyeball type. I can see it when the dogs are lined up in the ring, standing about loose or gaiting during competition. My eye tells me, "that dog has type."

Soundness? I can eyeball that by taking the dog down and back, and by watching it move in a circle. Is the movement adequately true? Does the front grab? Is the hindquarter "skittery" or without purpose and weak? Or, does the dog have purposeful movement with the front reaching out and the rear "driving," and all parts working together in a fluid, efficient manner.

But correctness is more evasive. My mother always insisted that two wrongs didn't make a right. My mother was wrong.

If you have a fairly straight-fronted Poodle with an equally straight rear, you may very well end up with a dog that while *not* correct according to the breed Standard, can handle itself very well and move reasonably soundly. It looks right—but for the wrong reasons. The shoulder blade and upper forearm may not be of near-equal length, the front leg may be well ahead of the highest point of the withers (they are supposed to be under the withers), and the hindquarter when positioned to suit the eye may be so overextended that the bone from the hock to the rear pastern isn't vertical at all.

Or, consider the frequently seen good-footed dogs that result from a certain kind of incorrect (steep) shoulder. The foot looks like a little

Ch. Ascot Easy Does It was Glenna Carlson's homebred PCA National Best of Breed winner in 1990. Her dam, Ch. Ascot Olivia, resulted from a half-brother, half-sister breeding that traced right back to the foundation stock at Ascot. Olivia was mated to the outcross Ch. Graphic Good Fortune to produce the PCA winner. Easy already has two champions with several more pointed.

black walnut—but only because the shoulder is wrong. These aren't the worst kinds of Poodles to own, show or breed, but they are still several notches away from being correct.

What I'm saying is that *to assess a Poodle's correctness, there has to be a laying on of the hands to see if the pieces and parts fit as the breed Standard asks*, or whether a combination of problems are working together in a way that makes the incorrectness unapparent.

When I'm showing a dog, I place less emphasis on correctness. In the ring, finding it is the judge's problem. *When breeding dogs, we—not the judges—have to accept the problem and deal with correctness.* Dealing with it is a complicated task. Defining the problem really only takes a matter of seconds if you have a working knowledge of structural correctness in the Poodle and a pair of studious hands.

Temperament. The breed Standard gives us a good, working start. It says, "Carrying himself proudly, very active, intelligent, the Poodle has about him an air of distinction and dignity peculiar to himself. Major fault: shyness or sharpness." That definition is difficult to fault. But it is also somewhat difficult to assess. So many only somewhat-related factors seem to complicate our assessment.

I can adore a Standard Poodle puppy that is about to win a big Puppy class, until it does the porpoise-above-the-water act and soars above the handler's head. I am less tolerant of that kind of behavior in a mature dog who is a seasoned campaigner. I love watching a class of wham-bam Specials zero in on the bait their handler has and then fly around the circle when gaited. But at home, that kind of dog can drive me to distraction.

I abhor the recalcitrant bitch that must be nearly dragged around the ring and must have her head strung up with the lead to get even the most minuscule head carriage. But even more, I abhor the exhibitor or handler that made the bitch that way and wasn't smart enough to keep her out of the ring until she got comfortable on a lead.

Is the flash-and-dash, sockem-rockem show dog really what we want in Poodle temperament? Or is there truth in Bud Dickey's words when he says, "too many top show dogs are really only three notches short of crazy?"

Think about it. If a dog in the ring seems aggressive and growls, we would consider excusing him from the ring. What if the same dog behaved in an identical manner when an intruder entered his home? We'd give him a treat.

I think what we're all looking for is a dog that is mentally sound (not something that has to be taught to lie on the grooming table every time it is put on one) and behaves in a manner appropriate to the environ-

No dog appreciated a good win more than the all-time Top-Winning Standard Poodle bitch, Ch. Lou-Gin's Kiss Me Kate. Kate's exuberance is shared here with her co-owner, Terri Meyers of SWAG Kennels.

ment. And we have to factor in the impact that humans have had on the dog's life and temperament.

I've watched one particular handler bring puppies that he had to drag around the ring for years. When they finally knuckled under and did move somewhat adequately, that handler had to string them up to get any semblance of head carriage from them. His string has been that way for years—and probably always will be.

I was always so proud of the old Postmarc dog (even when he wasn't old) because he would be a show dog in the ring. You could put him on a table and let people push and prod on him by the hour at a show, and he'd take it all with tail wagging. At home, he was always up for a run in the park or a ball game, but in the house, he piled down on the floor beside me and looked like an unmade bed. And when people came, I could say, "Be an end table, Marc," and he'd quietly go in the crate at the end of the couch in the family room. He had a temperament that allowed him to behave in an appropriate manner in any situation. If he was lacking, it was that he was rarely the clown and was never devious.

Ch. Syntifny Piece of The Rock stood as the all-time Top Producing Toy sire for many years with 63 U.S. champions plus 23 additional in other countries. Whelped in 1975, Rocky was sired by Ch. Amberly's White Rock of Delnor X Am. Can. Ch. Adiona of Aurora. Bred and owned by Jane A. Winne, Rocky revamped the type of white Toy Poodles. A few days before he was six years old, he and a promising son were stolen from the kennel and never heard from again. His champions list and influence might have been much greater had he remained in Jane's care.

If you can assess type and soundness with your eyes, and correctness with your hands, assessing temperament is the most difficult. You have to use your eyes and your mind, you have to factor in previous treatment that might have made a lasting difference and you have to see the dog in some range of situations that enables you to make a reading.

Type is the starting point, but following right behind are soundness, correctness and temperament. Each of the four figure importantly in the breeding strategy you develop.

Ch. Aizbel All About Angels, a specialty Best of Breed winner and the dam of 6 champions has had a tremendous influence on Miniatures through key producing sons and their offspring. Angie was a littermate to Ch. Aizbel Headstudy In Black. The full brother, sister breeding produced three champions, including Ch. Aizbel The Knockout, who sired 19 champions. She was bred and owned by Luis and Mary Jo Aizcorbe.

NOW, TO SOME OF THE STRATEGIES— BREEDING FAMILIES

I want to make one point that I believe has the potential to be the most positive step you can take in dog breeding: *Don't breed dogs; develop a family.*

Every dog has a family; some make more sense than others. Hopefully, when you selected your foundation female or females, you "bought into" a family of dogs that resulted from a long-term breeding program developed by breeders who believed in judicious use of linebreeding and maybe some inbreeding—with an occasional outcross (again to a family—not a dog). Families that are developed in that manner have a fairly

179

concentrated gene pool, and consequently can be expected to perform in a more predictable manner than an animal that results from the mating of an unrelated sire and dam.

Look at it this way. Let's say you have a bitch who is the result of a half-brother, half-sister breeding. The pedigree would look like this:

                              Duhbigwinnah

                Hesadog

                              Notherfinegirl

    Whatabitch

                              Duhbigwinnah

                Classicgirl

                              Stillanother

The genetic makeup of your bitch, Whatabitch, comes half from the sire, Hesadog, and half from the dam, Classicgirl. Now moving back one generation, each of Whatabitch's granddams (Notherfinegirl and Stillanother) contribute 25 percent to Whatabitch's genetic makeup. But because both granddams were mated with Duhbigwinnah, he contributes 50 percent. So in that generation, the genetic makeup comes from three animals rather than four, and you have doubled the influence of Duhbigwinnah.

Let's suppose we breed Whatabitch to her grandsire, Duhbigwinnah. Now he contributes 50 percent as the sire, plus 12.5 percent twice as the two great-grandsires (each generation a dog moves back in a pedigree his influence is cut in half, e.g., 50 percent to 25 percent to 12.5 percent to 6.25 percent and so on), so fully 75 percent of the genetic influence of that litter comes from Duhbigwinnah.

Let's hope you like him and that he is from a linebred family that can be counted on to reproduce itself. And perhaps we should, at this point, clear up the terminology just a bit. Rather than turning to an animal breeding text written by a geneticist, let's, instead, turn to one of our master handlers who has also successfully bred Toy Poodles under the Carnival prefix and Standards under the Ale Kai banner, Wendell Sammet.

In the May–June 1989 issue of *Poodle Review*, Wendell discussed the two this way.

> Poodle people often talk about the benefits of outcrosses vs. linebreeding. Most breeders tend to prefer linebreeding. That's because the chances of getting the quality you're looking for—in just a few generations—will be much better if you consider a family that is linebred or inbred.
>
> First, we need to make the distinction between the two. Inbreeding

Ch. Dassin Daniella is the spearhead of the Dassin Farms Miniature breeding program. The dam of 14 champions, she is the result of a half-brother, half-sister breeding. Her sire, Dassin Dickenson, and her dam, Dassin Danska, are both sired by the Australian import, Ch. Proudaire By Golly. In limited showing, Daniella won an all-breed Best In Show. She was bred by D. Gammon and Joseph Vergnetti and owned by Vergnetti and F. C. "Bud" Dickey.

Ch. Dassin Dansabelle is a Daniella daughter with six champions to her credit to date. Sired by Ch. Penchant Paladin and owned by Joseph Vergnetti and F. C. "Bud" Dickey, she portrays the lovely balance and type, feet and presence that are most frequently part of the Daniella family.

181

involves mating a bitch to one of her close relatives, no further separated than one generation in her pedigree. This will be her son, her brother, or her half brother. Linebreeding is accomplished with relatives that are a little more distantly related.

Many successful breeders favor linebreeding. A common example would be breeding your bitch to her cousin or nephew. By linebreeding you are trying to accumulate the genetic contributions of one outstanding ancestor. If in future breedings you keep linebreeding to this common ancestor, the ancestor's outstanding qualities will express themselves in future generations. It usually takes three or four generations before you'll see strong evidence that the linebreeding is working in your favor.

Now, about inbreeding. It's tricky. And it isn't something novices should attempt without considerable help from experienced breeders.

Inbreeding—breeding to one of your bitch's close relatives, no further separated than one generation—will be her sire, brother or half brother. Inbreeding concentrates the genes of one or more particular individuals and reduces the overall number of different hereditary combinations that can enter the germ cell.

Inbreeding is likely to concentrate good qualities in some puppies and poor qualities in others—within the same litter. The individual puppy inheriting a double dose of these genes—whether they're faults or virtues—is apt to be prepotent for these characteristics and will probably pass them along to its progeny.

Inbreeding fixes type quicker than any other method. Unfortunately, it fixes the faults as firmly as the good qualities. If you do inbreed, you must be prepared to be very, very drastic in culling the inferior progeny. Otherwise, it is all to no avail.

16

How Much Is Enough?

H OPEFULLY, from the very start of your interest—right after you successfully gained your personal concept of type—you made some hard and fast decisions about how "big" you were going to be in dogs. **"Too many dogs" is a constant problem for every breeder.** Some reach that point when the second dog joins the household. For others the number is higher.

Once you begin showing—even at the match level—you will come face-to-face with a closely related problem: How long are you going to be out on the road at dog shows? If you have the foresight to consider that question—and the discipline to stick with it—you will soon discover a marvelous fact about showing your Poodles. You can be happy and satisfied with any level of showing—as long as you have considered how active you want to be and set some realistic goals.

In the acknowledgement section of this book, I credited Mockey Chaney for some valuable help she gave me early in my career with Poodles. Mockey has enjoyed a lifetime with our breed. She showed what she bred, she only attended local shows—rarely driving more than two hours to a dog show. She finished one champion. She started showing dogs before I did. She is still active in her local kennel club. She would be quick to say that her involvement with the Poodle has greatly enriched her life for more than thirty years. She has enjoyed Poodles as a part of her life as much as anyone I know.

At the other end of the continuum are the people who make entire careers of showing, breeding and handling Poodles. Their dogs are a nearly around-the-clock involvement for them. And they enjoy Poodles as a part of their lives as much as anyone I know—even Mockey Chaney. And there are Poodle people at all points along that continuum who have found their niche and have a level of involvement with the breed that enables them to enjoy what they're doing to the fullest extent.

But such is not always the case. Often, people get enthralled with the sport, increase their involvement once, twice and several times more and suddenly find themselves on a treadmill from which they can't get off. Family members feel neglected, nondog friendships end, and the central designer of the activity soon asks, "Why am I doing this."

You'll probably enjoy your involvement most over a longer period of time if you make some decisions about how much you want to be involved. Discuss your options with your significant others, and get some guidelines on paper to help you remember what made sense when you made the decisions.

Leave yourself some leeway. If a new dog seems capable of a significant place in the national standings—and that is important to you—revisit your plan, and consider a revision. Again, discuss it with your significant others. The objective is for you to make the decisions about

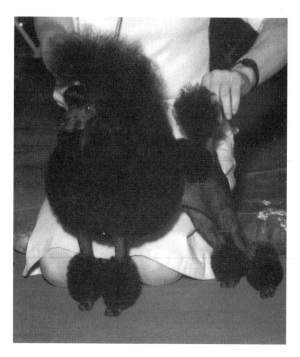

Ch. DeLorch This Love Of Mine not only won Bests in Show and was the top-winning Toy in 1983, she spearheaded a family whose influence is now felt beyond the U.S. "Dinah" held up well thoughout her lifetime and made several successful appearances as a Veteran. She is sired by Charade Brown Bear X GER's Windsong of Edirret and was bred and owned by Ginger Thompson.

184

DUSTY, age 14

Learn the Basics of Drawing in Year Round Classes
Color Pencil • Inking • Watercolor • Portraits • Cartooning • Oils • Acrylics
Weekends, Evenings & Homeschool Classes Provided
Small Classes & Affordable Rates

KIDS CAN
DRAW
ART
CLASSES
AGES 7-18 YRS.
531-6491

BEFORE

AFTER

MELISSA, age 11

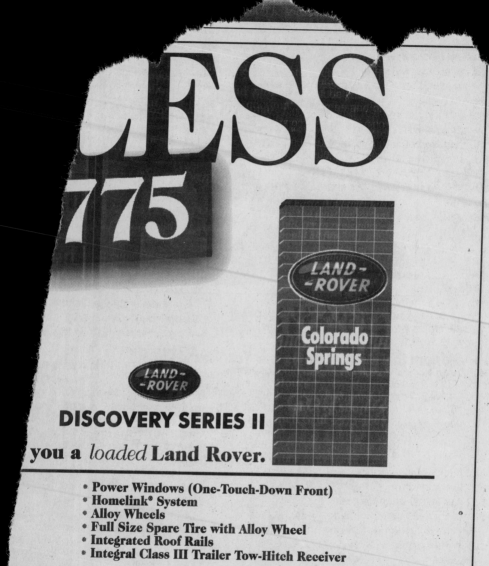

ESS

775

DISCOVERY SERIES II

you a *loaded* **Land Rover.**

* Power Windows (One-Touch-Down Front)
* Homelink® System
* Alloy Wheels
* Full Size Spare Tire with Alloy Wheel
* Integrated Roof Rails
* Integral Class III Trailer Tow-Hitch Receiver

GS in Motor City **636-9199** www.LandRoverCS.com

LAND-ROVER
Colorado Springs

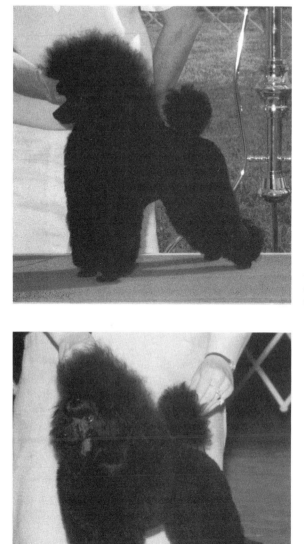

Ch. DeLorch Love Me Tender, a son of Ch. De-Lorch This Love Of Mine sired by Ch. Bandy-Cha-rade Hot Shot, gave the De-Lorch family of black and brown Toys international reach. "Elvis" stood high in the top-winning and top-producing ratings for several years and is the sire of 40 champions in the U.S., Japan, England and other countries.

Am. Jap. FCI Ch. DeLorch Its My Turn, an "Elvis" son, was the No. 1 Toy Poodle in Japan in 1989 and 1990 and won 19 Bests In Show. His dam, DeLorch Flash Dance is the dam of six champions. He was bred by Ginger Thompson and owned by Mima Shima-mota in Japan.

how you will be involved rather than discovering that decisions have been made on a day-by-day basis with nobody accountable for having made them. That way, you have decided where you will place yourself on the continuum. It can make all the difference in the world in your long-term enjoyment with the breed.

Am. Irish, Scot. Eng. Ch. DeLorch's The Turning Point quickly finished his English title with owner Leslie Howard of Grayco Poodles. "Turner" is sired by Am. Jap. Ch. DeLorch Its My Turn and is the first U.S. Toy champion to become an English champion. He was bred by Ginger Thompson and completes four generations coming down from Ch. DeLorch This Love of Mine.

USE YOUR HEAD AS WELL AS YOUR HEART

Your involvement will result in a considerable number of expenditures—some totally related to dog showing costs, some at least partly chargeable to the notion that dog showing is your form of recreation. Once you establish how involved you want to be, you can begin to anticipate what your expenses will be on an annual basis, so that you begin to get a handle on that information before you are overdrawn.

Let's look at the categories of costs that you will encounter so that you can begin to plan what your venture into showing might cost at various levels. And here, we're looking primarily at the costs of taking a group of dogs on the road to show. We are not considering the costs of operating a breeding program and facilities at home.

Transportation

At one level of involvement, the family car will provide all you need. Put the crates in the backseat, put the grooming table, exercise pen and tack box in the trunk, and go. But be prepared. As you increase your involvement, you will need more room. Will it be a station wagon, minivan, a full-scale van or a motor home designed to accommodate your dog show needs?

You may make the move to a station wagon and escape attributing the entire cost as a showing expenditure. But when you make the move to the big van—or especially a motor home—that's a dog show expense and you can't escape it. You'll feel pretty silly picking up the kids after school in a motor home. They don't fit the drive-through window at the bank, and it is pretty senseless to use one to pick up the week's dry cleaning.

Housing on the Road

As you begin, an occasional night at a motel (one that accommodates dogs and allows you to back up to the door) will be most affordable. But as you think about making seventy or eighty shows a year, those motel bills really add up. Motor homes keep you in closer contact with your dogs without hauling crates night and morning, and they allow you to integrate your morning routine into your dog work schedule, which beats having to be ready to leave the motel at 6 A.M. to get set up at the show and be ready for the first class. Another motor home advantage is that once you have one, you are eligible to be members of the motor home fraternity that meets each weekend on dog show grounds. It is a marvelous fraternity that facilitates looking at puppies, watching dogs work, watching others trim, gossiping and exchanging theories, all capable of adding a kind of richness and education to the dog show experience. I think the fraternity is called Alpha Grabba Pooper Scooper, and there is no information about a telephone number for the national headquarters.

Motor homes are great, but they are also expensive and they require routine servicing and maintenance. If you don't take care of those aspects of motor home ownership, motor homes get more expensive. You'll find yourself basking in comfort along the interstate when your Open dog should be in the ring, and by Group time, you'll be back on the road—*if* the garage had all the parts you needed.

Food Costs

You'll really be forced to make a lifestyle choice to begin to assess how you will estimate these. Some stalwart exhibitors are perfectly happy with dog show coffee in the morning, a dog show hot dog at noon, and a quick stop at a fast-food place at the end of the day.

Others enjoy studying the fine restaurant scene where shows are held. At the end of the year they can tell you where to find black bottom pie in Meridian, Mississippi, ribs in Indiana and an entire host of food items that they have enjoyed with dog show friends. Such spots become part of the annual pilgrimage and are as important in determining where to enter as the breed judge that day.

One final point. Motor home dwellers have some opportunities to manage their food costs that motel and restaurant people just don't have.

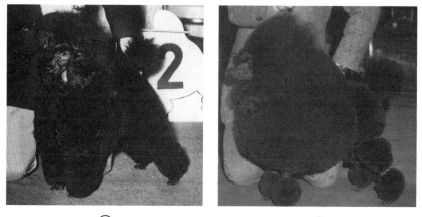

The accompanying four pictures depict a Miniature bitch that had a long-lasting ring career and a producing career that included six champions. (A) Ch. Cutler Ebony Wysteria earned 12 points toward her championship and several Group placements from the Puppy class. (B) She started her specials career at less than two years of age, wearing the big coat that was fashionable at the time. (C) She became a multiple all-breed Best In Show and Specialty winner with a PCA Variety win, a Group 2 at Westminster Kennel Club and a Group 1 at the International Kennel Club show. She whelped two litters and returned to the ring for her most successful year. (D) At nearly nine years of age, after four litters of puppies, she returned to the ring once more as a Veteran at the Great Lakes Poodle Club show. She won Best of Breed under Derek Rayne, and was the first bitch of any Variety to win a Specialty from the Veteran class. She was bred by Mrs. James Cutler, owned by Del Dahl and Josephine McCool and shown by co-owners Dahl and Peggy Hogg.

Entry Fees and Photographs

These two seemingly unrelated costs group together better than it might seem, because the more you show, the higher they go. If you're attending six or eight shows a year, with one dog, you're looking at an annual entry cost of $90 to $120. But if you're making 70 shows a year with a string of several dogs, at $15 per entry, you should anticipate an annual cost of nearly $3,500. Two photographs a year might cost $50. But if you average one photograph a show, a 70-show year might approach the $2,000 mark.

You begin to establish what these costs might be as soon as you decide how actively you will participate in shows.

Expendable Supplies and Equipment

At the beginning, you'll have a water spray, a conditioner spray and a few more items, and that will be that. The longer you go, the more you will be likely to carry special shampoos, conditioners, protein packs and a dozen other items that get used up over and over again as the year rolls by. As your involvement increases, these difficult-to-define-and-measure costs can amount to several thousand dollars.

Crates, a table and a tack box with a minimum of items probably marks the start of it all for most newcomers to the dog show scene. But as the number of entries increases, you need more crates and more tables. An exercise pen becomes a must, and you may choose to have more than one of them. Then you need pooper scoopers, and so it goes.

At some point you will decide you need a dryer to take on the road with you. And the first time you want it and can't find a power source, you'll go the route of the big people and start looking for a generator. And, of course, the day may come when you will want your own tent.

With a little planning, the cost of such major pieces of equipment can be phased in over a period of years. And while an entire set of matching crates—cabinet-quality, no less—is a real smash at your setup, you could get by with airline shipping crates until you phase-in the cabinetry a little later when your cash-flow situation permits.

It will be helpful if you have a set-aside equipment fund so you aren't in a state of panic when the dryer breaks down and every credit card is at the limit. Dryers, clippers and the like don't last forever. And leave the wrong dog in a new crate, and you'll need a new one as soon you catch the dog in the morning.

Evaluate your situation with the people involved and decide. Don't simply let things happen as they do. You'll stand a far better chance of enjoying what you do—perhaps for many years or a lifetime.

Do Poodle champions have fun? Even with all that hair? It never bothered Ch. Nevermore Jillian UDT who was always ready for a game of ball all during her ring career. Jillian was bred by Sue Henly and owned by Miriam Hillier. She is sired by Ch. Nevermore Gable UD X Ch. Nevermore Earhart CD.

17

Conditioning—
In the Broadest Sense

A RELATIVELY NEW BREEDER wrote one time to ask what I thought were the most common mistakes made by owner-handlers. Without hesitation I had an answer: They show their dogs before they are ready. It is as simple as that.

Too often, owner-handlers don't win because their dogs aren't ready to win when they come to the ring. They aren't in hair. They aren't in condition regarding muscle and weight. And owner-handlers who show dogs that aren't ready always have reasons. "He lost weight when my bitches came in season." "She scratched her topknot out just this week." "The weather has been too bad to get the dogs out."

Nobody cares. The dog is either ready or it isn't. The professional handler or owner-handler (*both can be professional* in my opinion) leaves dogs at home if they aren't ready—whatever the reason. But owner-handlers tend to think that judges will ask, "Are your bitches in season?" "Did she scratch out her topknot after you entered her?" "Have you had a lot of rainy weather?" It never works that way, and the owner-handler who tries to explain most often comes across as a novice who is making excuses. Nobody cares.

IN CONDITION—THE INGREDIENTS

To many Poodle enthusiasts, the term "condition" is spelled h-a-i-r. That's part of it, but if you define condition as hair, what are the Greyhound people talking about when they use the term? There's a more expanded line of thinking that contends that conditioning has to do with bringing dogs to the ring that are *well-muscled*, that are *in weight* and that are *in hair*. In this chapter, we'll deal with muscle and weight. In Chapter 19 we'll take on the task of bringing dogs to the ring in full coats—regardless of the dog's age or the trim.

Be prepared: Most experienced and dedicated breeders and handlers are fully convinced dogs brought to the ring should be ready to win. Otherwise, they come to the ring when they can be easily beaten. And that makes no sense.

Thinking About Muscle

There's only one thing I remember about the first Poodle Match I judged. By the time I finished the last variety, I absolutely hated to reach in to check the muscling of the dogs' hindquarters. It was like grabbing a tube of toothpaste about three-quarters full. It felt awful. It really gave me little hope about how the dog would move. It made me look for the elusive dog that would come under my hands with a hard feel that told me, "This dog has muscle. This dog could work in the water or in the field."

I felt I learned something that day. I never wanted to be on the end of the lead with one of those squishy-reared dogs.

Poodles come by their lack of muscle honestly. Their owners place such high priority on growing hair that the dog's muscle development is neglected. Sometimes, the urban kennel facility isn't conducive to muscle development. And there are other reasons. There are some excellent reasons for assigning priority to muscle development. Try these for starters.

1. Poodle movement will often improve if dogs have a chance to get out, use themselves and develop a bit of muscle on their own. If your dog—or your entire show string—spends a considerable amount of life on the grooming table or couch, or in a crate or exercise pen, he may not be moving nearly as well as if muscle development was part of your conditioning program.
2. Dogs with restricted physical activity frequently lose their appetites. They simply don't do enough to work up an appetite. Having dogs in proper weight—filled out and firm but not necessarily fat—makes them feel a great deal better to many judges. Coupled with good muscle development, such dogs often feel

better when judges go over them. That can make a world of difference in their placings.

The trick is getting the dog to eat well enough to maintain that kind of body weight. Exercise may make a difference. It is a whale of a lot better than force-feeding.

3. Finally, Poodles in good physical condition often feel better, are more alert and exude the kind of energy that makes a Poodle "Poodley." The soft, couch potato Poodles too frequently walk into the ring with tail dutifully where it should be—and go where they are taken—but really have their minds on getting back to the table or crate and sleeping away the rest of the day.

Providing Exercise

What will work for you is really going to be determined as much by your lifestyle and facilities as by what the dog really needs. If you're a small breeder with an eight-to-five job and no kennel help, you're going to have to look for what you can make work for you. You'll have to put together a program that will work for your dogs, but here are some general approaches that have been successful for many breeders

In-Run Exercise. If you have a series of long, narrow runs, use them to get your Poodles to exercise themselves. Dogs often "run the fences" whether we like it or not. Place dogs next to each other that either play well together or hate each other. Some handlers use appropriate-sized jumps to put a little more muscle in the hindquarters.

Ch. Ted-El American Beauty finished in three shows—the PCA National where she won the Toy variety from the classes, Westminster and the Houston Astrohall show. She was bred by K. Jones and owned and handled by Robert N. Peebles. Proving that good ones really last, "Erica" has won the Toy Variety at the PCA Veterans Sweepstakes in 1992 and in 1993 at nearly 10 years of age.

Because hair-coat is such an important part of Poodle presentation, we hesitate to put more than one dog in each run. But try some dogs in pairs or small groups. If they don't destroy each other, you may find that small groups result in more activity while the dogs are out. That builds muscle.

While the dogs are exercising, you can do any of a dozen other things, so this form of exercise has the potential to demand less of your time than any other form. **Leave the Dogs Out.** The intent is not for them to relieve themselves so their crates stay clean. It is exercise that builds muscle and it doesn't happen in ten-minute periods twice a day.

Some cautions. Be aware of the temperature and the sun. Both are a potential danger during hot weather. A covered run offers protection from both the sun and a fast-breaking thunderstorm that can drench a show coat quicker than you imagine. And keep an ear tuned for scrapes. Some groups of dogs will get along for days—and then the scraping begins. Break them up before it blossoms into a full-fledged fight.

To the Field. When I can make it happen, this is my favorite way to exercise dogs. You just take a dog or two—or as many as you can manage—to a favorite secluded park or quiet, grassy, fenced area and turn them all loose. Once they get hard, they'll romp and run for a good thirty to forty-five minutes, and then crawl back in your van with their tongues hanging out.

You have to stay on hand and call them in as they play so you know if the neck hair on the black bitch is getting chewed. So take a hefty supply of bait with you. While you're checking on this and that, you can also be managing a bit of bait training. And you'll reinforce good behavior that will help assure the dogs will come when you call.

The marvelous thing about this form of exercise is that it is totally natural and not at all forced. The risky part is that you never know when a stray dog will enter the area, or when one of your dogs will suddenly depart for places you cannot see. You will need to keep tabs on things in this kind of situation.

This form of exercise demands more of your time, because you have to be out with the dogs while they're running. The time demand is real, but it can be tremendous fun, and watching dogs develop and come together is really a satisfying by-product of the time spent.

Finally—Road Work. If you're a jogger, this form of exercise for your dog may really fit your lifestyle. A surprising number of people use this approach to tone up the dogs for a show. They usually turn to it when they discover they've got movement problems with a dog, and then admit the dog has not had adequate exercise. If you're not a jogger, use a bicycle, a horse or your car or van. Just go slow and accustom your dogs

194

Ch. Tebach's Halo Jet Setter had a sensational puppy career including Best Puppy In Show at the PCA National, an all-breed Best In Show, a Specialty Best of Breed and four Group wins. His correct balance and lovely reach of neck were evident at an early age.

to the approach you're using, and take care that the dog doesn't get injured or frightened. One aspect of road working bothers some people: It doesn't provide a natural approach to developing muscle tone. It is forced. Still, it is probably better than nothing—especially if you go slow.

You have to learn to "read" your dog from the very start of road working. When movement becomes labored or the dog shows any other signs of tiring, quit. Another way to gauge how much is enough and how much is too much is to keep an eye on whether your dog seems to enjoy road work: At the first sign of weariness or that the activity has ceased to be fun—just call it a day.

Follow the same route day after day so you can keep track of how far you went when the dog showed signs of tiring. Work at that distance for three or four days and then gradually add to the distance.

Don't feel you have to road work your dog every day—at least not in the beginning. Every other day is plenty of exercise at the start, and it may be enough throughout your conditioning process The most important caution about road working is this: Go slow and read your dog. Don't overwork.

With any form of exercise, remember that the program will take time. Dogs don't get muscle overnight, so don't wait until the entries are in to begin exercising. It just doesn't work that way.

Thinking About Weight

Chapter 11 provides an overall look at feeding strategies throughout the various stages of a dog's life. Everything said there would apply here. But the focus in this chapter is really on the dogs you are conditioning who are being fed in an adequate manner but are still too thin for the show ring.

Unless the dog is horribly thin, I'd hold off seeking veterinary attention until I had an exercise program in place and was certain that lack of exercise wasn't the problem. As you make that determination, you should also have a stool sample checked for worms. Then I'd try slowly increasing the amount of fat in the diet. Corn oil is a frequently used approach. Cheap (high fat) ground beef is another. Fat is fat, so it really doesn't make any difference. The single advantage of ground beef is that it may entice the dog to eat more than he has been eating.

Remember, as you increase fat, do it slowly, and spend more time watching the dog's stools than is amusing. If the stool is too soft, you're pushing too hard. Reduce the amount of oil or ground beef and try it again.

If none of this works, it is time to check in with your veterinarian. Explain your concern and advise the veterinarian of what you have tried to this point. If a problem surfaces, get it treated, and continue as your veterinarian advises.

18

Growing Hair, etc.

Now, to the final component of conditioning—growing hair. Even the most disinterested dog show visitor can tell you that "all that hair" is one of the most distinctive features of our breed. So obviously, bringing dogs to the ring in full coat will be a goal for the exhibitor of one dog just as it is for the professional who is showing an entire string.

Breeder judge James E. Clark, Surrey-Rimskittle Miniatures and Standards, often contrasted rose shows with Poodle shows. No rose exhibitor would come to the ring with a battered stem and explain that because of last week's dreadful rain and hailstorm, all the petals had been beaten off the rose. That exhibitor would simply forfeit the entry because it wasn't competitive.

Poodle owners, however, bring Poodles to the ring minus ear and/or neck hair and topknot nearly every weekend. And except for offering an occasional excuse, they think nothing of it. That's not how we want it to be.

TOOLS OF THE TRADE

If you're going to grow hair, you have to have both the tools of the trade and the know-how to get the job done. A pin brush (pins set in a rubber cushion) is an essential item, as is a fine slicker for Toys and

Miniatures and a larger slicker for Standards. In addition, you'll need a Greyhound comb and a wide-tooth comb. You can buy dozens of other kinds of combs and brushes, but for many breeders and handlers, that's the core of what you need.

In addition, you'll need a dryer, a pair of clippers and attendant blades. For your show trims, most of your work will be done with the #40, 30, 15 and 10 blades. The #40 blade gives a surgical cut, and the smaller the number, the longer the cut. The #07 and 04 blades are used to leave a blanket of hair and are used almost entirely for convenience trims. In addition, you'll need blade cleaner and clipper cooler spray if you're putting your clippers to extensive use.

By all means, get a supply of knitting needles to part hair, get a half-dozen spray bottles, and, although they aren't used to grow hair, invest in a good tooth scaler, blunt forceps and nail clipper. And as soon as possible, invest in a nail grinder. You'll also need some additional supplies to be effective in growing hair on your Poodle. Shampoo, creme rinse and coat oil lead off the list. Add to those, ear powder, nail clotting powder, wrapping material and some strong rubber bands.

Your clippers (about $200), blades (about $20 apiece), dryer (about $250–$300) and grinder (about $60) will be your most expensive items. As you visit with breeders, ask if they order various kinds of supplies by catalog and where they seem to be getting the best price. Order their catalogs, and soon you'll be able to do some comparative pricing right in your own home.

As you progress, you'll add to this basic collection as you learn some "tricks" other breeders have effectively used. But rest assured, you can get the job done with the items mentioned.

THE BASICS OF BRUSHING

A key practice essential to growing hair is brushing. Anybody can do it and do it well if they think through what they're doing and are meticulous about it. There's no "only way to do it," but there are some guidelines that apply to any approach you use.

Teach your dog to lie on the table on its side and stay quiet until you ask it to move. Be direct and firm in teaching the dog, but avoid frightening. The grooming table is a key part of a show dog's environment. The dog will be groomed there, trimmed there and examined by the judge on a table unless this is a Standard. Make all associations with being on the table positive, but be firm. Your work will be much more pleasant, and, ultimately, your dog will probably fall asleep while being brushed as most Poodles do.

198

The corded Poodle is a rarity in the U.S. today. But Pat Aloe Stauber discovered that the coat of her apricot Standard bitch, Torquay Emerald Isle, really wanted to cord. So she quit brushing it, and the cords develped—skinny as a "crow quill pen" as Lydia Hopkins prescribed in her writings.

I always brush the dog's right side first so the last side (left) is the one the judge will see during the judging procedure. It really doesn't make any difference for at-home brushing, but why not do it the same all the time?

Develop a logical pattern for brushing. Many of us start at the neck, sectioning off small areas as we work our way toward the tail and finally—section by section—work down to the belly. Always brush the hair up toward the backbone. Some do just the opposite at home. Start at the belly, work toward the backbone and always brush down. Brushing up makes sense when the dog is being brushed for a show, but at home either approach will work.

Part each section with your fingers. Make certain the part is clean clear to the skin, Then lightly mist that area with a water spray, a diluted creme rinse or a light oil spray and brush each section with a pin brush.

Then use your comb and your ears to double-check yourself. Tangled hair will result in a noise from your brush as it pulls through the tangles. Brushed-out hair lets the brush go through without a whisper. Use your Greyhound comb to check that all the tangles are out. If it pulls, rework that section with the pin brush.

When you start, follow this rule: Use a **pin brush** on the long hair you want to keep growing; use the **slicker brush** on short hair (the belly) and scissored areas (packs and puffs). As dog and coat mature, and as you gain experience in brushing, you'll find you can use a slicker on the longer hair without any problem. But initially, use the pin brush. You'll pull out less hair.

Getting Through

You don't just drag or pull the pin brush through the hair. Loosen your wrist and use a light, easy touch, but be certain you brush all the way to the skin. Each part and each section you brush should produce a skin line free of crossed-over hair or tangles.

If you hit a matted area, slow down and think. Try gently breaking up the mat with your fingers. A light oil might cause the mats to break up easier. Once it seems fairly pulled apart, go back to the pin brush. When it brushes out easily, double-check yourself with a slicker to move out the tiny balls of hair that you often find after working through a mat.

Each coat is different, but most experienced breeders and handlers say you should never brush a dry coat. Always use a water spray or a variation of it.

Topknots and ears are generally wrapped on the show Poodle or put up in rubber bands. Remove the wraps or bands and gently pull apart the

The 1993 PCA National Best of Breed winner Ch. Maneetas Del Zarzoso Fuego Fatuo brings an international dimension to the U.S. Poodle scene. He is bred by Laura Hand and owned in the U.S. by Dr. Mark Harrison and Ashlyn Cannon. He is sired by the Swedish-bred Eng. Ch. Harbovi's Heaven Can Wait for Vanatonia X Spanish-bred Del Zarzoso Boquita Pintada at Maneetas. While Spanish and English influences are up front in his pedigree, he traces back to Primetime, Valhallas and Eaton lines from the U.S. "Gordon" earned his U.S. title with Dennis McCoy handling.

hair that was enclosed. Then mist lightly and brush. You'll break less hair than if you just unwrap the dog and start raking through it. I usually do the wrapped areas last and then rewrap them when they're brushed out. It keeps the hair out of the way and reduces breakage.

How Often Should You Brush?

So many variables affect the answer. But think about it this way. You are trying to grow hair. Removing mats removes hair. On the one hand, you don't want to spend your life brushing your Poodle, so let the dog go until you are nervous that mats will begin to develop. Then brush. If you find mats as you go through the process, you've waited too long.

Young puppies and really mature coats can often go a week without matting. Keep a close check that the wraps aren't tangled, but if they will go a week, brush those dogs once a week. At certain stages of coat development (the change from puppy to a more mature coat) you may find you have to brush once a day or even twice a day on some dogs. That's not true of every dog, and you may only need to do such frequent brushing for a three-week period.

After you've brushed a dog a few times, you'll know where its mats most frequently develop. From that time on, if you're astute, you'll check those areas with your hands to see how they're holding up. Brush at the first hint of a problem. And each time you handle a dog, check the wraps to see if there's a hint of a mat forming at the skin line or just below the wrapping material. If there is, take the wraps off and brush them.

The goal is to go as long between brushings as possible—as long as the dog hasn't started to mat.

EAR, TOOTH AND NAIL CARE

Ear care can affect hair growth. Teeth and nails don't. But caring for ears, teeth and nails should be an integral part of the grooming routine, so let's deal with them here.

Dirty, gunky ears—sometimes infected or infested with mites—can drive a Poodle to distraction. They hurt and they itch, and the Poodle does what a Poodle should never do. It scratches. When a Poodle scratches— especially wrapped areas—the same thing always happens. Hair mats. You'll never grow hair if you have to demat the area every time you brush.

Start by using your forceps to gently remove small amounts of hair from the ear. Don't get the points of the forceps so deep in the ear you hurt the dog, but do try to remove all the hair you see in the ear canal.

Use your eyes and especially your nose. If you only get a little bit of hair, everything looks clean and nothing smells, you're in good shape. Once you remove all the hair, either use an ear powder or Panalog to keep the ear healthy. Many of us flood the ear with rubbing alcohol or hydrogen peroxide, but if you've removed considerable hair from the ear, consider waiting a day or two before flooding the ear. The alcohol may make the dog uncomfortable and cause scratching.

If you inherit an ear in trouble (or slip up and cause the problem yourself), your eyes and ears may reveal some problems that need quick attention—and maybe even veterinary care. Are you pulling out gobs of dark ear wax? That's not good. Does it smell foul? That's even worse. Is the wax a cookie dough texture or really wet and gunky? That's bad, too.

The first time you find that kind of an ear, go to your veterinarian or to an experienced breeder who can help you evaluate what you are seeing. What you really need to know is whether this is just a dirty ear, a dirty ear with an infection or whether it might be an ear mite problem. You need a veterinarian's help in treating ear mites. If it is just a dirty ear—or even one that is infected—you can probably solve the problem with some rubbing alcohol and Panalog.

You don't want to guess wrong. If you assume mites aren't part of the problem and use alcohol, the mites will likely be more difficult to treat by the time you change your guess. That's why you probably should get veterinarian help until you're experienced in making that judgment.

If you decide to try treating it yourself, clear the outer ear of any hair and see if some of the wax and hair from within the ear can be removed easily. Then flood the ear canal with alcohol and massage the channel under the ear with an up-and-down motion so you cause the alcohol to bubble up and out of the ear. Once you get that to happen, the gunk will come out with it. Use a Q-Tip to clear it from the outer ear, add some alcohol and do it again. Use your forceps to remove the hair that's surfaced, and just keep repeating the process as long as you can stand it and the dog seems comfortable.

You can break up the session and work on that ear twice a day or once a day until you feel most of the wax and hair is gone. Then use Panalog, an antibacterial, antifungal product your veterinarian can provide, to deal with any remaining problems. You can flood the ear with Panalog and bubble it out as you did the alcohol periodically, and within a week to ten days the ear should smell normal and the dark wax should disappear. But keep an eye on that ear. If the problem returns, hang your head and sheepishly visit your veterinarian.

It goes without saying that the best approach is to never let an ear get dirty. Check ears every time you brush your Poodle. Pull a little hair and use either a powder treatment, alcohol or Panalog. If you don't let it "get broke," you won't have to fix it.

ATTENTION TO TEETH

Look at teeth every time you brush your dog. As tarter becomes evident, remove it with your scaler. Don't just remove what you see. Carefully use the scaler to push up the gum line and remove what you uncover. Develop a gentle approach and try not to cause unnecessary bleeding. But don't panic at the sight of blood. Once you quit working and let the dog's mouth close, a lick and swallow a time or two and all of the blood will be gone.

If you get a dog with excessive tartar on the teeth, try using your ear forceps to crack off as much tartar as possible. Just press the tips against the teeth and squeeze the forceps together. Sometimes you can get a major part of the tartar off that way without putting pressure on the teeth. That is especially important as dogs get older and the teeth get loose. It is especially helpful with Toys where there is so little bone holding the teeth in place. Even if you use a scaler, always develop a gentle hand. Cleaning teeth can loosen them—especially on the smaller varieties. And again, teeth are easier to keep as you want them if you never let them get in bad condition the first time.

NOW THE NAILS

Nothing reflects your management more than the nails your dogs wear in the ring. Let your dog enter the ring with raccoon nails, and everyone knows you're responsible for letting them get that long. Chop them back, and they know you have neglected nails and then taken drastic measures, causing your dog considerable pain, to keep yourself from looking bad. Either way, you lose. That single sign of your ability to manage a simple task is enough to help people decide what to think.

Well, while I am on your case, you aren't the first. But it turns out that when we neglect nails, they get long. When we trim for the show, the long nails suddenly become evident. They may suddenly become evident, but they didn't suddenly get long. This isn't Pinocchio's nose we're dealing with.

If you're faced with the dilemma of long nails, look to your management and accept the responsibility for them. Do a little nail grinding or trimming two or three times a week for a month or so. The "raccoon" look will be gone, and you won't need to draw a drop of blood.

Let's think about an individual nail for a minute. The outer area is the shell, the inner area the quick. You can do anything you want to the shell without causing major discomfort to the dog. If your nail trimmers are sharp, it shouldn't hurt more than when you trim your own nails. But when you cut into the quick, it is a different story. As the shell of the nail grows out (the part you see), the quick comes right along behind. But if you nip back or grind the shell of the nail, the quick immediately goes into retreat. The more frequently you remove and shorten the shell, the sooner and farther the quick retreats.

There's no magic involved in keeping nails short. Use a trimmer or use a grinder. Just adopt a management program that assures you work on shortening nails two or three times a week until you get them as you want them. Once a week will be adequate after that.

Once you have them short, let's consider how we can make them pretty. To my eye, the chopped-off look—whether the chopping made the nails bleed or not—leaves the foot unnatural and unattractive. I never just chop off the end of the nail with a trimmer. I nibble at it. And the point of that is to do everything possible to retain a reasonably natural nail shape. Consequently, I generally finish trimming the nail with a grinder. Shorten the nail as much as you safely can with a trimmer. Then grind what's left to get a smooth, natural look—although, in truth, the end of the nail is a bit more blunt than when left alone.

I do one more thing that I think helps improve the attractiveness of any less-than-perfect foot. Just trim or grind away as much of the shell on the outside of the nail as you safely can without making it bleed. The nail won't be symmetrical—or natural—but nobody will notice. And the foot will look more attractive.

Once I've finished the grinding and bathed the dog for the show, I use a Magic Marker on black nails—and clear fingernail polish on the other colors—to take away the discoloration and dullness that results. I suppose that contributes to the natural look, but more importantly, it doesn't draw attention to the feet.

One special caution as you work with nails. Be especially careful with Toys and Miniatures. As they struggle against you, you stand a fair chance of putting stress on the stifles, and that can ultimately cause problems. Be firm, but after a point, be certain you lose the battle. Don't fight so long and hard that you put the dog's soundness in jeopardy.

TO OIL . . . OR NOT TO OIL

At some point—and perhaps fairly early in your involvement with showing Poodles—you'll learn that some people "oil" their dogs. Let's get an understanding of what it means and why they do it, so you don't ask, "Three-in-One?" and cause an outburst of laughter.

If you're only showing one or two dogs, and you have the time to stay on top of routine coat brushing and care, you'll probably never need to worry about oiling your dogs. But as the number of show dogs increases, or if you run into a dog with a difficult coat to keep, you'll soon be on the telephone learning all you can as quickly as possible. You'll be ready to put the dog in oil.

"Oiling the dog" is not an expression intended to help the moving parts move freely. Instead, it is the use of heavy conditioning oil for the coat that slows the matting process, reduces the amount of brushing needed and lubricates the hair so that it is less likely to break. Oil doesn't "grow coat." It just makes it easier for you to maintain the coat.

Most breeders and handlers use it to save brushing time, especially on dogs that aren't ring ready or those that are only shown periodically. They also use it on the difficult stages when puppies change coats and seem to mat as fast as you brush them. It is a time saver. But it isn't the be-all and end-all of dog grooming. It has some obnoxious disadvantages as well. Coats in oil pick up dirt and dust. White dogs soon become the same color as the rock dust in your kennel run. And when dogs come in the house, they're apt to leave oily stains wherever they lie.

Finally, when you bathe the oil out of the coat to trim or show, the dog goes through a period of several weeks when the coat tends to mat and do it quickly. During that period, you'll have to bathe the dog fairly frequently, brush even more often and watch every day to see that you're staying ahead of the matting problem.

What Do You Use, and How Do You Do It?

There are a host of products on the market, and more are available each year that are designed to check the matting process and wash out thoroughly so that matting doesn't follow. Some of the stalwarts still being used are Hagen Oil, Wu Pi Oil—both intended for dog use—and Alpha Keri, the bath oil used by people for years. But talk to some breeders and handlers. They may be using a newer product that works even better than the stalwarts. Most come with directions for mixing with water. If the dog is really matting badly, you make the mixture a touch more concentrated (and it will be harder to wash out). If you're simply protecting yourself, you can extend the dilution a bit.

Bathe the dog as you typically do to assure that the coat is totally clean. And be certain the coat is mat-free when you start. Then use the coat oil rather than the conditioner you typically use. Towel-dry the dog as much as possible before applying the diluted oil mixture, and if possible *put the dog in a pan that will collect the oil so you can pour it through the coat several times*. That's important. You want every inch of every hair totally covered. And if you miss a spot, you'll know. That hair will mat like crazy.

When the coat is saturated, let it drip dry and then towel-dry the dog. A brief turn-out in a sunny exercise pen will save you some additional drying time. Then put the dog on the table and dry the coat as you usually do. Expect to be confused. Oiled hair dries shiny and slick. When the dog stands, the hair hangs down like a Maltese. And that's okay. Once you've finished drying the dog, wrap it as usual, and then brush the coat starting at the belly and brushing down.

Brush the coat again the next day—probably more for you than for the coat. If all is well (that means mat-free), you've probably mastered the task and are ready to accept all the plus and minus factors associated with oiling.

COAT CARE BY LIFE STAGES

Babies need their faces, feet and tails clipped at fairly frequent intervals. And as the hair grows, you'll need to clip their backsides a bit, purely for hygienic reasons. Other than that, the only reason to brush them or do anything to them is to get them accustomed to the grooming process and to being handled and placed on a grooming table.

In fact, some breeders scissor the coat way back at about ten to fourteen weeks of age. They feel it encourages hair growth and ultimately results in a better coat. Families and lines may vary in the benefit gained, and the breeders who are most closely associated with your dog's family will have the most experience and be best able to benefit you in considering the cutting-back practice.

During the first six months the coat really doesn't need much attention. But the foundation you establish now, will determine how accepting the dog will be of grooming as an adult. They have so little hair that you can flick through them with a slicker brush in a matter of minutes. So periodically work at teaching them to lie on their sides and endure the brushing process.

At some point, you'll have to decide whether the puppies are damaging the hair to the point that you have to separate them to grow coat. I tend to let puppies play together as long as possible. They get the best kind of exercise that way, and puppies are supposed to play. But as they get older, you'll just have to watch and decide when it is time for separate accommodations.

Do make certain the puppies are bathed once a week, and use an

Ch. Magicstar Infiniti at 13 months wears about as much hair as you would expect on a Standard of that age. Miniatures, and especially Toys, carry a full, mature coat much earlier than Standards, largely because of the difference in size. This dog at 13 months is a good reminder that the Poodle can wear too much hair. At this stage, the dog's balance and proportion are perfectly evident and the hair he has is adequate to make an appealing outline. He is bred and owned by Roberta (Pepsi) Gilson.

all-purpose creme rinse. Especially work it into the neck hair, hocks, tail and topknot where you want hair to grow and where breakage is apt to occur. In conjunction with the bath, check ears, teeth and nails, and do what needs to be done.

At some point during the first six months, the topknot hair will begin falling into the eyes. Rubber band it loosely to keep it up. And if the hair on the ears is long enough, put a rubber band around it as well. Don't let the band touch the ear leather. You'll not only lose the hair, but you'll cut off circulation and lose part of the ear.

The Six-Month Mark

By six months, your puppy's coat will be developed enough that more frequent brushing will be needed between baths. It will be time to switch from the slicker to the pin brush. Watch the critical matting areas: behind the ears, the chest, elbows and over the shoulders. The topknot will need attention as well, and you may choose to start wrapping both the ears and topknot.

If the hair starts to clump up badly, you may want to bathe, rinse and condition as usual, then pour some of the diluted oil through the trouble spots. If your time is really short, you could give up and put the entire puppy in oil. That usually isn't necessary until the puppy goes through a coat change at about ten to twelve months.

You wrap puppies just a bit differently than adult dogs for two reasons: they have less hair and they are more apt to goof around with the wraps than an adult. Get some tiny latex bands like the orthodontists use. They may be able to supply them or tell you where you can get a supply. Section off two small areas by dividing the front one to one and a half inches of the topknot in half from front to rear. Catch up the hair in those two sections with a latex rubber band set reasonably close to the skin. Then do the same—always creating small sections—over the rest of the head and down onto the neck. Use your knitting needle to section off the hair, and keep the area clean where the hair is parted. If you don't, you'll find the hair mats at the part.

The latex bands make the hair groupings much easier to work with. Now you can apply a conditioner, protein substance or cholesterol to the tips of that hair to encourage growth and reduce breakage. If you're using rubber bands only, just put two or three rubber bands on each section, and tie the sections together with a rubber band to keep the overall topknot up and away from the face. *Never let a rubber band be so tight that it pulls at the eyes or the skin.* Your puppy will fuss with it and you'll get breakage and matting every time.

If you choose to put plastic strips on the sectioned areas, you'll need to do a bit of shopping first. Go to a beauty supply house and ask for "Webril." It is a cotton strip that you can put around each section of hair to reduce breakage. Don't cut it; just pull it and it will tear into whatever length you choose and meld together when you put it in place. Then go to a hobby shop and ask for some lightweight plastic. That works fine, but so do plastic garbage bags if you can find them in a light grade.

After you put on the latex (which you don't have to use; it just makes handling the hair easier), wrap a small piece of Webril around the section of hair and then put a cut strip of plastic over that. The plastic should be just wide enough to go around the section of hair with a little overlap. And it should be long enough to extend beyond the length of the hair you are wrapping.

Make all of your wraps tight so they don't get sloppy and fall apart. But don't wrap them so tightly that they irritate and cause the dog to paw at the wrap or bite at the ears.

Then take a rubber band (I really like the kind horse suppliers use to band horse manes), fold the hair wrapped in plastic into a neat little package and put two rubber bands around the entire thing. Why two rubber bands? In case one breaks, you'll still have the hair secure until you spot the problem.

If the puppies leave their wraps alone, your job is complete. If they fuss or play with them, section off another piece of Webril, put it on the outside of the ear and douse it with Bitter Apple to discourage future chewing. If the Bitter Apple doesn't deter them, try Tabasco sauce straight from the bottle.

Keeping a Routine

So far, there's been no magic. You bathe, brush and wrap—on a routine basis. If something goes amuck, you adjust your routine. But then one day—perhaps as early as ten months—everything goes amuck. Mats appear where they never have before, and rematting occurs soon after you've brushed out the mats. Coat change is underway.

In some cases, increasing your brushing and bathing routine with the heavy application of a creme rinse will get you by. But if you get the feeling you can see the mats form before your very eyes, you better consider the oiling routine. White Standards are perhaps the worst, but it can become necessary in every color in all three varieties.

Just monitor what is happening, rely on oil, check the coat every day, and solve the problems as they emerge. Mix up a dilution of the oil you're using and put it in a spray bottle. Use it to work out the matted areas.

Stick with the oil routine, but back down the brushing and bathing schedules as much as you can. When everything seems unbelievably good, you can even try eliminating the oil if you prefer. But remember hair just out of oil has to be watched carefully. And you solve the problem by frequent bathings (detergent is the best shampoo at this point) and more frequent brushings.

Constant attention and problem solving are the best answer. Don't give up. Don't put off solving the problems until tomorrow. Tomorrow they will be worse. And several weeks later, you'll notice that the hell you've been going through is somewhat lessened. The coat change is beginning to end, and you have survived.

The Twelve-Month Mark

At twelve months, and maybe before if your puppy isn't being shown, you can put your Poodle in an adult trim and get rid of even more hair. Dogs that won't be shown in the immediate future can be cut back a bit—rosettes, puffs and everything that will have time to grow out—and you'll reduce time spent caring for the coat even more.

But keep in mind throughout the entire process, you're constantly checking the condition of the coat. Then you're brushing and bathing only as frequently as necessary to keep the coat from matting. As the coat matures, you can expect to extend your bathing interval to as much as two weeks. When the coat is fully mature, it may only need weekly brushing.

Your experience and constant checking will help you decide how much is needed and how little you can get by with.

If you stick to a thought-out routine religiously, there's no reason why you can't bring every dog you want shown to the ring or to your handler in plenty of hair and ready to win. If you've also taken the steps to assure muscle development and have the dog in good weight, the basics of conditioning are all attended to. Your dogs will be ready, and you will earn the respect of fellow breeders and handlers.

One point should be made. *If you want to reduce the amount of time you spend brushing* and taking care of puppy coats, *keep the dog scissored*. Once you cut off all the hair you don't need, you don't have to work with it anymore. A tightly trimmed puppy requires less time to keep up than one with hair hanging from everywhere.

Ch. Barking's Shimmer of Wildways, a Scintilla daughter sired by Ch. Wilhoit Whoodeni, followed her dam's ring career with many Specialty and BOB and all-breed Best In Show wins for owners John Long, Chris Zaima and Dorothy Hageman. She was forever an energetic showdog with the ability to capture ringside with her Poodley antics. "Riva" repeated her dam's Best of Breed win at the Poodle Club of America National and they are believed to be the only daughter-dam of any Variety to win Best of Breed at PCA.

19

Getting Your Dog Mentally Ready to Show

PEOPLE WHO HAVE SHOWN DOGS for years, the real old-timers, still get lumps in their throats when they look across the ring and see one of those givin'-it-her-all show dogs that simply won't quit. And we can remember dogs from the past who were great show dogs as well as if we saw them last weekend. For me, Frank Sabella's return to the Westminister Kennel Club show with Ch. Tedwin's Top Billing, is as clear in my mind today as when it happened. Frank's voice and eyes could control his tail. Mrs. Erlanger stood aside to avoid interfering with their stellar performance. It was unforgettable.

With each new dog we bring to the ring, we bring the hope that they too will be that kind of great show dog and turn in their own unforgettable performances. Those dogs are few and far between. But there is a lot we can do to move us toward the kind of performance that Frank and Billy gave so many years ago. And as mentioned in Chapter 13, it all starts when the puppies make their first toddlin' little trips away from the whelping box.

NEVER LEAD BREAK A PUPPY

The very term "lead break" carries exactly the opposite connotation of what we want to happen when we begin working with a young puppy hopeful. I want the two of us to always have happy times. If a confrontation seems apparent, I give in. If a fight develops, I lose as quickly as possible. Nothing is more important to me than for puppy hopefuls to believe that every time that lead is put around their necks, good things happen. Food appears. They get to go see stuff—and if they want to spend time looking at it, or playing with a leaf, they can!

In the beginning, the puppy makes no mistakes. Confidence grows. Trust grows. The puppy wins all the mental confrontations and we avoid all physical confrontations. And soon, that pup owes me. So if I want to go the other way, and a bite of turkey or hot dog or cheese helps us make the turn, the puppy owes me. Because that dog likes me and trusts me, we will soon discover we have shifted the balance of power. We went from the pup having all the decision-making responsibilities to me having them. And the puppy never noticed.

You don't need a lead to lead-train a puppy. A little walk you take together will do just fine. Then add the bait. And then add the lead.

But that's not the way it happens for some puppies. The lead goes on the first time they're plunked on a grooming table. We twist the front leg to toe in, we shake pups to make them stand still, and we chuck them under the chin—all during the first session on a lead. If a puppy has a positive mental attitude after all that, it is nothing short of amazing.

Then it is down to the floor and a sharp chuck on the lead to get them moving. They brace, somebody pulls, and the fight is on. If the puppy does start moving, it must be in the manner the person on the other end of the lead chooses: "Let's do a down and back; let's try the triangle." And if the puppy sees a clump of interesting hair gently blowing across the training area, there is another chuck on the lead because the pup has lost his/her focus. In this case, a pup may not only have lost the focus, but be about to lose attitude as well. So far, from the puppy's point of view, nothing has been fun. And if that's how time on the lead is viewed from the start, we've got nothing but disappointments ahead. The probability of your pup changing her mind is slim.

And it is all so senseless. Who cares if the puppy goes a straight line or a triangle when you're just starting at home? Even if he does do what you ask, nobody is going to award points toward a title. There will be no Best of Breed ribbon. Group judging is not scheduled for later that day. The goal is not to go in a line or in a triangle. The goal is to produce a happy puppy who has the world by the tail and enjoys proving it.

And you can help her think and feel that way by keeping your hand and pockets full of favorite treats. Your puppy gets one almost whenever she is not making a mistake. And since you always agree to do what she wants, she never makes a mistake. You can encourage thinking and

Ch. DeLorch Hey Look Me Over and handler Diane Artigues demonstrate the interaction everyone hopes to have when they enter the ring with their Poodle. "Prissy" is animated while standing still, and is left to present herself all on her own. She won the Toy variety from the Bred-By-Exhibitor Class over 43 champions at the 1988 PCA National. She is sired by Ch. DeLorch Love Me Tender X DeLorch's My Diane. She was bred by Ginger Thompson and co-owned with Dianne Connell.

feeling that way by avoiding fights. At the first stop, or drop of the tail, or the first lowering of the head and neck, you have seen the first sign that the puppy is winning the fight. You are losing. Your hopes of this puppy being one of those great show dogs is being dashed before your very eyes.

WHEN TO SHOW

I always hated it when good judges came along just as my new puppy turned six months old. There was always such a temptation to try and win the first time out, and I knew that my puppy would come to the ring wild as a March hare and totally creative when it came to staging a performance. That's how I wanted them at that point. They'd had some basic work in being set up and gaiting, but they were full of themselves and they were naughty.

I left them more creative and naughty than I wanted them through the first several shows until I was convinced that they thought being a show dog—even at a dog show—was fun. Once I had confidence that they felt that way, I gradually started getting control, and gradually had things my way so we could begin to get competitive.

I always appreciated the judges who understood Poodle temperament enough to know where we were in our development as a team, and were willing to tolerate that "normal-but-naughty" behavior. Anne Stevenson, a long-time breeder and respected judge, could lose her heart to that kind, and if she could see enough to judge what she needed to, she came close to ignoring the little hay-ding-a-ding routines puppies would go through as babies.

I made every effort possible to "read" what those puppies were telling me. And at the first signal that the puppies weren't having fun, we backed up a notch or two and went back to "their way." Fighting with a puppy is always a fight you will lose. You may win an individual skirmish, but if your puppy loses the notion that being a show dog is fun, you've lost the fight.

ABOUT TABLE TRAINING

I always viewed table training as consisting of two outcomes: First, the dog learns to stay on the table during grooming and on show days; second, the dog learns how to be "stacked" for the judge to examine. I like dogs as much at home on the table as they are on the ground. And that means I like the dog mentally comfortable with the notion that during individual examination, I'm going to twist this a little, twist that and pull and poke on a variety of things. The dog who is comfortable on the table is going to be a lot less concerned about those happenings than the one who is also worried about being "way up there."

So babies go on the table as soon as they are toddling about. I "bait" them with bits of hamburger, tweak their noses and in general do

216

anything that seems fun while they're on the table. As they get older, I occasionally pull their tails, hold their chins and make passing attempts to set up their little bodies as I will someday in the ring. *But I never point their toes forward, screw their front legs into place or shake them if they move.* Their little fronts can be totally "eastie-westie" as far as I'm concerned. I just want them comfortable on the table, comfortable with me pickin' at them, and confident that everything is okay.

Obviously, you stay very close at hand so you can snatch them up as they toddle about. A fall is the worst thing that can happen to a puppy at this stage. It could injure them physically, of course, but it could also mark them mentally for the rest of their lives. So I let them play and spend time on the table, but I always guard that they don't fall off. I generally tuck the table in a corner so at least two sides are protected.

As the puppy gets accustomed to "penthouse" living, increase the frequency of setting up the dog *on* the table. Forget the details, just steady the chin, lift the rear and extend the hind legs by putting two or three fingers in the puppy's crotch. Do lots of "good boy" and "nice girl" each time you do it. And if they squirm and decide to crawl up your front, let it happen. It may remind you of what Poodle puppies are all about— in case the dreams of first points have caused you to forget.

As long as the puppy is totally comfortable on the table and reasonably willing to be set up, you can keep adding some details to the process. Grasp the chin . . . lift the hind legs out behind . . . rearrange a front foot, for example. Remember, use the elbow to move a front leg (if you move the elbow it is fairly certain the leg under it will follow) and the hock to move a hind leg. Puppies hate having their feet touched, so why bother?

At about this point, add one little step to your setting-up routine. Do whatever you have to do, and when you're finished, reach up and apply a gentle pressure to the tail. We want the tail up and a sustained pull backwards. You'll find that the puppy almost instantly leans forward just a bit and you can control leaning. The harder you pull, the more your puppy will lean.

If you tug just the right amount, the brisket (or chest) will be more evident. The elbows will fold in against the chest, the topline will brace up a bit and you'll feel the muscles contract in the hindquarters. The hindquarters may bend just a bit more as well. Tug too gently and nothing will happen. Tug too much and the feet will go flat, the toes will go out and you will see a "panic ranch" look because the puppy is afraid of being pulled off the table. This training tip works a lot like prescription medicine. A reduced dosage will do you no good. The right dosage can cure you. Overdose yourself and you might die. So go easy.

At the Westminster Kennel Club Show each February, the spectators give real meaning to "ringside seats." They are right there. Handler F. C. "Bud" Dickey competes with the photographer for the attention of the 1993 Best of Variety winner, Ch. Reignon Knight Delight, a multiple Best In Show winner and contender for all-time top-winning brown Miniature. She is sired by the Australian import, Ch. Marsden Black Knight, and out of Ch. Jay-En Trixie Delight.

That gentle lean forward you're striving for is what makes puppies "stand over themselves" or "use themselves" on the table. Without it, they look "plopped" on the table like dirty laundry, and they don't feel nearly as impressive when you go over them. The use of their muscles makes all the difference in the world about how they feel.

When started early, some puppies brace up and use themselves in response to the first little tug. A mature dog may not respond much at all. Give the dog some time, but if you don't seem to be making progress, try setting the hind legs very near the edge of the table. Pull back steadily and firmly enough to actually drag the hindquarters off the table. Don't let the puppy fall, but do let back feet hang off the edge of what you hope junior thinks is the veritable brink of death. Then put the puppy on the table and try it again. Ten to one, the first little tug produces the forward lean you were hoping for.

Once the puppy knows what the tug means, always add that as your last step in the routine. This becomes nothing but a signal that it is time for the puppy to brace up and tuck in all the pieces and parts so that he looks and feels as much like the breed Standard as possible.

CULTURAL ENRICHMENT IN GENERAL

Once the puppies have had their shots, you owe it to them and to yourself to **expose them to as much of the world as possible**, whether they ever enter the ring or not. They'll be a great deal more willing to approach new situations and new people with an adventurous flair than if you keep them "protected" in your back bedroom until they are four months old. Puppies treated that way will be like I was the first time I crawled off the plane in Zambia. It was culture shock—pure and simple.

For that reason, trips to the park, to the street where school kids walk after school, to the shopping mall and to handling classes are all experiences that can enrich a puppy's development. Provide those opportunities, but stay in charge. Don't let the puppy be overcome by what is happening. If a kid comes running up, stop the child before the puppy trips out, and use that opportunity to teach that child how to approach any animal to love or play with. While you're teaching that lesson, the puppy will gradually learn the world is not falling in, and the kid may learn something, too. Get the youngster to sit on the sidewalk or the grass and give the child a piece of your bait-of-the-day. Soon the puppy will be wagging her tail and crawling all over her new friend.

People with new puppies often inquire about the value of handling classes. They can be great. They can be awful. Again, you take control.

Explain what you want from the classes for your puppy, and swat the first instructor that twists the front leg if you elect to put the puppy on the table.

Some of my puppies spent most of their first night at handling class in their crate and in a quiet corner where I let them look and listen and eat a half pound of garlic-baked liver. Nothing hurt them, nothing frightened them, the liver was as usual and so was I, so what could possibly be wrong with a handling class and the dogs and noises that are part of them? But I've been in handling classes where the instructor wanted to play "How to Go Best in Show," and expected everything from seasoned show dogs to beginning puppies to play the game. And I've taught handling classes when owners would bring babies in and *they* wanted to learn how to go Best-in-Show and do it now.

That won't work, and it won't help your puppy. Handling classes can be a tremendous help, but before you enroll, consider what you want out of the class for your puppy or dog, and then simply explain that you've paid your money and want to play the game by your own rules. If you have a seasoned dog and your intent is to improve your own handling capabilities, play by the instructor's rules. He or she might be really helpful—but only if you let them teach the way they want to teach it.

In summary though, I'm convinced that many of the "won't show" and the "isn't a gangbuster show dog" problems that we've all heard about are a result of starting too late and of failing to make the puppy's right to have fun our highest priority.

Play with them from the start, gain their trust and confidence and then fine-tune their creativity. With all that and about thirty-five pounds of garlic-baked liver, you've got a chance of having a dog that will do to me what old Top Billing did so many years ago.

20

Getting Ready
for the Ring:
From Topknot to Tail

Y OU'VE DONE YOUR HOMEWORK. You're at the
show and your Poodle is all brushed out and ready to be put together to
take into the ring. And what's more, you've planned wisely and have
time to get the job done. Okay, let's wrap it up.

First, put the lead on the dog's neck and bundle it up so it fits neatly
and tightly under the chin. That's one place a puppy can't manage to
chew it. Teach yourself to make that the first step in your routine. If you
don't, you'll find your dog all ready to go to the ring and—you guessed
it. No lead. Not only is there no lead, there's no good way to get one on
him unless you destroy the topknot and a lot of the work you've done.
Forgetting the lead is a mistake many people make only once.

Now, stand the dog up, and, holding the nose, use your Greyhound
comb to pull all the hair on the top and upper sides of the dog "up and
forward," in layers from the top of the head to the rear of the pack. All
you're doing at this point is getting the hair "up and forward" where
you'll want it as you continue getting the dog ready. When that's done,
it's time to start putting up the topknot.

Ch. Halcyon Helena demonstrates how this topknot done up for the show ring frames her attractive face and enhances the appearance. The "bubble" emphasizes the stop. The double rubber bands give the topknot a bit of lift off the face, and the gentle drape of hair to each side flows into the ears and completes the frame. Helena was sired by Ch. Longleat Alimar Raisin Cane X Ch. Eaton Evita. She was bred by Daniel Augustus and Mark Shanoff and owned by Margaret Durney.

THE TOPKNOT—COMPLETING THE PICTURE

While it is only hair, the topknot is often the component of Poodle presentation in the ring that makes the entire picture come together. For that reason, we're going to spend considerable time thinking about how to help owner-handlers find ways to get the job done with the same smashing effect that our most skilled professional handlers are able to do day after day. Nothing completes the Poodle picture like a smartly done topknot. But there's nothing more disheartening than to set the first rubber band at a dog show and know it has to be reset. That's a sure sign of what's to follow and it won't be good.

On the other hand, there's real satisfaction when you begin putting the rubber bands in, setting the "bubble" and working the hair—and suddenly discover, "this bitch is prettier than she's ever been." When done effectively, the topknot can make your dog prettier . . . more glamorous . . . more elegant. When viewed from the front, the topknot is an important determinant of your dog's expression. The "bubble" is actually a part of the dog's head, and the hair above it creates the setting for the face—much like a frame for a picture or the background for a piece of sculpture.

Face-to-Face with the Rules

Putting up the topknot is also a key point because it brings each of us face-to-face with fairly heavy questions: How ethical are we going to be? What rules will we wink at? What rules will we follow to a T?

Hair spray is a "foreign substance." It is not permitted. The use of more than three rubber bands or rubber bands beyond the occiput is not permitted. The use of switches—little bunches of some other dog's hair that is bound together and fastened in place with rubber bands—is not permitted. Enhancing the hair color with anything from a chalk to a permanent hair coloring is not permitted.

And so it goes, not only when dealing with the topknot but throughout the sport. A ten-and-a-half-inch dog is a Miniature; a fifteen-and-a-half-inch dog is a Standard. Do you show them as a Toy and a Miniature? Or do you follow the rule to a T and show them as a Miniature and a Standard?

I suspect that across the nation, all breeders, exhibitors and handlers have found it necessary to deal with such situations in two ways: as an ethical matter and as a practical decision that gets made time and again on a day-to-day basis.

And each of the practices is viewed differently by the individuals making the decisions. Some will not color a dog—but will show one slightly oversized. Some follow the size limits to a T but will enhance color. As far as rubber bands and hair spray are concerned, many make that decision on a day-by-day basis depending on who is judging. I do feel that today's astute breeders admit that decisions they make on a day-by-day basis are, in addition, a statement about their ethics. Avoiding that admission is a failure to look at things the way they really are.

Creating Each Topknot—One Size Does Not Fit All

The goal is to fashion the topknot in a manner that improves the face as a judge sees it. No, you can't work miracles. You can't make a bucket head into a classic Poodle head. But, you can create a bit more stop. You can slightly alter the eye shape, and you can, to a certain degree, mask some cheekiness you wish didn't exist. If the head is a bit coarse overall, a bit of extra hair creates a larger "frame" for the head. The head won't be less coarse, but to the judge who only has two minutes per dog, it might seem a bit more refined.

The topknot—along with the neck hair—also has some important functions when viewed from the side. When used effectively, that hair can make a dog seem shorter and higher in overall balance and proportion. It can make a dog seem neckier and can visually shorten the length of back.

Each of us has our own "look" that we're trying to create. But regardless of what we're after, we're basically creating that look with two or three things: hair, rubber bands and a substance that holds the hair in place once we get it where we want it.

Because of the widespread use of hair *spray*, we'll talk about using it in a limited manner. But understand, if you follow the rules to a T, you will do otherwise. If you use it—be discreet. Excessive use always creates an artificial look. It may be sticky or may flake. A few light touches in critical places and a light overall misting as you finish should be adequate and should not be offensive.

Rubber bands? Believe it or not, three of them really will do a pretty good job of providing the control you need to produce the look you want. The original ruling said "no more than three—and none back of the occiput." There's been some loosening up on the number of bands tolerated these days, but placing them behind the occiput is still a no-no.

Finally, *hair*. If you're really eager to present your Poodle as effectively as possible, wait until you have—without question—plenty of hair to work with. It really is hard to achieve the look you want if you're trying to make each hair do the work of two or be twice as long as it really is. If your dog has plenty of hair to work with, you can experiment with several approaches to rubber-banding and working the topknot hair. If there is barely enough—or not quite really—you'll find that you're more limited in what you can do.

The Look and How to Get It

We photographed a white Miniature with plenty of hair to work with (Photo A). She's an attractive-headed bitch and our intent is to use the

224

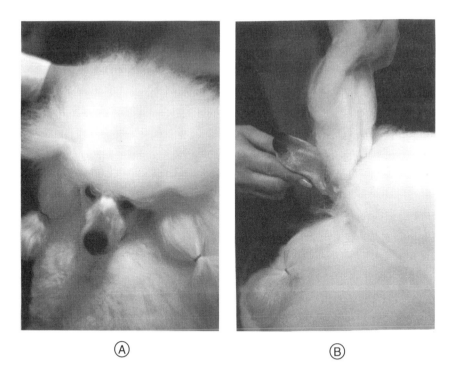

(A)   (B)

following series of photographs to show some various approaches and to illustrate the "look" that many try to achieve.

Let's *start by parting off the front section* of the hair as shown in Photo B. That line begins well behind the eye—maybe a half inch on a Toy; three-quarters inch on a Miniature; and an inch-plus on a Standard.

One exception to the "well-behind-the-eye" guide: On six-month-old puppies, you may have to set that line barely behind the eye. They just don't have enough hair as babies. The other alternative is to not use a rubber band. Instead, you just comb all the loose ends up across the front and use a spray to hold them in place. That is preferred to setting a rubber band in hair so short that the rubber band invariably pulls at the eye.

Use a knitting needle to run that part across the top of the head to the same point behind the other eye. The knitting needle works well in producing a clean part. A clean part won't mat, remember.

Now gather up the parted-off hair and *place a rubber band* around it (a strong latex orthodontist band works well) as close to the head as possible, and right in the center of the sectioned-off area as shown in Photo C.

Now *repeat that process* by sectioning off a second area with the line crossing the head just in front of the ears. Repeat the process one more time with the final line running across the occiput.

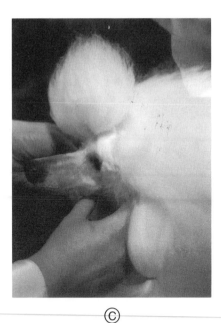

Ⓒ

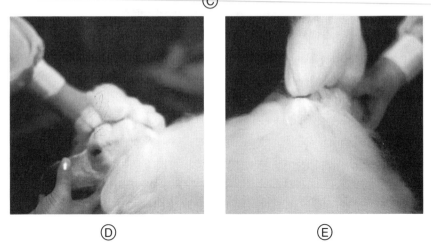

Ⓓ   Ⓔ

You now have three sections of hair as shown in Photo D.

One point about the last section. Set that rubber band toward the front of the third section rather than the center (see Photo E). That helps bring the hair on the back of the head toward the front where we will ultimately want it.

Next, *take a comb* (Photo F), a knitting needle or your fingers and pull that rubber band back—BUT NOT UP! As you do it and release it, the "bubble" will emerge as in Photo G. But keep the rubber band close to the head. That's important in creating the side picture shown in

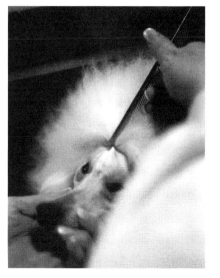

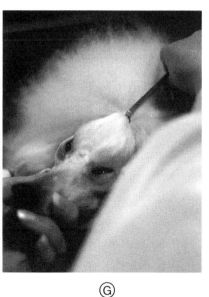

(F)   (G)

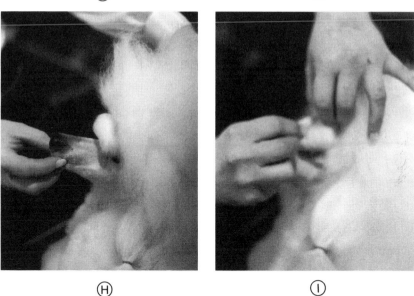

(H)   (I)

Photo H. If you don't get the sharp curves shown there, your bubble will produce a stark, harsh, expressionless look every time.

You may need to pull out some hair to shape the bubble and to ensure that you don't have an eye pulled askew, creating a wild surprised look. Notice in Photo I that while one hand pulls to shape the bubble, the other keeps a firm grip on the rubber band so it isn't pulled away from the scalp.

Photo J shows what we've accomplished so far: a neat bubble that sets out over the eye and enhances the overall expression.

If you don't get the look that suits you, cut the rubber band and start over. It will be more difficult to correct as the process proceeds.

If you have some loose ends, wet your finger and brush them into place. I also like my old typewriter brush—it's a lot like a toothbrush, but with a soft, fine bristle to brush those loose ends in place. A light touch of spray (be certain to cover the eyes) will keep them in place.

Working with the Hair

Now you're ready to begin working the hair. Think three things at all times: forward . . . center . . . up. If every hair you move is in those three directions, you'll greatly improve your chance of the hair ending up where you want it. If you don't, you'll probably find the topknot and neck hair "falling apart" even if you use too much spray. It won't be pretty.

So, working thin layers of hair from front to back, you begin combing the hair in the front section forward, to the center and up, as in Photo K. When you get it there, a light touch of spray deep in the hair and next to the skin will hold it in place. And a few quick strokes with a pick, such as the one in Photo L, will give a smooth, nonsectioned look. Remember that spray sometimes leaves a spray mark, especially if you use too much.

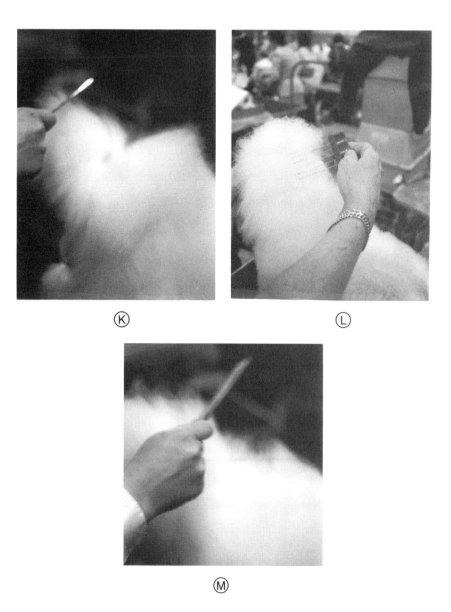

Be certain you also work up the hair over the sides of the shoulders. Be especially certain that you do as well on the dog's left side as you do on the right side.

Layer by layer—make that small layer by small layer—you come forward, center and up. Use a light touch of spray . . . and keep picking lightly to produce the smooth, natural look you see in Photo M.

You continue that process across the top of the head, down the neck and the back, almost to the back of the pack. The shorter the hair, the

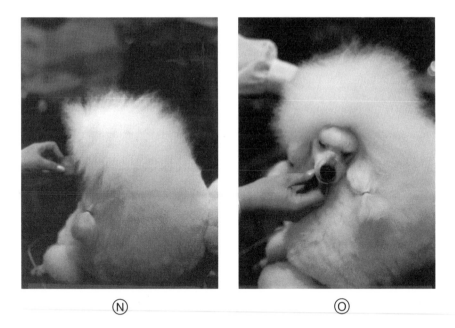

N   O

less spray you will need, and the back half of the pack may not benefit at all from the use of spray.

When the process is complete, you should have an end result that looks like Photo N from the side and Photo O from the front. Notice the difference in expression between Photo A and O. You've come a long way, baby.

Now, if you have plenty of hair up front—and an attractive head that you really want to accentuate—you might try for the effect shown in Photo P with a double rubber band in front.

You can stick to the three-band limit by eliminating the one just ahead of the occiput. You simply set the two bands and create the bubble as described earlier. Then—above the rubber band behind the bubble—section the hair in half from side to side. Combine the front half with the hair above the bubble and put another rubber band around that hair. On Toys, the top band is about a half-inch above; Miniatures, three-quarters; Standards, the short side of an inch.

This approach does let the head be evident, and it gives some extra control at outdoor shows. But beware: Rubber bands almost "eat" hair. The more you use, the less topknot you'll seem to have. Photo Q shows the effect from the side, and you can compare it with Photo N to see the difference the second rubber band makes.

I suppose my prejudices are showing, but let's take a look at a double-banded topknot such as the one just described, but let's work the

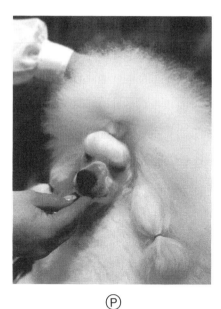

(P)

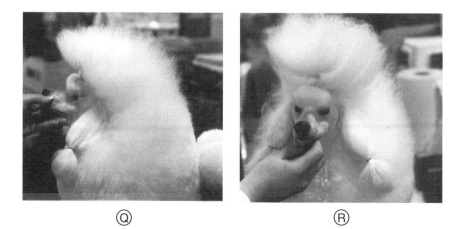

(Q)   (R)

hair up and backwards rather than forward. Photo R shows the look, and it was the type of topknot that was frequently seen in the late 60s and 70s, and is still seen in the ring today.

It has some advantages. It probably gives about as much height as any topknot, if you're trying to create an illusion of more neck. And if you're dealing with a classic head, it certainly gets the hair away from the face so it can "all hang out." If this look appeals to you, simply *reverse the section . . . spray . . . pick* process described earlier. Get somebody to hold the head for you, and starting right behind the lead, lift that hair up and give it a touch of spray. Come ahead of the lead and do the same with the next section. When you get to the front of the dog, arrange the hair above the second rubber band in an attractive fan shape, back-comb it tightly and you are done.

My prejudices again: It shows the head but harshens the expression. Compare Photos R and P to see the difference. I've also seen what happens when that approach is overdone. Some dogs achieve a mohawk effect; others appear to have glazed flower pots on their heads. I much prefer the expression that results when hair is pulled forward, and the more natural look that results.

Obviously, all of these approaches work best with full, well-grown topknots, and that's the kind we should bring to the ring. But puppies often haven't had time to grow hair, and occasionally older dogs get shown when they really don't have all the hair you wish they had.

For any of those reasons, there is one other approach that will get you the advantage of the second rubber band and still help you maintain the most good from the hair you have.

Photo S shows the first band and bubble created, and the hair sectioned off for the second rubber band. But let's cheat a little as in Photo T. Instead of putting the entire section in a rubber band, let's peel off a thin section of hair on each side from front to back. Pull the center section forward (Photo U) and fasten the two sides together behind it as in Photo V. Pull the sections in opposite directions to bring the rubber band down to the scalp (Photo W). The hair in front is not shortened by rubber

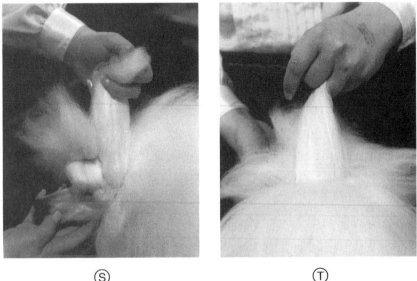

Ⓢ   Ⓣ

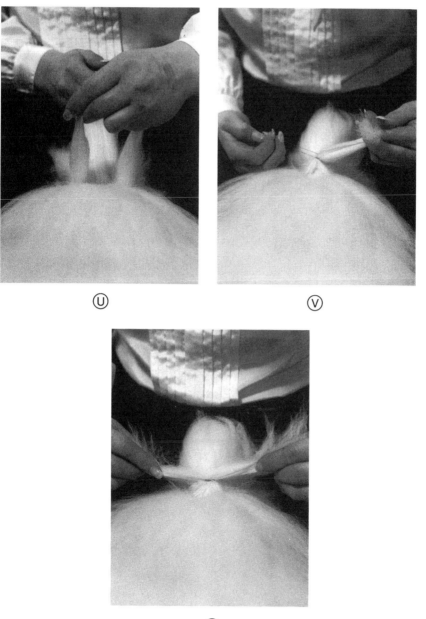

(U)　(V)

(W)

banding, and the two side pieces banded together will force all that hair to stay forward.

The big advantage of this approach is that it lifts the hair off the side of the face . . . it forces the hair forward . . . and it does those things without shortening already short hair.

These are some of the basic approaches and strategies for putting up topknots several different ways. And there's room for you to adapt each approach to suit your own taste and eye.

Once you've finished, hold your dog in a show stance and look at the picture from both sides and from in front. Use your pick to create a smooth and natural look. Then take out your scissors and do a quick over-the-top scissoring to *make certain that the topknot you've constructed blends in with the rest of the body coat.*

If you have space in your setup, unwrap the lead and let your dog get down on the floor. Invariably dogs will shake, and at this point, that's good. When you put the dog back on the table, you will probably find some loose ends have surfaced. One more quick scissoring will eliminate those loose ends and give your trim a more final look.

If the topknot seems to have loosened too much, or a part of it is not where you want it, use your comb to back-comb it and lock those areas into place. If you've been judicious in your use of a spray, a light mist will further help assure that everything holds together. Use your pick on any section that looks sprayed or that needs to look more natural.

If you have adequate help, have someone hold your dog's chin until you are ready to go to the ring. The more the dog moves head and neck, the greater the chance that your back-combing will loosen up and your topknot will begin to loosen. While the head is being held, you can use your comb to lift out the puffs, scissor some more or go to the bathroom before you leave for the ring. And you might as well. You and your dog are ready for the ring.

21

The Dogs Are Ready— Let's Worry About You

THE POODLE is a people dog. Whether a show dog, Obedience dog, water retriever, companion to a senior citizen or a full-fledged member of an all-American family, Poodles are most artful about figuring out the needs of people and carving out a niche where they can meet them.

In all but a few unfortunate circumstances, Poodles are loved. And that is how it should be. In fact, in many cases, they are able to endear themselves to the extent of being pampered and somewhat spoiled. None of that is a bother. They serve people well, and if people pamper and spoil their Poodles in return, that action simply reflects the strong feelings people have for their dogs.

That type of symbiotic relationship is admirable and workable in almost all situations. The one place where it is definitely troublesome is when the Poodle joins the owner-handler in the ring. Everything goes amuck.

I've suffered the consequences myself, along with hundreds of other owner-handlers who found their most loved potential show dog "so silly." "He just won't settle down. I can't make her stand. He grabs at my slacks when we gait. She's just so silly."

On the surface, it sounds like those puppies have a real problem. But after it happened to me several times, I finally got to the root of the problem: It was me. It had to be. Either that, or I was consistently picking the most obnoxious puppy in the litter as my next great hope. None of the littermates were as "silly" as the one on which I had pinned my hopes and to whom I had given my heart.

Finally, I figured out that I was doing something wrong. I had been unable to establish a "social distance" with the potentially great puppy and maintain it in such a way that it understood that when we worked, we worked, and when we played, we played. When I played, they played. And when I wanted to work—at home, at a training class or in the ring—they continued to play. The problem rested with me. I had been so busy loving them, coochy-cooing them and playing with them, that I'd overlooked the need to communicate, "sometimes we're together on a business trip."

Don't get me wrong. Poodle puppies need to be fun-loving and vivacious. Given equal equality, I'd always rather show the one that walks out to the end of the lead, surveys the world and makes a creative judgment about how to be. That kind is a great deal more fun (and easier to win with) than the methodical puppy who is always good but never has a creative thought. Those that don't show aren't any fun at all. The creative ones are fun. They may also be more than a beginning owner-handler is really willing to tackle.

Keep this clearly in mind. Teaching a puppy that "sometimes we work" shouldn't be interpreted as the process of drubbing all the fun out

The Andechez white Miniatures are well known throughout the nation in conformation and Obedience. One of the breed's most experienced exhibitors, Rebecca Tansil developed the Andechez program with her sister, Blanche. At 93, Rebecca still enjoys being part of the Bred-By Exhibitor competition at the PCA National Specialty.

of your new hopeful. When the fun goes, so does your chance of winning. You can have "work shifts" and still love the dog. It shouldn't be any other way.

WORK AND PLAY

As I see it, you can group all the things you do with a show prospect into two broad categories that determine the social distances you establish with that puppy.

First, there's physical handling. When it is time to go to work, you need to strive for a matter-of-fact or contrived indifference attitude. That's the approach I use when I do any "work" with a pup. I take a puppy from the run (no emotion and no chitchat) and put the dog on the table (with more of the same).

Even with puppies or new dogs, I give credit for intelligence. I put them on their side as with an old Special in the twilight of a career. I expect them to behave that way. It is amazing how often it works. If it doesn't, I add a degree of firmness and a harsh-voiced command, usually "Stay."

Then I cheat a bit. I brush, but I don't do a very good job because I skip the parts that dogs usually don't like (between the front legs, for example) and parts that allow puppies the freedom to move (the hind legs among others).

The point is this: As you start working with a puppy, consistently use a matter-of-fact, unemotional approach, and avoid situations that allow the dog to make a mistake. And take advantage of the converse. If a puppy is resting quietly, I'll brush the same spot for three minutes just to give the puppy additional chances to do things right.

But you've got to believe that puppies are intelligent and smart enough to know when they are pleasing you. That's the approach you use with every task you do. Be matter-of-fact. Create chances for puppies to succeed. Eliminate chances for puppies to make mistakes. I find I generally have to talk only in a command voice, and it is really best if I talk as little as possible until we rather routinely work when we're "working."

Just before I put the puppies away, I always stack them. I don't care about the details; I want to know if the puppy agrees to doing this without play. If the dog stays up on his feet with the tail up, I may cheat a bit at the end with a "good dog" just to see if I can get the tail to quiver a bit. Later, I fill in with foot placement and all of the rest of the details.

Now let's think about some mental maneuvering we can do to gain a social distance and eliminate the silliness we only see when "Mommy has me."

Jessica Wiwi won the Junior Showmanship competition the first year it was offered at the Poodle Club of America National in Pennsylvania. Mrs. James Edward Clark judged. Later Jessica scored another big victory by winning the Junior Showmanship competition at Westminster Kennel Club show.

Try this. Put a puppy (one you aren't emotionally tied to) on a table and without saying a word, smile, squint, wink, mouth words and tilt your head. Use everything about your face and head—except sound—to communicate with that puppy. Unless the puppy is a real dullard, she will begin to respond and come as close to "giggling" as a puppy can get. That's enough to convince me that dogs read our faces, our eyes and our bodies in general—even when we don't say a word.

I watched my son walk through a park with two three-month-old puppies. They were leaping at his mittens (unworn in cold weather) that hung from the strings his mother used to assure he didn't lose them. That scene reminded me of every Poodle I've ever seen watch the handler's swinging hand (sometimes with bait in it) during an individual gait.

What could be more logical? The hand and bait were as inviting as an engraved invitation. Your eyes and smile can issue similar invitations to puppies—and it isn't their fault. We almost issue invitations to be "silly," and then we complain about it. So the puppy gets sillier, and we decide to scold by wagging a finger at him and chatting about how bad he's being. Sounds like fun to me, and so it goes.

We've all known some dogs that have almost astounding levels of intelligence. But all things considered, the human mind really has a considerable advantage when we use it rather than being ruled by our hearts.

If you're having one of those "too silly" problems, you can bring them to an end if you are willing to accept the blame and are willing to do some problem solving to pinpoint the trouble and begin working on the solution. These are the things you will need to do:

- Identify the stimulus that triggers the undesirable behavior.
- Avoid exposing the dog to the stimulus so you don't provoke the behavior.
- Be careful not to reward the undesirable behavior, not even accidentally.
- Avoid using punishment, particularly when the behavior is related to stress or anxiety. It will produce wilted tails and flat feet like you've never seen before.
- If you resort to punishment, do it while the undesirable behavior is in progress.
- If possible, use a form of punishment that can't be directly associated with you or the handler.
- Make rewards immediately following the behavior they are meant to reinforce.
- Vary rewards from time to time, and once the behavior is firmly established, begin reducing the frequency.

Solving behavioral problems with dogs got much easier for me when I finally learned this: I am most often the cause of the problem because I am sending the wrong signals or I am unable to maintain what I call a suitable social distance—especially with puppies I really like.

Like many other problems, this one is another that is easier to avoid than to solve. And the problem is worth working on because its successful solution lies at the heart of what makes owner-handling a really fun part of our sport—in both the conformation and Obedience ring.

If you can put together a package that will enable you and the dogs to work together as a team, you'll have a considerable advantage over many of the owner-handlers in the ring—even those who have been at it awhile.

PLANNING YOUR SHOW DAY

But there's more, so let's consider some other aspects that will help assure that you get a good start and have a successful career as an owner-handler. All of this assumes that you will have your homework as complete as possible before you start packing the car or van. Your dog is in condition, trained, trimmed and ready to win before you leave. Now, leave early enough so that you have time to do all your work and that you don't have the stress of being rushed.

You can start planning how that will happen as soon as you get your judging schedule. List all the things you will have to do at the show, and start back-timing how your day will unfold. That way, you'll know when you need to do each thing and you'll know you have time to get them done.

Although quarantine requirements make it difficult for Poodles to move back and forth between Hawaii and the mainland, a strong contingent of Hawaiian breeders maintain a hotbed of activity in that state. Multiple Best In Show winner Ch. Bragabout Polynesian Vamp has earned both top-winning Poodle and top-winning Toy status in Hawaii for owners Bradley and Arlene Odagiri. Vamp is sired by Bragabout Rocknroll X Bragabour Snow Solus. Her sire is by Ch. Syntifny's Piece Of The Rock, and her dam goes back on both sides to the important white Toy line produced by Pamela Ingraham's Sassafras Kennels.

When you get to the show, find a place to set up, and get unloaded and organized. Next, get a catalog, find your ring and your judge and watch the ring procedure your judge is using. Where does she start the class? How does he prefer dogs on the table? What gaiting pattern does she follow? Observe all those things, and then look at the ring and envision yourself with your dog in the ring going through the entire procedure. Go through that process mentally until you've got it and know you've got it. Now you can go in the ring with some confidence.

You know what you're doing and you know you are capable of doing it. Each item you check off as you go through the day can give you a boost of confidence, and entering the ring confident rather than nervous makes all the difference in the world.

Finally, it is time to go to the ring. Make a check of the area outside the ring. If there is room to put your dog down on the ground outside the ring, go up a few minutes early so the dog has a chance to relax—and so will you. Let him know you have bait. Check that your number is secure and that you have the squeaky toy, bait and comb you will need in the ring.

When your class is called, review the routine you will follow one last time and in the ring you go. Unless you have a reason to do otherwise, pick a spot about the middle of the class and line up there. That will give you a little time to settle yourself and will keep you from the tail end of the line where every new person really wants to go.

Remember, when you paid your entry fee, you really bought two minutes of time. It is yours. You show dogs because it is challenging and it is fun. You bought the time, so use it your way.

Tim Brazier demonstrates how effective handlers fade into the background and let the attention focus on the dog. Here is Ch. Graphic Constellation at the Westminster Kennel Club show, totally in charge of her appearance and stance. She was sired by Ch. Aliyah Desperado X Ch. Graphic Helvetica. To date she has produced seven champions. Her dam has 15 and her sire has 49.

22

Choosing and Using a Handler

THERE'S NOTHING more satisfying than a pleasant handler-client relationship, and there's nothing more frustrating than a bad one. It has always amazed me how a handler or client can have so much satisfaction in one situation and so much difficulty in another.

EXPECTATIONS—ON BOTH SIDES

I'm convinced that, in many situations, there's a chemistry that makes a handler-client pair work or not work. But chemistry aside, a good part of what makes the relationship work is simply a matter of met expectations.

A client expects a handler to do certain things; perform certain roles. When it happens, the relationship is good. A handler has a similar set of expectations. Clients who meet them are good; those who don't are the other way.

So to assure that expectations are clear to both parties involved, you really need to have a clear understanding of what each expects before you form a handler-client relationship. And these are some of the key areas that need consideration.

Rates

We expect a rate card to clearly identify board and handling charges for each variety—including charges for Group appearances, placements, wins and Bests in Show. That's long been the norm.

But today, with the high cost of supplies and the high cost of going on the road with a group of dogs, many handlers have opted to offset their costs in a variety of ways. Some, probably most, charge prorated mileage. Some charge for special products such as conditioners, protein packs and the like. Still others add airport travel costs for bitches coming to be bred, as well as charges for trips to the veterinarian.

There's no single "right way." But it is essential that the handler and client agree on the charges beforehand. The practice will eliminate the chance of a surprise that too often leads to frustration.

RING PRESENTATION

Before you start negotiating a handling arrangement, spend some time at shows noting how a handler's string appears day-in and day-out. Some handlers' trims and ring presentation will ring your bells. Others won't. It makes sense to consider those who suit your tastes rather than to assume the handler will change his or her ways when you become a client.

Remember, your handler is your agent. He or she represents you. Your choice should, in part, be based on whether you're being represented the way you want to be.

A word of caution: Some clients force handlers to show dogs long before they are really in hair and condition. If the bulk of the dogs in a handler's string is well presented, but one or two lack topknot or neck hair, it may not be the handler's fault. With some clients, it is just easier to knuckle under and take their money than it is to explain that dogs that aren't ready to win rarely do.

AT SHOWS—BUT NOT IN THE RING

For many clients and new people, this is one of the most difficult aspects to evaluate when choosing a handler.

Clients aren't at the show at 5:30 or 6 A.M. when some handlers arrive and begin the day's routine. They aren't even there at 9:30 when

Ch. Yerbrier Done To Perfection and her handler F. C. "Bud" Dickey were a real team. Her career included many all-breed and Specialty show wins and made Whimsey the top winning Poodle carrying the Yerbrier prefix. Skillful handlers can often pick up a dog at ringside and turn in a creditable performance.

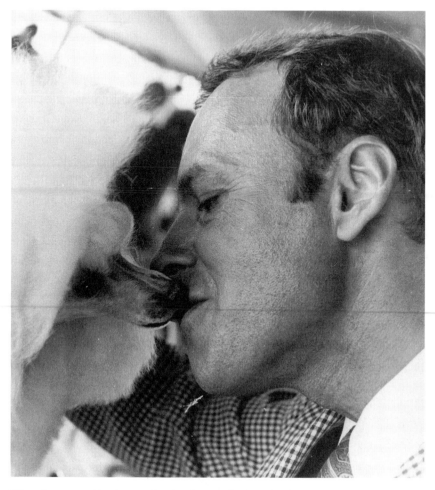

When the competition is over for the day—and when the ring career ends—there's still a special bond between the two team members. Whimsey was sired by Carliclan The Roadrunner X Du-Rant Maple Candy. She was bred by Betty Yerington and Marilyn Horn and owned by Betty. Following her ring career she gained Top Producer status and was the dam of three champions, two of which became Top Producers and the third also produced champions. Whimsey remains a force in Yerbrier pedigrees 20 years after she was whelped.

other handlers arrive and begin slinging things around and "throwing dogs together" before they head toward the ring.

Usually, the early risers are also the handlers who leave late after everything is brushed out, carefully wrapped, fed and exercised. Those who arrive late often make up for it by leaving early. They flip two rubber bands in a hair spray–ladened topknot, and pitch the entire string into a few exercise pens for a few minutes while they dump a little semimoist food into the crates. Once the dogs are back in their crates, those handlers are gone—for party time.

Again, you can learn a lot about a handler's operation if you go early and stay late.

FACILITIES AT HOME AND KENNEL

This is another hard-to-assess part of choosing a handler. Some clients have worked with handlers for years without ever having been to the handler's kennel. Some handlers have handled for years without runs and stalls. Crates, exercise pens, grooming tables and one sizeable room are about the extent of their facilities.

If you send a dog out for majors and all goes well, and quickly, such facilities will be perfectly adequate. But a lot of dogs go to the handler for conditioning and their entire ring career. Hair may grow in such facilities, but I have trouble seeing how muscle development can take place in an exercise pen or on a grooming table. And what about cleanliness? I'm not talking about compulsive cleanliness—just the kind that reflects good management and offers some promise that parasites and other management-related problems are under control.

It boils down to this: The longer you intend to leave a dog at a kennel, the more important it is you know what the facilities include and whether they will really provide what your dog needs over the long haul.

SPECIAL SERVICES

Some handlers operate businesses that focus entirely on getting dogs in the ring and finished. Others provide a host of varied special services—depending on their talents and interests. They maintain brood bitches, manage stud dog careers, plan breedings and even raise the puppies.

You need to think carefully about what services you want from a handler, now and in the future. Then explore the handler's interest and willingness to provide such services should the need arise. If you align yourself with a handler and haven't even begun to explore the handler's willingness, you may be in for some unsettling situations down the road—and you will be as much at fault as the handler. "I just assumed . . ." may be a true statement on your part. It usually isn't a solution to the problem of the day.

Sometimes a handler that might be a perfect match for your needs at another time, simply can't take you on as a client—or shouldn't—

because of previous commitments to another client. At other times, the problem that keeps you from riding into the sunset together is another dog, a good dog that promises to be in the ring for a while. Such is life. Timing is everything. Again, you have choices: Look elsewhere, or take your place in line.

ANOTHER PERSPECTIVE—HERE'S LOOKING AT YOU

It may surprise you to know that as you are going through the process of choosing a handler, the handlers under consideration are making choices as well. They're looking at you and evaluating you as a client. Handling is a hard life. But frankly, the problems of managing the dogs that are an obvious part of a handling operation are small, when compared to dealing with the problems of managing the people.

In a sense, dealing with people is as much a part of a handler's job as dealing with dogs. Clients who one way or another are a pain in the patoot, sometimes just aren't worth the hassle, regardless of how many dogs they have or the quality of their dogs.

After nearly thirty years of working and hanging around handlers' setups, and handling myself for a good number of years, I've come up with the "big four" pet peeves that are discussed within handling circles, and they all relate to clients, not dogs.

1. Clients Who Don't Have a Realistic Appraisal of Their Own Dogs. Clients with this problem set unrealistic expectations for what the dog can do in the ring, and when a dog will be ready. Most handlers are used to hearing the breed Standard recited when they ask a potential client what a dog is like, and "dripping in coat" is often part of the description. Far too often, the dog that comes out of the crate only moderately resembles the breed Standard. And while the hair may "drip" in some places, the neck hair may have been raked out at least eleven times and there's precious little there to "drip."

    If the dog is far less than the one described, and if the coat is far less, the handler may totally revise the estimate about how quickly the dog can be finished.

2. Clients Who Make Financial Commitments and Then Don't Follow Through. That means they don't pay their bills. Be honest about your ability to pay. Find out what the charges will be. Most handlers understand how quickly bills add up, and many are willing to work out arrangements. But agree on what is

acceptable, and then abide by it. One reason some people have switched handlers so frequently is that they still owe the last one, or four in some cases. If you can't stand the heat, get out of the kitchen.

3. Clients Who Want to Dictate Where a Dog Will Be Shown. So often, they want to make the decisions on the basis of what judge put them up when they were showing the current dog's grandmother seven years ago. Forget it. Occasionally, one of those situations happens, and admittedly, it is special. But for the most part, handlers know best where they can win, and under whom. You pay handlers for their strategy in entering your dog, as well as the actual presentation. Don't tie their hands.

That doesn't mean it isn't appropriate to tell a handler if you'll be attending a show well in advance of entry closing. Unless it is really a bad entry, most handlers will try to arrange their string to include your dog.

4. Clients Who Are Insensitive to Their Use of Handler's Time. This problem happens both at home and on the road. The handlers I've worked with and respect go to shows early and they have a jam-packed routine that dictates dogs being in the ring at a specific time that is not flexible. If Toys start at 10 A.M., they start at 10 A.M. You either make it or miss it. That schedule continues throughout the day until the Groups are over, the dogs are cared for, the van is packed and you are finally on to the next show or staring at the highway during the long trip home.

In the midst of all this your client comes in. Having arrived fashionably early to get a good seat to see her single entry, the client is waiting for the big moment to come. She's chatting a mile a minute about things you would be interested in at another time. You're shown pictures as you set one topknot and are offered watercress sandwiches as you scissor the puppy. And all the time, the clock is ticking, and Toys are in the ring at 10 A.M.

It just isn't fair, and it isn't necessary. When you as a client get to the show, check in at the setup, unless your dog goes bonkers when you arrive, and then check out until the Variety judging is finished. That means *all* the Varieties and breeds your handler is showing, not just the variety in which you have an entry. There's often a break between Variety and Group judging, and that's where you can offer the sandwiches and iced tea.

But it can be just as bad as the home kennel. This example isn't farfetched; it is really fairly realistic:

The handler pulls in the driveway at 2 A.M. after six hours on

While many Poodle owners enjoy showing their own dogs and do it well, Arlene Scardo recognizes the satisfaction that comes from watching her dogs in the ring with a handler. Here she shares "out time" with Ch. Arlrich Halcyon Days after winning Best of Breed at the Watchung Mountain Poodle Club. "Esa," on the other hand, is ready to let down after a hard day's work.

the road. The dogs are let out, exercised, put back in their runs and the water bowls are checked one last time. Finally, at 3:30 the handler puts on "jammies" and goes night-night.

At 7 A.M. the handler drags himself down to the kennel to start a full day's worth of catch-up work that includes bathing one dog to ship and breeding two bitches. All that has to be done by 9:30 when it is time to leave for the airport. But the phone starts ringing at 8:07, and six clients call in rapid-fire order—each eager to learn how their entry fared during the weekend.

That's fair. With a marked catalog by the phone, anyone who answers can provide the weekend results. Make sense? Maybe so, but it won't work. The six clients want to talk with their handler about their dog, about a new litter, about what the old champion caught down in the apple orchard and any number of other things.

By mid-week, when all is settled and before preparations for the next weekend are in full swing, that kind of chitchat could be interesting—or at least the handler can fake it. But on a busy Monday morning, the timing couldn't be worse.

Handlers need clients, and they are willing to talk to them. But timing is everything. Even the most considerate people will make this mistake because they've never had the responsibility of getting a full string of dogs in the ring on time, looking right.

Even if you've shown two or three dogs at a show yourself, you probably don't have a good appreciation of how it feels to leave your setup when Toys start and realize you won't get back until Standards are finished. Sometimes it happens that way.

TO CONCLUDE . . .

Do your homework as you choose a handler. Look for someone who is doing things the way you like them done. Talk about your immediate needs and explore their interest in your long-term needs. Be clear about your expectations and encourage the handler to do the same. Be clear on the matter of costs—all of them.

Keep an eye out for the chemistry. Sometimes it's there; other times it isn't. Remember, it may not last forever.

Above all, try to move forward in a businesslike and professional manner. You become a handler-client team when you hand over the first dog. Becoming friends takes longer, often much longer. It usually happens when two considerate people are both having their expectations met in a satisfactory manner.

Always trimmed and presented with the same attention paid during conformation competition, Am. Can. Ch. Ravendune On The Lite Side Am. Can. UD always heeled in perfect position with full attention to his owner handler.

23

Obedience and Your Poodle

T HE POODLE consistently ranks near the top among all breeds in terms of popularity. Of course, many Poodles are owned by people who consider themselves breeders and are deeply involved in the sport of showing and breeding Poodles. But by far, the greatest number of Poodles make their way in life by being the pet and companion of an individual or a family.

Having a Poodle as a companion, even for long-term breeders, is probably the Poodle's most important role in society today. And through the years, the breed has proven its marvelous suitability for that important task.

But like children, the Poodle needs manners, to learn to behave and adapt itself to the realm of propriety as a family member. And indeed, that's how most Poodles are viewed.

Poodle owners are a great deal more fortunate than parents. While an abundance of references exist on both child raising and dog Obedience training, the task of raising and training a Poodle is generally accomplished during a considerably shorter period of time. That is not to suggest that the Poodle is quicker to learn than the child (although I've had some days when I believed that without question). Instead, it is simply an indication that Poodles reach maturity a great deal quicker, pass through fewer developmental stages and really have far fewer demands placed on them than children on the way to taking a place in society as an adult.

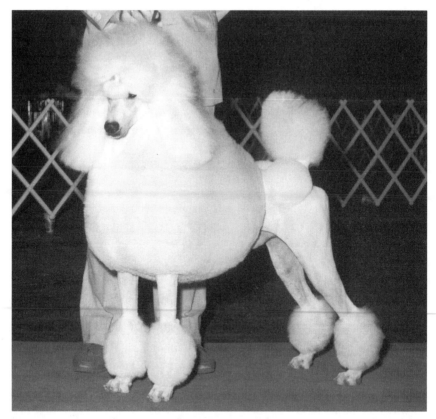

Am. Can. Ch. Ravendune On The Light Side Am. Can. UD earned his conformation title wearing the Continental trim. Once his conformation career had ended, owner Cheryl M. Bailey set out to begin Risky's Obedience career. His sire is Ch. Ravendune Manilow and his dam is Oakgrove Naive. He was bred by Todd Patterson and Jerry Edwards.

So for most people, Obedience training at some level is an essential part of owning a Poodle. As a matter of fact, it is essential for the well-being of the Poodle as well as the people involved. The basic commands "Come," "Sit," "Halt" and "Stay," for example, in some cases are required to keep the Poodle safe. Some owners accomplish the minimum basic training at home on their own on a piecemeal basis. Often that is all that is required to enable the Poodle to manage an acceptable behavior, enable it to fit the home situation and stay free from harm.

But some people don't have the skills to make dog training a do-it-yourself project. Some dogs present problems that are more taxing than expected, and the owner needs some professional training help. Some owners are astounded at how quickly their Poodle learns. They want to challenge their pet's ability to learn, and in doing so learn the satisfactions that come from Obedience training.

In any of those situations, the Poodle owner is likely to move beyond the level of reading about dog training and begin looking for local training programs where they can learn and their dog can be challenged.

FORMAL COMPETITION—IN THE BEGINNING

Interestingly, the entire Obedience movement in the United States began with the interest and efforts of a member of the Poodle fancy back in the early 1930s. Helene Whitehouse Walker imported three Poodles from England and began breeding Standards under the Carillon banner. Because the dogs had come from England, Ms. Walker was a staunch reader of the English dog papers, which at that time were reporting work with Obedience tests being held there at that time.

The Carillon Standards were shown in conformation competition and had early wins at Westminster. In fact, Eng. Ch. Whippendell Poli of Carillon won Best of Breed at the first Poodle Club of America show.

But Ms. Walker's acquaintance with the English Obedience Tests was not forgotten, and soon she began to develop similar tests here in the United States. In fact, the first all-breed Obedience Test was held at her father's estate in 1933. In 1934, Blanche Saunders, who ultimately became her renowned associate, answered an advertisement for kennel help. Together, the two women pioneered the entire U.S. Obedience movement. Their early training guides and books on Obedience remain important references today.

In addition, the women undertook a series of activities to increase awareness of Obedience training and to popularize the activity throughout the nation.

When the American Kennel Club took over the responsibilities for Obedience competition in 1936, as a result of Ms. Walker's leadership and encouragement, the two were free to devote more effort to popularizing the sport. They put together a ten-week trip that covered 10,000 miles, and off they went with their dogs, training materials and equipment to blanket the nation. That trip and more of the early efforts are well documented in Ms. Saunders's book, *The Story of Dog Obedience*.

But without question, Poodles and their people were at the heart of the development of Obedience training in the United States.

OBEDIENCE COMPETITION

Today, most communities are home to kennel clubs with Obedience programs, or clubs that focus entirely on Obedience. Some owners will enter a basic Obedience program that meets once a week for eight to twelve weeks and then the dog and owner graduate. But for others, that kind of a program is only what gets them "hooked." Soon, they are members of the club and begin training on a continuing basis. And for some, that step is logically followed by entering shows where Obedience competition is offered.

Club members will help you learn of Obedience trials or matches in the area, both recognized AKC shows where your Poodle can qualify to earn an Obedience title, and matches where you and your dog can go solely to gain experience (and you can gain confidence). Matches are helpful starting points as you begin to get serious about competing. Match wins, however, do not contribute to the process of winning an Obedience title.

Let's start by considering the various classes offered in Obedience competition, and the progression of classes that lead to the Obedience titles offered.

Novice. In Novice, your Poodle will be required to Heel both on and off the leash. The dog must **stand for examination**, do a full ring length off-lead **recall** as well as the Group exercises, the **long sit** and **long down**. Those exercises are done with the handlers standing across the ring facing their dogs. They are called Group exercises because at least six but not more than twelve dogs perform the exercises at the same time.

Scoring is done by giving each competitor 200 points, the perfect score, to start. But points are taken off for faults committed. To qualify, your dog must earn more than 50 percent of the available points for each exercise and must retain at least 170 of the 200 points. When your dog qualifies three times under three different judges at different Obedience trials, the Companion Dog title is earned. From that time on, the letters **CD** become a part of the dog's registered name at the American Kennel Club.

Open. Open competition builds on the foundation work your dog learns in Novice competition, by adding the requirements of jumping and retrieving. As you enter the ring with your dog, you hand over the leash and dumbbell to a steward and go to the designated starting point for the Heeling exercise.

All work will be done off-lead. Your dog will be asked to **heel, drop-on recall, retrieve on the flat, retrieve over the high jump** and

Except when "Risky" was hard at work doing the Retrieve over the High Jumps, his tail never flagged, even when the going got tough as he completed his Utility Degree. "Risky" is a multiple High-In-Trial winner, and the kind of all-around dog that does much to enhance the popularity of the Poodle.

do the **broad jump.** In addition, it will have to do longer Sits and Downs, and handlers will not be across the ring. They will be out of the ring and *out of sight.*

Again, three successful efforts in Open competition will earn the CDX (Companion Dog Excellent) for your Poodle, and the American Kennel Club will add that designation to the official registered name. Because you must earn a CD before you compete for CDX, only the most advanced title is used.

Utility.   Utility is the highest level of Obedience work and depends entirely on the Poodle's ability to respond to hand signals for the **Heeling Signal Exercise,** the **Moving Stand for Examination** as well as some for the **Directed Jumping, Directed Retrieve** and **Scent Discrimination.** Obviously, this level of competition is only for the person willing to devote considerable time to training, and for the Poodle that has demonstrated considerable ability.

The **Signal exercise** requires a full Heeling test and halting, with the dog remaining in a standing position while the handler goes to the far end of the ring. Then a series of hand signals are used to ask the dog to drop to a down position, Sit, Come, sit in front and then finish to the Heel position.

Scent Discrimination requires the dog going to a cluster of articles into which the judge has placed only one object that has been touched by the handler. The dog must quickly locate that article and bring it back to the handler. The exercise must be done twice, working once with a leather article and then a metal article.

The **Directed Retrieve** exercise requires the Poodle to follow handler directions to retrieve one of the three white cotton gloves placed across the far end of the ring.

In the **Moving Stand and Examination** exercise, the dog Heels until the handler stops the dog in a standing position. The handler then moves another 10 to 12 feet and halts. After the judge examines the dog, the dog is called to a Heel position.

Finally, comes the **Directed Jumping** exercise where the handler sends the Poodle down the center from one end of the ring to the other. At the far end, the dog must turn and sit. Then, on instruction from the judge, the handler will send the dog over either the Bar Jump or the Solid Jump, placed midway in the ring. The exercise is repeated over the second jump.

Again, when your dog has qualified three times, the UD degree replaces the CDX already listed after your Poodle's registered name in all official records.

WHAT WILL YOU WIN?

If your dog has one of the top four scores in the class at a licensed trial, you will be awarded a ribbon that indicates the placing: blue for first, red for second, yellow for third, and white for fourth. If your dog earns a qualifying score but doesn't place, a green robbon will be presented to designate your achievement. Following completion of three qualifying scores, the American Kennel Club mails a certificate designating your dog is a holder of the appropriate title.

Once your Poodle earns a CD, you may no longer compete in Novice, but you may continue work in Open and Utility—even at the same time.

Dogs who earn the Highest Combined score in Open and Utility are awarded a blue and green rosette. If your Poodle earns the Highest Score in Trial, you will receive a blue and gold rosette.

At Specialty shows and sometimes at all-breed shows, special awards will be given. Such awards may be trophies, merchandise or even cash. Their availability will be noted in the premium list when you make your entries.

OTCh. Claude De Fabian, a Miniature owned by Gabrielle Fabian, was named Highest Scoring Dog in Trial at the 1988 Obedience Trial held at the PCA National show. Claude is no stranger to PCA Obedience competition, having won the event in 1983 and 1985.

POODLE OBEDIENCE WINNERS OF THE PAST

Obedience competition was first held at the Poodle Club of America show in 1948, and the highest scoring dog in Open B and Utility Combined was the great Ch. Carillon Jester UD, owned by the Carillon Kennels. He repeated the win the next year, and Obedience competition was underway.

Ch. Davroc Bronzed Bliss UDT, owned by Jean Combs, is not only a study in Poodle femininity, but is also an excellent example of the impact of the dilution gene on the brown Poodle. Born a rich, red brown, she became a lovely even, pale color when mature. The typical darkness on the face makes expression so evident and the slightly deeper brown color remains on the ears. She is sired by Bel Tor Don't Tread On Me X Ch. Bel Tor Blissful. Having won a championship as well as all Obedience titles and a Tracking title, she is proof that function can follow form.

Bobbie Jacoby's first OTCH. Andechez There Goes Timothy attained his first High in Trial at 8 months and the coveted OTCH. at age 2. As he matured, his reliability increased to 98%. He retired after 6 years of competition, winning the 1984 Gaines Super Dog competition, earning 3 perfect 200 scores, 82 High in Trial awards, 110 High Combined Scores and 2000 lifetime OTCH. points.

In 1951, Cassandra Young's Cartlane Gobelin Int. UD pushed the scoring level to the 393.5 mark, a record that stood until 1954 when Dorothy Bach's Blakeen Champagne Deborah UD scored 397. The very next year the high score went to 397.5 as a result of Mrs. Martin Meyer's Chevalier de Bouffeurs v d Mrn's efforts.

That score remains the highest earned at the PCA National, although it was tied in 1961 by Dorothy M. Bach's Champagne Dulcie UD.

In 1967, Cygnette des Fabian UD appears as the winner for Carlyle S. and Gabrielle Fabian, a win he would repeat four consecutive times (1967–1970) and again 1974. Gabrielle F. Fabian has been a consistent competitor since that time, scoring the top win in 1977, 1978, 1983, 1985 and 1988.

In 1989 and 1990, the winner was the silver Miniature, OTCH. Merene T. J. Finnegan owned by the late Barbara Jacoby. Alice Hartman's white Miniature, OTCH. White Crest Bingo, a white Miniature scored the win in 1991 for the owner.

1992 saw a black Standard back at the top, Syrena Debonaire Reginald CDX was the winner for Kathleen M. Joffe, and the most recent winner was again Alice Hartman in 1993, with another white Miniature,

OTCH. White Crest Hard Hitting Hannah UD. Hannah is the 1991 winner's graddam!

OBEDIENCE—THE BENEFITS

Obedience aficionados may also work in Tracking at two different testing levels, TD and TDX. Obviously, the AKC Obedience competition program is comprehensive enough that you can spend many years in competition with only your house pet. Not only do you gain the satisfaction that comes from the focused interaction with your pet, but you will gain an entire friendship circle with a common interest in Obedience work and a diverse set of other interests that always comes when you meet new people.

It is important to remember that Obedience work can be satisfying at any level, from teaching your dog to respond to commands that just make pet ownership more pleasant, creating a safe environment for your dog, and all the way to striving for the OTCH title. Your personal interest and willingness to commit the time and effort should guide your decisions.

One other point. There is nothing more thrilling than seeing a happy, Obedience trained Poodle and an owner enjoying the opportunity to do things together, whether it is walking in the park or competing at the Poodle Club of America National show. The condition and appearance

Can. Ch. Nevermore Pandora, a brown by Am. Can. Ch. Nevermore Newman X Ch. Nevermore Kelly is living proof that Standard Poodles are willing to work on land . . .

... and sea. She was bred by Sue Henly and represents the kind of Poodle that harkens back to its roots as a working dog. Pandora is owned by Sally Engebretson.

But enough is enough, and once the championship was obtained, Jillian successfully set out to earn her Obedience degrees in her "working clothes." Here she is on the track of something important . . .

of the Poodle reflects pride of ownership. The joyous attitude of both the dog and owner reflects the satisfaction that each of them have from their work together. And the wagging tail is a certain sign that the Poodle enjoys the work.

That is Obedience at its best.

But some owners and trainers—often because they are so intent on achieving a title or a qualifying score or absolute compliance to a specific

... Jillian retrieves what she was after and comes out of the grass with the same joy and enthusiasm she showed playing ball in her Continental trim. The switch from an adult show trim to a convenience trim is most often for the convenience of the owner rather than of the Poodle. They really don't care.

command (in the ring or at home) use forceful approaches that sometimes achieve the action desired, but in doing so destroys the essence of the Poodle.

This can happen to dogs in conformation judging *or* in the Obedience ring. It can happen to dogs in their own homes. To my mind, it is a certain sign that the Poodle has lost confidence in the owner or trainer and that she may live with an element of fear on a day-by-day basis.

That is Obedience at its worst . . . dog shows at their worst . . . a disappointing scenario when you see its signs in the Poodle's home.

Whatever level of obedience training you settle on (or show ring training for that matter), use your eyes to constantly assess your Poodle's attitude toward the work you are doing. At the first sign of a dropped tail, ask yourself, "why?" Alter your approach to gain the Poodle's confidence and assure that your dog approaches his or her role as an Obedience-trained dog in a totally positive manner.

The joyfully wagging tail is an absolute indicator that all is well between you and your Poodle.

24

The Poodle Is Not Perfect

COUCH-BOUND POODLES with large protruding eyes and Best in Show or PCA Best of Breed winners generally have one thing in common. They are dearly loved by the people who own them. And as you think about the versatility of the breed—family member, show dog, Obedience competitor, Tracking and field worker, companion to the handicapped or elderly—it is easy to say what so many have said before us, "The Poodle is a perfect breed."

And that is true in so many cases.

But the Poodle has two attributes that unfortunately make it less than perfect. First, most Poodles do not live as long as their owners. When the Poodle's life comes to an end, a great deal of sadness follows, despite the memories of all the good years that came from the shared lives between dog and owners. Fortunately, for most, the grieving process ultimately comes to an end and we reach the point where we can remember the dog we lost for the richness added to our life rather than the sadness resulting from its death.

The second aspect in which the Poodle is less than perfect is that the breed (as are all breeds and people for that matter) is subject to several heritable diseases that not only have an unfortunate impact on the dog involved; they also have devastating effects on the owners and breeders who developed the breeding strategies, produced the dog and then made its genetic influence available to the fancy.

Heritable diseases are not new to Poodles—nor to other breeds. But in the early stages of U.S. Poodle breeding little was known about the diseases, and, in particular, the heritability of the condition was an unknown factor. So it follows that any number of dogs who ultimately had tremendous impact on their variety contributed what they had to offer, including, in some cases, the genetic inclination to have a heritable disease.

Many of the relevant problems result from recessive patterns of genetic transmissions so they are difficult to detect. Even worse, some conditions do not manifest themselves until the dog is well into his breeding career and the bitch may very well be at the end of hers. But today, at least, there is knowledge to suggest that these conditions are heritable. At this point, they are not treatable.

MAKING PROGRESS

It seems that Poodle breeders, scientists and the dogs involved have progressed through several stages as they have interacted during the past more than thirty years.

In the first stage, problems were reported to the veterinarian and little was done because little was known. But veterinary science and its supporting research programs ultimately began defining the myriad of problems that exist, and soon their heritability became known. That led to the second stage—total trauma.

In this stage breeders who initiated the various testing procedures available almost fell into two camps when they learned that they had an afflicted animal. Some eliminated all of their breeding animals and started anew or went out of dogs. Others ignored the problem and kept very hush-hush about it all. Devastation affected both camps, and the new category of dog breeders, the witch hunters, was born. It was a most taxing era in which to be breeding dogs. So little was known. Concern was so great. The ignorance of the times and its impact on breeding programs was overwhelming. But gradually, the shift began to a new era. Gradual enlightenment is probably the best way to describe the era.

Hip Dysplasia

Standard breeders seemed among the first to make progress in dealing with such conditions. For some time now, canine hip dysplasia has been definable. Today all conscientious breeders work with their veterinarians to do preliminary X-rays of the hips and then to do the final X-rays when the dogs are at a prescribed age. Results of those X-rays are sent to a clearinghouse where the X-rays are graded and the dog is assigned on OFA number that may be used in advertising or any other way to indicate that the individual dog is free from the condition.

Dysplastic dogs still exist. Promising puppies occasionally make their ring debut and then vanish from the show scene because "they didn't X-ray." When that happens, there is most often some openness and willingness to talk about it.

In general, Standard breeders have moved their breeding strategies away from animals that produced the problem. The generations of X-raying that has taken place has not eliminated canine hip dysplasia, but it has reduced its frequency and it has reduced overall the probabilities of the condition occurring in a planned breeding.

PRA

Progressive retinal atrophy (PRA) has been slower in its progress. In the early years entire kennel breeding programs were brought to an end because of the disease. While such an effort was commendable at the time—and understandable even today—most breeders today would not take such dramatic action.

Because the disease is fairly widespread within Miniature Poodles, and is very much a problem with Toys and to some degree with Standards, most breeders today would be much more inclined to work to determine where their problems exist within their pedigrees. Some will launch a continuing testing program with both an ophthalmologist's examination and assessment by electroretinogram. Based on what they learn, they will find the animals that seem least likely to be carriers and select mates for them with believed high probabilities of being clear or, at the worst, carriers.

An *ophthalmologist's examination* can indicate that the dog does not have the disease on that day. *An electroretinogram* can indicate that the dog does not have and will not have the disease. Even that test does not answer the question of whether the individual dog is a carrier.

But research is underway to provide answers to that question, and this is another place where the Poodle Club of America, through its Foundation, is providing not only leadership but financial support.

OTHER HERITABLE DISEASES

At one point, canine hip dysplasia and progressive retinal atrophy were the major heritable diseases that concerned Poodle breeders. But in the 1980s attention was shifted to conditions related to the *immune system*, and researchers in several fronts began work and developing testing systems to help identify dogs more prone to the problematic condition. And as the decade drew to a close, *sebaceous adenitis*, a menacing skin condition, surfaced primarily in Standards, and attracted considerable attention.

While each of these conditions—and there is no intent to say there are only four heritable disease problems in Poodles—are very different, there does seem to be some commonality in the manner of dealing with them.

First, they are not problems that can be dealt with by any one of the actors involved. Breeders can't solve the problem. Practicing veterinarians can't. Research scientists have to be part of the mix that contributes to the solution.

Second, avoidance, or ignoring the condition, is not an acceptable manner of dealing with a heritable disease. Left unattended, the problems will only become more widespread. The process has been gradual, but today breeders are a great deal more inclined to share their problems and experiences rather than hide them.

Third, breeders have come to recognize that *no breeding program is totally free*, or guaranteed to be free forever, of the possibility of a heritable disease. Consequently, instead of abandoning entire breeding programs that may be very successful on many fronts, breeders are gathering the information available and picking their most usable animals from within their existing breeding program and moving ahead with planned caution.

Fourth, the scientific community is continuing to work at various testing and diagnostic programs that might very well provide the breakthrough needed to pinpoint individuals who are carriers well before they reach breeding age.

Finally, organizations have formed—embracing both the breeder community and the scientific community—that are documenting available information and providing breeders a way to publicly verify the results of the various testing programs of which they have been part. An OFA number or a CERF number, for example provides other breeders a higher level of assurance about information on a dog than a simple "eyes checked clear" statement.

We can generally agree that we do not live in a perfect world and still find a way to live in it. But none of us hesitates to be frustrated that the "world" of heritable diseases affecting the Poodle is not perfect.

It is not perfect. But it is far better than it was thirty years ago when problems such as PRA and Canine Hip Dysplasia virtually brought an end to some great kennels because those breeders—at that time—felt they had no option but to discontinue even lifelong efforts.

Today there is more openness among breeders, and with that openness comes support. There is more information in the scientific community. There are organizations focusing attention on genetic problems and providing funding to contribute to their solutions. Our own breed club, PCA, is at the helm in such efforts.

Most importantly, there is hope. Several breakthroughs seem reachable within the not-too-distant future that could go a long way in helping breeders greatly reduce the probability of producing litters capable of manifesting a particular disease.

Ours is not a perfect world relating to the genetics of the Poodle, but it is really not any worse than the situation facing other breeders. And most important, it is improving.

Normal temp 101°